CHRISTOPHER MICHLIG
FILE UNDER: SLIME

WENDY
CLELLA
FRIEDA
ON Y VA!

1930	1940	1950	1960	1970	1980	1990	2000	2010	2020
1931	1941	1951	1961	1971	1981	1991	2001	2011	
1932	1942	1952	1962	1972	1982	1992	2002	2012	
1930	1943	1953	1963	1973	1983	1993	2003	2013	
1934	1944	1954	1964	1974	1984	1994	2004	2014	
1935	1945	1955	1965	1975	1985	1995	2005	2015	
1936	1946	1956	1966	1976	1986	1996	2006	2016	
1937	1947	1957	1967	1977	1987	1997	2007	2017	
1938	1948	1958	1968	1978	1988	1998	2008	2010	
1939	1949	1959	1969	1979	1989	1999	2009	2019	

FILE UNDER: UNDER: S LIME

HAT & BEARD | LOS ANGELES

CHRISTOPHER MICHLIG

With a Foreword by
JAN TUMLIR

There are several friends and colleagues to whom I owe a great deal of gratitude for their critical feedback and vital encouragement. I first presented a talk on slime at the University of Oregon in 2016 in a visual studies course taught by Farhad Bahram who encouragingly inquired about my goal for the research, compelling me to pursue the topic in greater depth. In 2017 Peter Zellner graciously invited me as a guest lecturer at the newly-formed Free School of Architecture in Los Angeles where I presented a further developed lecture on slime over two days titled "Semiotics of Slime." Following my experience at FSA I realized that the scope of my research would be most productively sited in a book. Itza Vilaboy was exceedingly supportive at critical moments during my writing process when I reached out to her for support. Marc Lowenthal provided thorough and challenging feedback at a moment when I considered this project to be near completion, urging me to further my analysis of key concepts and precedents. I have had the incredible good fortune to have Jan Tumlir as a mentor, friend, colleague, and collaborator since first working with him when I was a student at ArtCenter and Jan's enduring editorial support and guidance during my writing process was central to keeping me mostly on-piste. Tobias Menely enthusiastically offered to read my manuscript as it neared completion and provided feedback that helped to draw out and clarify critical thematic trends within the research.

Brian Roettinger—without Brian, no book. Very special thanks to Wendy Heldmann for her patience, thorough copy editing, editorial vision, and critical engagement with this project, without which I would still be stuck in the slime. Special thanks to the University of Oregon Center for Art Research for their support. Lastly, thank you to J.C Gabel and Sybil Perez at Hat & Beard Press making it happen. ¶

Acknowledgements

JAN TUMLIR
Foreword

What is slime?

We are well acquainted with its
qualities in conjunction with certain things from
which we tend to recoil but to which we are also at
times fervently attracted–namely, things to which
we can assign the adjective "slimy." But what about
slime as a thing in its own right, considered ontologically? The problem that is immediately confronted
in any attempt to grapple with this question is that
the thing-ness of slime is precisely that of a no-thing,
not by any means nothing, but rather a thing that
says no to things. Amorphous, abject, disgusting,
slime is the perennial anti-object. The words we
employ to describe it all carry prefixes that speak
directly to its elusive nature, placing it outside of (dis-
), away from (ab-), against (a-). Slime, as a concept, is
by definition hard to grasp, but this is precisely what
makes it worth writing about, as this book stands to
amply demonstrate. Its author, Christopher Michlig,
takes up the challenge that slime poses to thought–
that is, not only to the attempt to think it through
in its particularity, but to thinking in general–with
conspicuous zeal. There is a pointedly philosophical
side to his project in that it orbits intently around
that which is most aporetic. If slime can be readily
deployed as a foil for thinking about thinking, which

would have to be the ultimate aim of philosophy, it is entirely due to its objective-empirical faults. In other words, slime does not suggest itself as something to be thought *about*, but rather thought *on*.

The book opens with a meditation on Sartre, a philosopher whose quite prodigious literary talents are too often overlooked, especially when it comes to the description of mental operations, which he consistently drives deep into the dark and humid zones of the viscera. Sartre's equation of existentialism with a kind of nausea might come to mind in this regard, yet Michlig latches on to a more obscure item from this author's thought-world: skiing. This would have to be seen as a quite challenging opening gambit, yet its purpose is clear: to straightaway detach slime from its most available reference points, to expand its theoretical scope. The subject of skiing, and moreover snow, would initially seem to be irreconcilable with slime, for here we find ourselves in a world of crystalline geometry rather than muck. In a section excised from most volumes of *Being and Nothingness*, Sartre expresses his enthusiasm for the sport in terms that bear a distinctly "Cartesian" (his word) orientation as a mode of projecting oneself, downslope, along a sightline. But when it comes to considering the composition of snow itself, his thoughts also admit some degree of ambiguity; it is something that can only be understood by the body passing over it, and therefore only understood partially. "The snowy space is massed underneath implicitly," he writes; "its cohesion is that of the blank space understood in the interior of a circumference, for example, when I look at the black line of the circle without paying explicit attention to its surface." In an ensuing section, Sartre will launch into a proper analysis of slime, precisely by attending to its surface. It is, he notes, an "aberrant fluid" where "fluidity exists in slow motion; there is a sticky thickness to its liquidity." Slime is viscous–"*visqueux*" is a word that repeatedly appears in Sartre's writing, and when it is assigned to objects other than slime per se, this word is often rendered, in the English translation, as "slimy." Inasmuch as skiing is also a phenomenon of "viscous drag," as Michlig points out, we are alerted to an opportunity missed by Sartre to connect the dots between his thoughts. Michlig seizes upon this "lapse" as an invitation; his project begins there.

Julia Kristeva and Georges Bataille are brought up further on as more familiar grounding points in the discussion of slime. Anyone who went to school in the eighties and nineties—and more specifically art school, which is where Michlig went—would have encountered these names as staple items on their reading lists. Here, slime is insistently connected to the realm of abjection, always pointing toward that which resists appropriation, an uncontainable excess before which the body balks and the mind reels. For both of these authors, horror of slime is at the crux of its ecstatic promise: to redirect us outside ourselves. Yet this outside, which is reached through a kind of non-metaphysical transcendence, a sensual convulsion, nevertheless risks devolving into generalization as always the same place. Here, the example of Sartre on snow proves particularly auspicious: "I have it well in hand," he writes. Could it be that slime is hard to grasp as a concept precisely because one can actually grasp slime as such? Unlike water or air, for example, which truly are indifferent to our touch, slime has a mass that can be felt, held, weighed, and assessed. It is entirely due to the fact that its formal ambiguity *is formed* that we can distinguish different kinds of slime, a variegated field of the slimy.

This book takes us on a tour of the horizon of slime, and one that constantly gravitates toward the outer reaches. Yes, slime always relates to something internal that has seeped through or overflowed its borders and now is manifested in external space–or better, is *demonstrated* there, to place etymological stress on the demonic and monstrous aspect of this showing. Substances such as spit, semen, blood, vomit, rot, etc., are readily characterized as slimy, and Michlig attends to these with due diligence, but generally also by way of unexpected detours. Accordingly, we are invited to consider how slime factors into the drooling caricatures of Garbage Pail Kids stickers; the phantasmagoric extension of the "cum-shot" in the proto-porn of *Behind the Green Door*; the alien mass that bleeds through the screen in the bargain-bin science fiction of *The Blob*; the coughed up "protoplasm" of female mystics in paranormal photography; or LSD considered as an agent of sensory putrefaction. Can we see the lysergic phenomenon of the visual trail as a slime trail? The art of the sixties would seem to confirm this view, as Michlig points out. Periodically veering away from everyday popular culture on an avant-garde tangent, he notes the exacerbation of Jackson Pollock's drip-painting technique into a succession of ever more freeform and voluminous pours in the works of such figures as Robert Smithson and Lynda Benglis. These are instances of an art once devoted to opticality becoming clogged with matter, congealing in "slow motion," to return to Sartre. The reader is encouraged to draw such associations casually, in passing, sliding by like the philosopher on his skis. From the great unwashed enclaves of hippie counterculture to the buttoned-down "white cube" of the art gallery, and then, via another sharp turn, to the Canadian game show for kids *You Can't Do That on Television*, where contestants are regularly showered with goo–this is a slalom course.

It has to be said that Michlig's account of the slimy alternates somewhat recklessly between the poles of the gross and refined, but this is as it should be. At the highest echelons of good taste–in food, for instance–the gag reflex is necessarily tested. A certain bravura is required to take this connoisseurial plunge, which ultimately is enormously pleasurable. In writing, no less than in cooking, it would seem that the supreme thrill is to put high-mindedness to the test of that which is impossibly low. Ideational mischief is also the lure of this text for the reader, but this is not to say that we are only having sloppy fun here, for slime, in even its most cartoonishly anarchic iterations, is never but a short distance away from the *doxa*. At every turn in this narrative, ideology reappears in the most oppressive sense, and this might begin, however paradoxically, with the anti-ideology of Bataille and Kristeva, which, in the end, is no less entrenched than what it opposes. After all, it takes some measure of gastronomic refinement (read: social breeding) to slurp up an oyster, because the slimiest foods are often also the most "classy." The fabled vomitoriums of Rome were reserved for the rich, as we know. The conversion of what is most common into an aristocratic privilege is the rule, not the exception, within the social process. And more generally we can say that the borderline zone marked out by slime is always beset by competing powers, repulsive and attractive at once. Here, we can experience the democratic free-flow of molecular independence while at same time being drawn toward the nucleus of the molar, monopolistic, and fascistic "one." Debased or exalted, slime remains dangerous, an existential threat. The "one" that is "oneself" is advised to proceed with caution.

Sartre characterizes slime as "a liquid seen in a nightmare." The free-flow of liquidity is arrested in slimy viscosity, and turns back on the subject, as though mounting an indictment of anyone who believes himself to be free: "all of its properties turn back against me." "Slime," Sartre declares with finality, "is the revenge of the In-Itself." The "self" that is "it" is apparently gained at the expense of my own self, which it somehow appropriates. Here again we might be reminded of the phenomenon of viscous drag, where that which is slippery can also stick. To grasp at slime is simultaneously to feel its cling, and in this its "revenge," which travels up from the hand to wreak a psychic havoc. In the exchange with the borderline substance that is slime—when the "In-Itself" is effectively on me, and has taken hold of me—I am transformed into a borderline personality. No more possibility of clearly distinguishing inside from outside, slime sets off an internal crisis, and one that projects, that subsumes the whole world to its symptomatology. Michlig's text bears down on its furthest flung flashpoints: in the "snow" that once graced off-air television as well as the floating flakes of radioactive fallout, to cite just two examples. To consider such things as slimy takes an imaginary leap, to be sure, but one of the chief benefits of this book, and perhaps its author's greatest accomplishment, is that it prepares us to do just that. It is in such seemingly idiosyncratic passages where the greatest analogical hurdles are encountered that the inherent *gravitas* of this project is most acutely felt. Periodically, and with mounting insistence, Michlig connects slime directly to technological power—that is, the power that our machines produce as well as consume—and this always is to invoke a catastrophic notion of progress. The inarguable sliminess of fossil fuels permeates the auto-scape, and will continue to do so even after our turn to the electrical car. That there is no such thing as "clean energy" is one insight that this book brings into sharp focus. The electricity that irradiates us through our TV sets, and now through computer flat-screens, still channels the sludge of decomposing dinosaurs. And nuclear fission, the "big bang" in reverse, threatens to decompose the world and everything in it back into the one thing that is also no-thing, a vast, undifferentiated "In-Itself" of primal ooze.

This book can be read as a file on slime, miscellaneous by definition. It is broken into a series of short sections, mini-chapters, each one devoted to a discrete variation on its overarching theme. One can delve in at any point, episodically, guided by pre-existing interests, and in this way treat the whole as a reference book. But I would advise reading from start to finish, because what is here proposed is essentially a passage across a terrain, which, in accordance with Sartre's Cartesian sightlines, has a beginning and an end. There are two ways that a file can be organized: taxonomically or chronologically. Michlig has opted for the latter mode. His organizing strategy is to divide different kinds of slime by the year of their emergence, which suggests that slime is a time-sensitive construct, but also one that changes and builds on itself. That the zeitgeist can be read into slime is an astonishing thought, but even more so is the thought that every zeitgeist could be a product of slime. At any rate, this is what we are here encouraged to think from the moment we occupy now–a moment where we find ourselves, as a species, definitely off-piste. ¶

Samuel Taylor Coleridge, *The Rime of the Ancient Mariner* (excerpt), 1834

Water, water, every where,
And all the boards did shrink;
Water, water, every where,
Nor any drop to drink.

The very deep did rot: O Christ!
That ever this should be!
Yea, slimy things did crawl with legs
Upon the slimy sea.

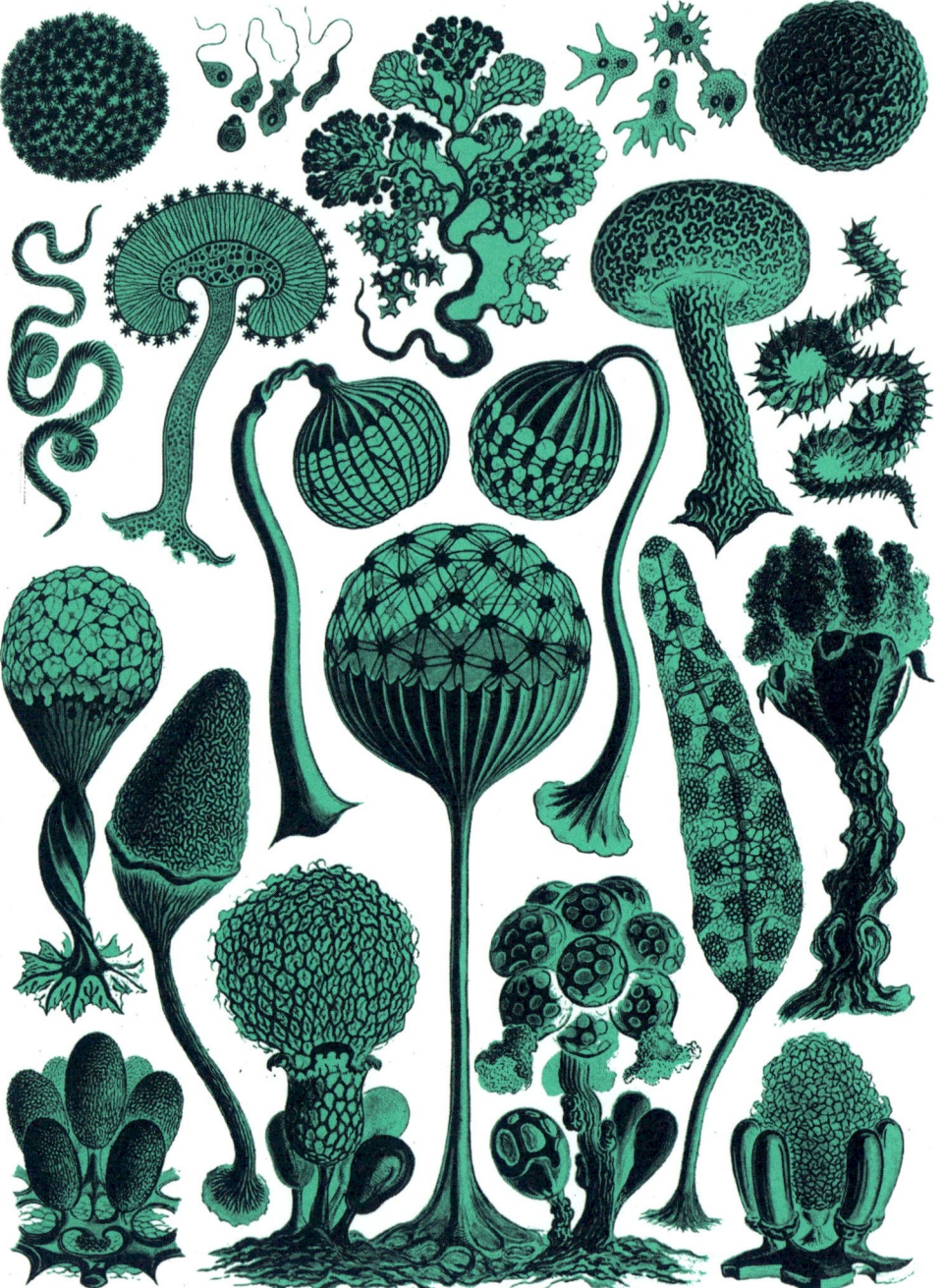

Slime's ambiguous qualities are accentuated by the fact that its "fluidity exists in slow motion"[1]; it makes a spectacle of its instability. Unlike water, which instantly absorbs into itself, slime does so slowly giving one the false impression that it is a substance that can be possessed. Slime is, therefor, read as a deceitful material. Its in-between-ness, its boundary-threatening attributes, provokes a base and horrible sublime experience.[2]

—Mike Kelley

NOTES

1. Jean-Paul Sartre, *Being and Nothingness: An Essay on Phenomenological Ontology*. New York: Washington Square Press, 1956. Print. p. 772.
2. Mike Kelley, "On the Aesthetics of Ufology" (excerpted from an interview with M.A. Greenstein), Blastitude, #13, 1997.

CHRISTOPHER MICHLIG
Introduction

Within the field of semiotics, slime could be described as a floating signifier[1], a reference without a referent performing a kind of free play in its varied visual and literary occurrences. The topos of slime in its enduring amorphousness has a culture-scale scope of signifying capacity, its meaning evolving with changes in social consciousness and zeitgeist. This project traces the chronology of written references and visual instances of slime ranging from early science fiction to contemporary precedents.[2]

In the fall of 2017, after two years of open-ended research into appearances of slime in visual culture, it became clear that to develop my project further would require concurrent theoretical and literary references to establish a dynamic chronology of slime's evolving significance. Around this same period of time, I also began research into the history of skiing and its intersections with art practice and literature. Having recently finished reading Simone de Beauvoir's memoir *The Prime of Life,* in which skiing is fondly recalled[3], I shortly thereafter came across a reference to de Beauvoir taking Jean-Paul Sartre on a skiing trip to Chamonix in the winter of 1934. *Being and Nothingness* was where I was pointed to find Sartre's writing about skiing. My 1965 Citadel Press edition of *Being and Nothingness* ends with the chapter "Being and Doing: Freedom," and to my disappointment, nowhere was there any mention of skiing. It wasn't until I took a closer look at the front matter of the book that I noticed the words "Special Abridged Edition," which in this case meant that the second section of "Having Doing and Being" was omitted. This missing section, "Doing and Having: I. Existential Psychoanalysis" contains lengthy descriptions of skiing as "a synthetic activity of organization and connection."[4] Sartre goes on and on about skiing and eventually goes so far as to say that "the act of skiing changes the matter and meaning of snow."[5] It is common skiing knowledge that the pressure of a ski on the snow lowers the freezing temperature of water, melting the snow directly under the ski. This creates a very thin layer of water between the ski and the snow, reducing friction and allowing the ski to slide very easily. This phenomenon also touches on a force known as viscous drag that refers to a particular type of surface friction between a medium such as snow and the material or equipment moving across or through it. Viscous drag has to do with the surface properties of a material and the medium over which it moves.

> To ski means not only to enable me to make rapid movements and to acquire a technical skill, nor is it merely to play by increasing according to my whim the speed or difficulties of the course; it is also to enable me to possess this field of Snow. At present I am doing something to it. That means that by my very activity as a skier, I am changing the matter and meaning of the snow. From the fact that now in my course it appears to me as a slope to go down, it finds again a continuity and a unity which it had lost. It is at the moment connective tissue. It is included between two limiting terms; it unites the point of departure with the point of arrival.[6]

Unlike physical change, the changing *meaning* of snow is related as much to a ski on the snow as it is to the actions of the skier engaged in an existential act of connecting a point of departure and a point of arrival through decisive movement across a field of snow that becomes such because of the skier's activity. In this way, "The snowy space is massed underneath implicitly"[7] and traversing across the snow on skis becomes a kind of possession and apprehension. Sartre continues:

> ... its cohesion is that of the blank space understood in the interior of a circumference, for example, when I look at the black line of the circle without paying explicit attention to its surface. And precisely because I maintain it marginal, implicit, and understood, it adapts itself to me, I have it well in hand; I pass beyond it toward its end just as a man hanging a tapestry passes beyond the hammer which he uses, toward its end, which is to nail an arras on the wall.[8]

Snow is Sartre's blank space and its implicit nature invites further consideration. The physics of viscosity enables and provides evidence of the movement of the skier, which also evidences the construction of meaning. There are traces of viscosity in the tracks of the skier, which to Sartre's dismay are not immediately concealed like the path of a water-skier, "How much better it would be if the snow re-formed itself as we passed over it!"[9]

Later in this same section Sartre launches into a discussion of slime aimed at articulating its peculiar mode of being and it is here that Sartre characterizes and lays the groundwork for ontological discussions of slime:

> What mode of being is symbolized by the slimy?
> I see first that it is the homogeneity and the
> imitation of liquidity. A slimy substance like
> pitch is an aberrant fluid... But immediately
> the slimy reveals itself as essentially ambiguous because its fluidity exists in slow motion;
> there is a sticky thickness in its liquidity.[10]

There is a near-overlap of the discussion of sliding and the discussion of slimy, our ability to slide across snow antithetical to slime as an ensnaring substance. Where the experience of skiing across snow is existentialism as radical Cartesianism, an experience of the slimy is existentialism as engagement, dialogue, and intersubjectivity. We slide across snow, but we get stuck in slime.

> At this instant I suddenly understand the
> snare of the slimy: it is a fluidity which holds
> me and which compromises me; I can not *slide*
> on this slime, all its suction cups hold me back;
> it can not slide over me, it clings to me like a
> leech. The sliding however is not simply denied
> as in the case of the solid; it is degraded. The
> slimy seems to lend itself to me, it invites me;
> for a body of slime at rest is not noticeably
> distinct from a body of very dense liquid. But
> it is a trap. The sliding is *sucked* in by the sliding substance, and it leaves its traces upon me.
> The slime is like a liquid seen in a nightmare,
> where all its properties are animated by a sort
> of life and turn back against me. Slime is the
> revenge of the In-itself. "[11]

The stability of snow on an incline can be disrupted through accumulation and changes in temperature, often with an avalanching effect wherein the sliding mass might simultaneously cover, ingest, and disperse objects in its path, skiers potentially included, their sliding *sucked* in. It is only in this way that Sartre's description of the movement of the skier or of snow might be haphazardly construed with a description of the movement of slime in its varied possessive and adherent qualities. It is tempting to somehow characterize snow as slimy, but it might be a stretch. While Sartre moves quickly from "slide" and "slimy," Hazel E. Barnes' translation of this section acknowledges the significance of Sartre's specific language. In a translator's note Barnes elucidates her choice of the word slimy:

> "French visqueux. This at times comes closer to the English 'sticky,' but I have consistently used the word 'slimy' in translating because the figurative meaning of 'slimy' appears to be identical in both languages."[12]

Sartre's visqueux translated as slimy is primary in laying the groundwork for the theoretical and visual characterization of slime as a restless idea, and his acknowledgment of its essential ambiguity leaves it open for further interpretation, which happens to be where *File Under: Slime* begins: "In one sense it is an experience since sliminess is an intuitive discovery; in another sense it is like the discovery of an adventure of being."[13]

Qualities of sliminess are further developed in the work of Julia Kristeva, who importantly connects her work on abjection to substances connected with life which also breach the border between the body and the world; living substances that can be separated from the body, that seem to have a life of their own, or some kind of afterlife. This is notable in the trajectory of precedents presented in this text as there is a tension between Kristeva, for whom slimy substances are sometimes expelled from the body yet stick around, and Sartre, for whom the slimy is something external that sucks and clings like honey or glue.

Synthesizing and in some sense formalizing differences between Kristeva's abjection and Sartre's slimy, Georges Bataille's writing about "informe" is taken up by Rosalind Krauss and Yve-Alain Bois in their significant 1996 exhibition and accompanying dictionary formatted catalog, *Formless: A User's Guide*. Their multiform project centers Bataille as a voice through which the concept and appearance of formlessness in the visual arts is explored, categorized, and indexed within a provocatively logocentric, alphabetic framework. Dynamic and intratextual in its structure, *Formless* seeks interpretation of Bataille's informe through general categories of "horizontality," "base materialism," "pulse," and "entropy," inflecting Bataille's anti-materialism and his predilection for "alternating rhythm"[14] over dialectics. Whereas Kristeva has particular interest in abject qualities, Bataille is ultimately concerned with the social and biologic mechanisms which bring about abjection.

For *File Under: Slime*, I have adopted a chronological scheme with the aim of sketching out a topos of slime, more a sequencing of appearances than a strategy of clarification. While the emphasis on

Bataille for Krauss and Bois is derived from a group of texts from 1930 titled "Abjection et les formes miserables," Bataille's own use of the word slime, which appears in a different and unrelated text, is not only anecdotally compelling, but also significant in its singularity and suggestive consequences. In his aphoristic *On Nietzsche* from 1944, Bataille wrote, "The communication of two individuals occurs when they lose themselves in sweet, shared slime ..."[15] This sentence is significant in relationship to my project in that it suggests dislocation, transference, and adjoining brought about by and experienced in slime. Bataille is speaking to us from the afterlife and we are caught in the slime of his texts posthumously.

Georges Bataille's Bataille's transgressive and vivid writing about laughter is also important within this project because of Bataille's deployment of the word "glissement" (slipperiness), which bumps against Sartre's visqueux and moves through and beyond references to slapstick comedy. In her essay "Georges Bataille's Laughter: A Poetics of Glissement" Bénédicte Boisseron wrote of Bataille's *Histoire de l'œil* that:

> The novel overflows with liquid imageries, often in relation to laughter. *Histoire de l'œil* is the tale of the tragic-comic sexual adventures of the narrator and his female accomplice Simone, as they embark on a journey to the end of abjection. The narrative is punctuated with a chronic flow of urine squirting either from the narrator or from Simone's sexual organ. Several times in the story, urine is mixed with sperm as the narrator releases a spermatic fluid after urinating on Simone or

has an orgasm after seeing Simone urinate. Urinating and orgasms become transposable but, in a diuretic fashion, urinating and laughing are equally interchangeable.[16]

Boisseron highlights Bataille's characterization of laughter as the point at which sliding occurs, a glissement of corporeal control as well as comprehension. The coupling of slime with transgressed boundaries and incomprehension is featured prominently in the history of slime.

Finally, much of the groundwork for *File Under: Slime* references an edited conversation between Mike Kelley and M.A. Greenstein that was published in multiple formats as "On the Aesthetics of Ufology."[17] Having studied with both Kelley and Greenstein at ArtCenter College of Design, Pasadena, CA, from 2004–07, I consider this project a kind of intergenerational exchange and continuation of that conversation, particularly in its emphasis on the ontology and aesthetics of slime. ¶

1. Jean-Paul Sartre, *Being and Nothingness: An Essay on Phenomenological Ontology*, trans. Hazel E. Barnes. 1943 (New York: Washington Square Press, 1956), p. 611. "Thus in the project of appropriating the slimy, the sliminess is revealed suddenly as a symbol of an antivalue: it is a type of being not realized but threatening which will perpetually haunt consciousness as the constant danger which it is fleeing, and hence will suddenly transform the project of appropriation into a project of flight."

2. Ibid., "Thus I am enriched from my first contact with the slimy, by a valid ontological pattern beyond the distinction between psychic and non-psychic, which will interpret the meaning of being and of all the existents of a certain category, this category arising, moreover, like an empty skeletal framework before the experience with different kinds of sliminess."

3. Simone de Beauvoir, *The Prime of Life*, trans. Peter Green, 1960 (Penguin Books, 1965) pp.206-207.

4. Jean-Paul Sartre, *Being and Nothingness: An Essay on Phenomenological Ontology*, trans. Hazel E. Barnes. 1943 (New York: Washington Square Press, 1956) p. 582.

5. Ibid.

6. Ibid.

7. Ibid.

8. Ibid. Sartre's description of the "blank space" in the circumference of a circle, as well as his example of the "arras" (a hanging textile typically used to conceal a space), allude to experience beyond and in some sense obscured by Cartesian experience.

9. Ibid., p. 584.

10. Ibid., p. 607.

11. Ibid., p. 609.

12. Ibid., p. 604.

13. Ibid., p. 611.

14. Yve-Alain Bois and Rosalind Krauss, *Formless: A User's Guide* (New York: Zone Books, 1996), p. 71. "For Bataille, there is no third term, but rather an 'alternating rhythm' of homology and heterology, of appropriation and excretion."

15. Georges Bataille, *On Nietzsche*, trans. Bruce Boone (New York: Paragon House 1992), p. 98.

16. Bénédicte Boisseron, "Georges Bataille's Laughter: A Poetics of glissement," *French Cultural Studies*, Volume 21, Issue 3 (August 2010), pp. 174-175.

17. Mike Kelley. "On the Aesthetics of Ufology." *Blastitude,* #13, August 1997, blastitude.com. Accessed November 9, 2020.

Introduction   29

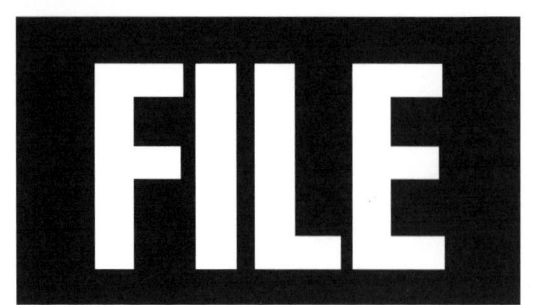

1932

1936

1939

The late 19th-and early 20th-century history of spirit photography coincides with the popularity of séances, spirit mediumship, and various other social gatherings themed on communication with ghosts. Commonly referred to as "ectoplasm photography" these images are significant for their visual representation of a gauzy substance purportedly evidencing threshold crossing and interaction with the dead. In her examination of the integral relationship between photography and ectoplasm, historian and mythographer Marina Warner writes, "Photography, as well as offering a deep metaphor for the relation between external matter and immaterial thought, also played an inestimable role in disseminating the mise-en-scène and the conduct of mediums from country to country."[1] Mediumship activities took place in low-light, the occurrence of ectoplasm as fleeting as the shuttered exposure of photographic emulsion to light required to snap a shot. Albeit eventually soundly debunked, there is nonetheless a non-photographic physical sample of ectoplasm from one such conjuring in the catalog of the archives of the Society for Psychical Research, now kept in the University Library, Cambridge. Though not referred to as slime at the time, the ectoplasmic depictions in these photographs set into motion some of the formal and conceptual parameters for what we now refer to as slime—amorphous, evidentiary of ghostly contact, and importantly manifested via female mediums.

The association of slime and femininity is later written about by Sartre in *Being and Nothingness* where he says:

> I open my hands, I want to let go of the slimy, and it sticks to me, it draws me, it sucks at me. Its mode of being is neither the reassuring inertia of the solid nor a dynamism like that in water which is exhausted in fleeing from me. It is a soft, yielding action, a moist and feminine sucking.... Slime is the revenge of the in-itself. A sickly-sweet, feminine revenge which will be symbolized on another level by the quality "sugary." A sugary-sliminess is the ideal of the slimy; it symbolizes the sugary death of the For-itself (like that of the wasp which sinks into the jam and drowns in it) ...[2]

These photographs, as well as written accounts, depict and describe extrusions of ectoplasm being coaxed from mediums' ears, mouths, noses, nipples, and vaginas. These photographs are more mannered than staged, the medium often in an apparent state of paralysis or ecstasy. Nearly a century later there is a tendency to read these images as pure artifice, humorous in their earnest portrayal of an experience through a medium that is no longer as convincing as it once was.

Artist Mike Kelley, in his essay "On the Aesthetics of Ufology," ties the unconvincing nature of these photographs to their mannered quality:

> The fact that these photographs strike us as funny reveals the fact that such overt sexual connotations are incompatible with spiritualist

imagery, that the "sexualizing" of an image is a form of defilement. On the other hand, our present problem with ectoplasm photographs could simply be that the displays of ecstasy depicted in them strike us as too mannered to be believable at this time—that they are not convincingly erotic. If it weren't for that fact, perhaps such imagery could maintain its transcendental value despite its sexual overtones. I prefer this second interpretation; if it is true, then my desire for erotic depictions of blob monsters is a possibility.[3]

Kelley goes on to connect his sexualized interpretation of these photographs as retrospectively foundational for the conceit of the "money shot" in pornography. In Kelley's words:

An amusing result of the rise of the money shot in pornography is the result it has had on the reading of earlier "spiritualist" photography, specifically the genre of photograph that depicts the medium exuding "ectoplasm," a white substance that is said to flow from the orifices of a medium in a trance. A photo of the medium Mary M., taken in Winnipeg in 1929, shows the cotton-like material caught in the female medium's hair, and pouring from her ears, nose, and down her chin onto her chest. Her eyes are rolled up in the ecstatic pose familiar from pornographic photos from the same period, a gesture that seems derived from ecstatic countenances found in Christian religious imagery. Another photograph depicts the material running from between the medium's legs into a heap on her

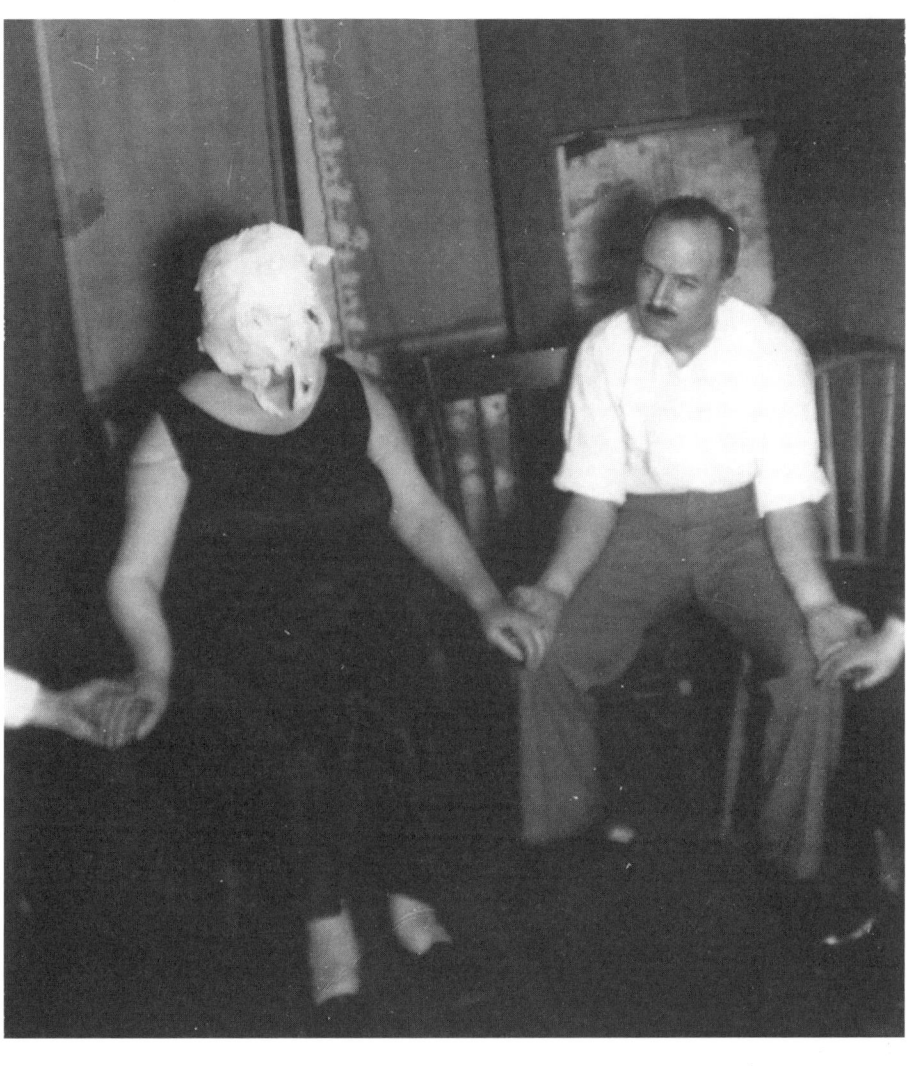

1932   35

feet. The sexual connotations of such imagery is so obvious that it could not be produced now without it looking like it was designed specifically to reference the money shot, a pornographic trope that was not even present in pornographic photography of the Twenties.[4]

Spiritualist photography indeed bears more than a passing resemblance to concurrent pornographic photography. The viscerality of these ectoplasm photographs has not so much to do with the ectoplasm itself, which reads more as membrane than viscous. Rather the origin of the extrusion of ectoplasm establishes a particular corporeal territory for the conceptualization of slime as well as a potent kinesthetic sympathy in the viewer because of the transgressive idea of one's body acting as a conduit for something unseen. ¶

NOTES

1. Marina Warner, "Ethereal Body: The Quest for Ectoplasm: Seeing is believing," *Cabinet*, Issue 12 / The Enemy / Fall/Winter 2003.

2. Jean-Paul Sartre, *Being and Nothingness: An Essay on Phenomenological Ontology*, trans. Hazel E. Barnes. 1943 (New York: Washington Square Press, 1956), p. 772.

3. Mike Kelley, "On the Aesthetics of Ufology." *Blastitude*, #13 (August 1997), blastitude.com. Accessed November 9, 2020.

4. Ibid.

There is early precedent within the zeitgeist of science fiction wherein explorers traveling to distant and often cold places encounter varied horrors, some of which are slimy. The roots of this theme derive from H.P. Lovecraft's "At the Mountains of Madness" that was published in 1936 in three serialized installments in *Astounding Stories of Super Science*. "At the Mountains of Madness" contains memorably hyperbolic, sensorially vivid descriptions of Shoggoth creatures discovered by the central characters while on a geologic expedition to an unexplored part of Antarctica:

> They were normally shapeless entities composed of a viscous jelly which looked like an agglutination of bubbles, and each averaged about fifteen feet in diameter when a sphere. They had, however, a constantly shifting shape and volume—throwing out temporary developments or forming apparent organs of sight, hearing, and speech in imitation of their masters, either spontaneously or according to suggestion.[1]

One can imagine an early reader going over these lines again and again in an effort to piece together an image of what is being described, the individual elements themselves difficult to imagine let alone the creatures' overall form. Aside from the Shoggoth's themselves who the reader is told were created for servitude by their tentacled "masters," Lovecraft also describes in detail the Shoggoth's geronticidal decapitation and slimy engulfing of their creators:

> And now, when Danforth and I saw the freshly glistening and reflectively iridescent black slime which clung thickly to those headless bodies and stank obscenely with that new, unknown odor whose cause only a diseased fancy could envisage—clung to those bodies and sparkled less voluminously on a smooth part of the accursedly resculptured wall in a series of grouped dots—we understood the quality of cosmic fear to its uttermost depths.[2]

True to the genre and comic-like form of publications such as Astounding Stories and Weird Tales, highlights from Lovecraft's stories were illustrated to accompany the published texts, and a fantastic full-color illustration of "At the Mountains of Madness" was featured on the cover of the first of the three issues in which the story was published. The issue's artist Howard V. Brown rendered Lovecraft's creature as ghostly translucent and green. The "normally shapeless" Shoggoths and their slimy, "accursedly resculptured" victims from "At the Mountains of Madness" belong to a larger shared fictional world of Lovecraft referred to as the "Cthulhu Mythos" in reference to an earlier story by the prolifically imaginative author where the creature Cthulhu is described as combining an "octopus, a dragon, and a human caricature…. A pulpy, tentacled head surmounted a grotesque and scaly body with rudimentary wings."

Careful to differentiate her own orbiting of these terms from Lovecraft's "misogynist racial-

At the Mountains

by H. P. Lovecraft   of Madness

The effect of the monstrous sight was indescribable! Some fiendish violation of natural law!

1936

Howard V. Brown, Illustration for "At the Mountains of Madness: Part 2," H.P. Lovecraft, *Astounding Stories of Super Science*. Street and Smith Publications, Inc. March, 1936.

nightmare monster Cthulhu (note spelling difference),"[3] Donna Haraway employs "tentacular" as an open taxonomy as well as a reference to networks of multiplicitous identities. Haraway's "Chthulucene" is a non-geochronic anti-Anthropocene characterized by disrupted categories of desire and interdependence of humans and animals rather than resource extraction and "ongoing terran finitude."[4] "'My' Chthulucene, even burdened with its problematic Greek-ish tendrils, entangles myriad temporalities and spatialities and myriad intra-active entities-in-assemblages—including the more-than-human, other-than-human, inhuman, and human-as-humus."[5] Whereas Haraway moves toward the slimy,[6] Lovecraft's characters are repelled.

The narrative unfolding in "At the Mountains of Madness" is as focused on the shape of consciousness as on descriptions of creatures and encounters. The story's explorers are in uncharted Antarctic territory making observations of incomprehensible specimens whose location in the ancient stratum are out of sync with geologic timelines: "Fabulously early date of evolution, preceding even simplest Archaean protozoa hitherto known, baffles all conjecture as to origin. Complete specimens have such uncanny resemblance to certain creatures of primal myth that suggestion of ancient existence outside Antarctica becomes inevitable."[7]

The progression of details in "At the Mountains of Madness" correlate to an archaeological, geological methodology of exploration and discovery, easing the viewer toward an experience of horror that is structured by scientific inquiry arriving at an impasse.[8] The story culminates in an escape and a warning to future expeditions to steer clear, the nonknowledge of the scene prioritized over fully apprehending what has occurred. ¶

NOTES

1. H.P. Lovecraft, *At the Mountains of Madness: And Other Tales of Terror*, 1936 (New York: Ballantine Books/Del Rey Books/ Random House, Inc., 1964), p. 69.

2. Ibid. p. 99.

3. Donna Haraway; "Anthropocene, Capitalocene, Plantationocene, Chthulucene: Making Kin." *Environmental Humanities*, May 1, 2015; 6 (1): 159–165. Haraway's "Chthulucene" is etymologically tied to "Chthonian" Greek subterranean/underworld deities, whereas Lovecraft's "Cthulhu" is a satiric, rhetorical misspelling.

4. Donna Haraway, "Tentacular Thinking: Anthropocene, Capitalocene, Chthulucene". (2016) e-flux 75. Paul Virilio fleshes out the synthesized violence of speed and weapons in The Speed of Politics.

5. Donna Haraway; "Anthropocene, Capitalocene, Plantationocene, Chthulucene: Making Kin." *Environmental Humanities*, May 1, 2015; 6 (1): 159–165.

6. Donna Haraway, "Tentacular Thinking: Anthropocene, Capitalocene, Chthulucene". (2016) e-flux 75 Although Haraway does not use the word "slimy," the wordplay in her tentacular list alludes to many of the qualities one might describe as slimy: "The tentacular are not disembodied figures; they are cnidarians, spiders, fingery beings like humans and raccoons, squid, jellyfish, neural extravaganzas, fibrous entities, flagellated beings, myofibril braids, matted and felted microbial and fungal tangles, probing creepers, swelling roots, reaching and climbing tendrilled ones."

7. H.P. Lovecraft, *At the Mountains of Madness: And Other Tales of Terror*, 1936 (New York: Ballantine Books/Del Rey Books/ Random House, Inc., 1964), p. 22.

8. Jean-Paul Sartre, *Being and Nothingness: An Essay on Phenomenological Ontology*, trans. Hazel E. Barnes. 1943 (New York: Washington Square Press, 1956), p. 610. "But the slimy offers a horrible image; it is horrible in itself for a consciousness to become slimy."

I worried about her flinching. Besides spoiling the
shot, this would mean hours of delay while Alice took
a shower, got a whole new make-up job, a hairdo, and
was fitted for duplicate clothes outfit.[1]

–Buster Keaton

NOTES

1.   Buster Keaton, *My Wonderful World of Slapstick*, (New York:
      Doubleday, 1960). p. 254. Buster Keaton describing his experience
      throwing a pie in the face of actress Alice Faye on the set of the
      1939 film Hollywood *Cavalcade*. Within the vernacular of film
      production, the "money shot" is the shot which is most expensive
      and technically challenging to capture.
2.   Giorgio Agamben, "The Face," *Means Without End*, University of
      Minnesota Press, Theory Out of Bounds v. 20, London, 2000. p. 96.

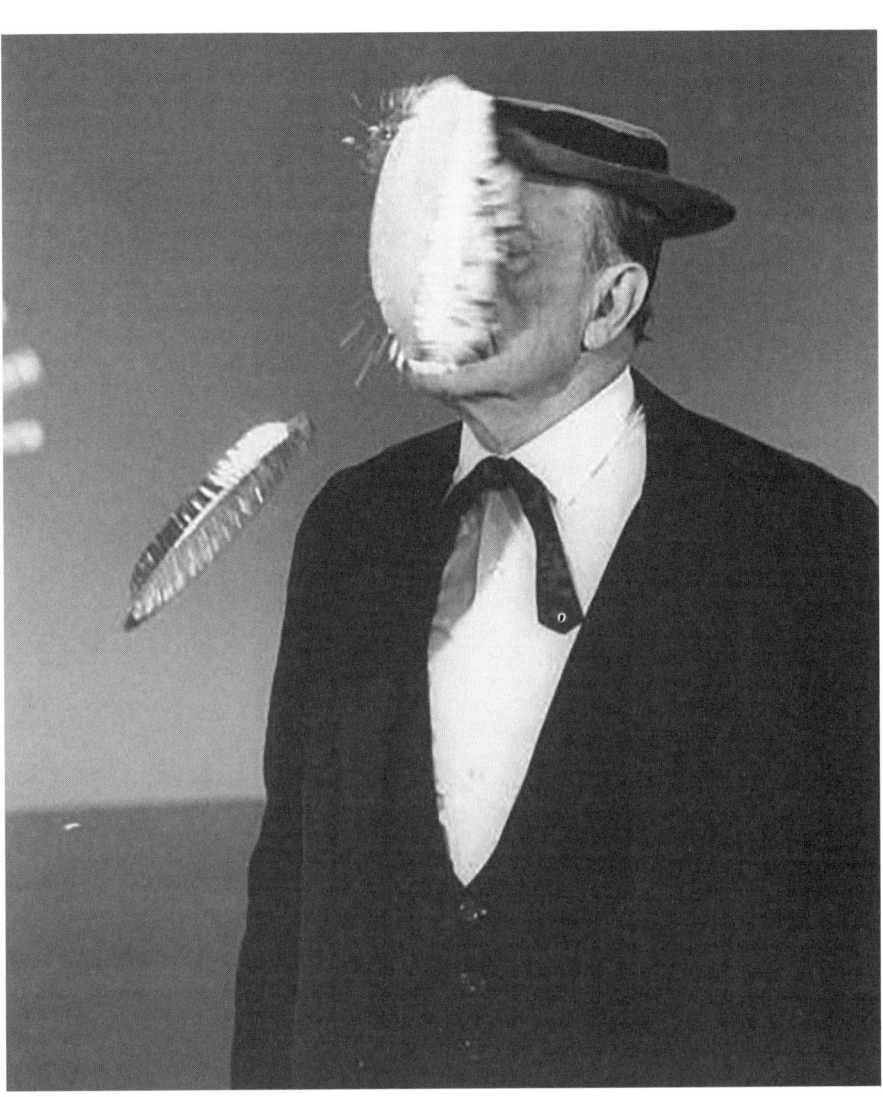

Buster Keaton rehearsing a skit for the Salute to Stan Laurel TV show. 1965. In reference to his default deadpan facial expression, Keaton was ofte referred to as a "sad clown," his face in a sense "always suspended on the edge of an abyss."[2] His neutralized expression already belying a state of meta-tragicomedy, the obfuscation of this same face with a pie is at once a highly mannered comedic gesture and a satirical anti-communicative act.

1939

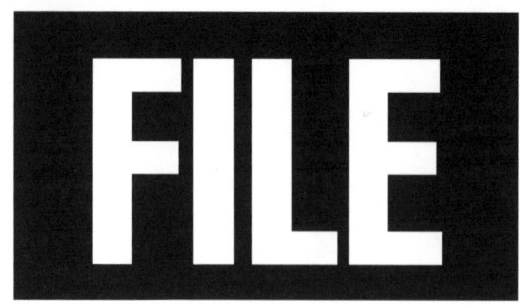

1942

1949

"Colonel James Marshall established the Manhattan Project on the 18th floor of an office building at 270 Broadway in Manhattan in June of 1942. The Army Corps of Engineers worked out of it, and New York City was peppered with physics laboratories, including a major one at Columbia University. Much of the United States' stockpile of uranium ore was in the city in warehouses or on docks, arriving from the Belgian Congo. This Army establishment was called the 'Manhattan Engineer District' after its location."[1] An abundant source of concentrated energy, uranium in its enriched form as uranium-235 is the only naturally occurring fissile isotope, which makes it widely used in nuclear power plants and nuclear weapons. Energy abundant aspiration and its intersection with a fear of nuclear annihilation lodge themselves firmly in the global zeitgeist following the discovery and development of nuclear fission technology. Nuclear fear is a fear of being molecularly reconstituted and reduced to slime. ¶

NOTES

1.   Gordon McDonough, Science Evangelist. "How did the 'Manhattan Project' get its name?" 2017. Bradbury Science Museum, Los Alamos, New Mexico. lanl.gov.

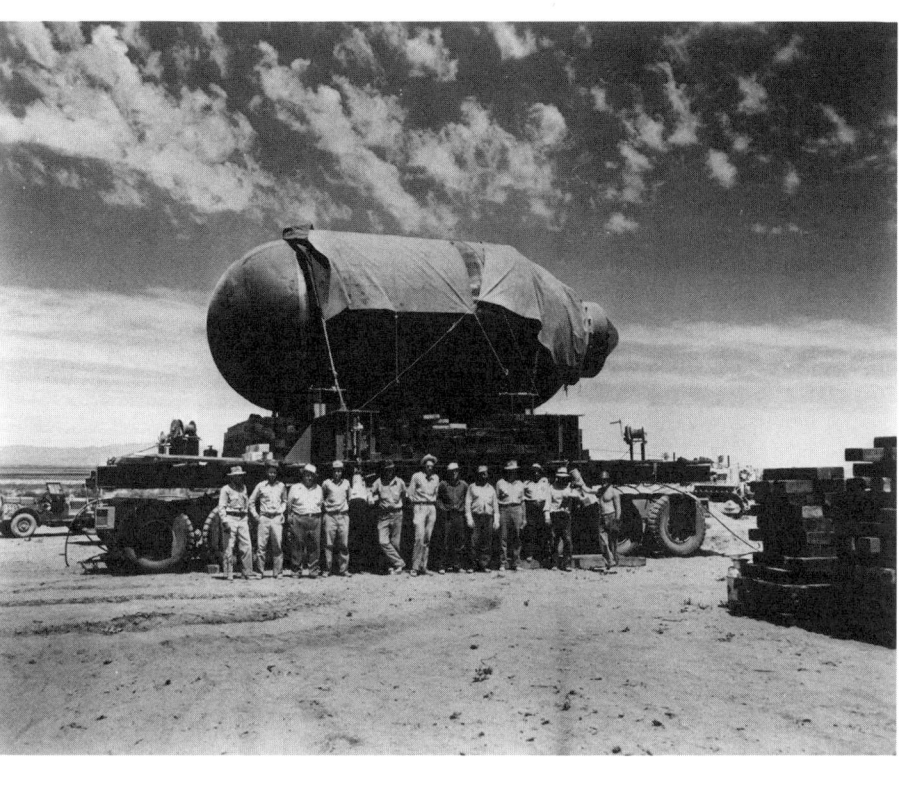

A Manhattan Project team poses with "Jumbo" or "Big Brother" prior to its detonation on July 16, 1945 in Alamagordo, New Mexico. This detonation marked the first controlled atomic explosion and began the atomic age.

1942

In Dr. Seuss' 1949 story *Bartholomew and the
Oobleck*, a king becomes bored with the predict-
ability of the seasons and their respective forms
of weather. The king expresses a desire to create
a new type of weather irrespective of the current
season, an impulsive expression of desire to effect
nature. The king's ambition lies beyond his magis-
terial power, and so he orders a group of wizards to
conjure something new. Arriving from a tower, the
wizards succeed in fulfilling the king's request after
a period of chanting in an unidentifiable language
reminiscent of mediumship psycho-babble, formalized as an incantation in couplets. The chanting
itself precurses the impending weather ooze in its
formlessness, neither articulating nor disambiguat-
ing. The new weather doesn't begin instantaneously,
but begins the following morning as a subtle, almost
imperceptible sprinkling. As a contemporary illustration of this detail we might point to the recently
observed presence of microplastics in our air and
atmosphere, indoor and outdoor, detected even in
France's Pyrenees Mountains.[1]

"Oobleck" continues to fall from the sky becoming
incrementally more disruptive and eventually over-
comes the entire kingdom, thwarting every effort of
the king's young page to alert the community. Once
all of the townspeople and castle staff have been
inundated with oobleck—the bell tower muted, the
trumpeter gooped, everyone stuck—the page is at
last able to implore the king to decry his arrogance

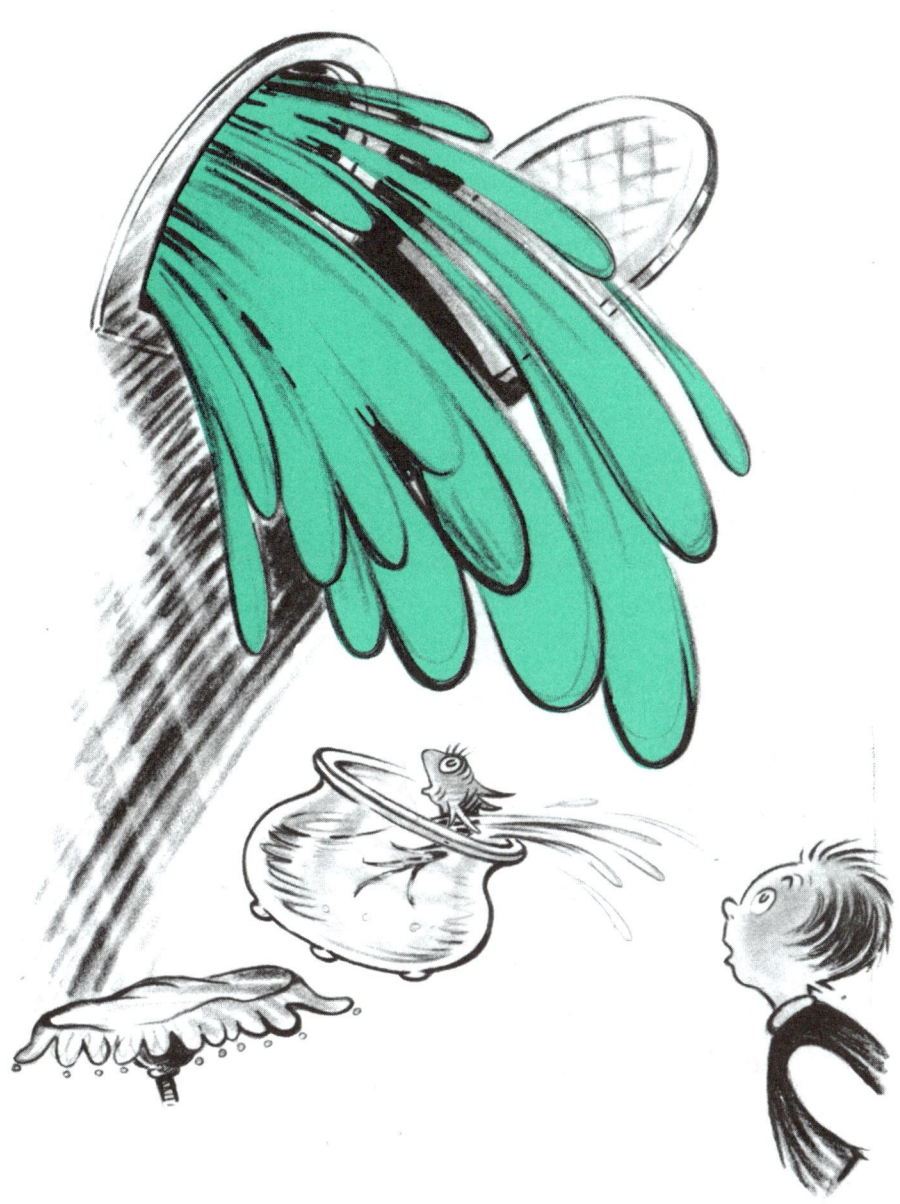

Theodor Geisel (Dr. Seuss), *Bartholomew and the Oobleck*, 1949.

1949

aloud by yelling, "Oh, Bartholomew, I'm awfully, *awfully* sorry!"[2] immediately after which the oobleck dissipates and everything returns to normal. This parable-like story reads like an illustrated interpretation of Sartre's highly characterized description of slime's effect, "The For-Itself is suddenly compromised. I open my hands, I want to let go of the slimy, and it sticks to me, it draws me, it sucks at me."[3]

In light of the current urgency surrounding conversations about climate change, this story reads like a harbinger, as our current global climate situation is recharacterizing a new meteorological[4] reality. Though not ordered by a king, our climate is being driven by a "droit du seigneur" of late capitalism. An at-hand illustration of this is the nebulous emission of container ships, just one of which operating 100k-ish horsepower low grade bunker fuel engines emits as much CO_2 per year as 50k automobiles. Says James Corbett, professor of marine policy at the University of Delaware, "Ship pollution affects the health of communities in coastal and inland regions around the world, yet pollution from ships remains one of the least regulated parts of our global transportation system."[5]

Seuss' introduction of oobleck is multifaceted, cementing existing ontological associations, and forward thinking in its representation of slime as vibrant green. The story is visually chromatic, progressive, and cumulative in its use of green, this single color increasingly axiomatic in its visual predominance. In this way, Seuss' story spills over into the realm of the production of the book itself, the offset press incrementally applying green to each page during the printing process, which is itself an expression of an industrial and ideological moment. One could flip through the book without reading anything and glean from its aesthetic dimension alone a cumulative progression of interruptive green amorphousness. ¶

NOTES

1. Christopher Joyce, "Microplastic Found Even In The Air In France's Pyrenees Mountains." *Environment*. npr.org. April 15, 2019. "Surprisingly high amounts of microplastic are raining down on a remote and seemingly pristine part of France's Pyrenees Mountains, according to scientists who say such particles could potentially be floating everywhere."

2. Dr. Seuss, *Bartholomew and the Oobleck*, 1949 (New York: Random House, 1976.) p. 43.

3. Jean-Paul Sartre, *Being and Nothingness: An Essay on Phenomenological Ontology*, trans. Hazel E. Barnes. 1943 (New York: Washington Square Press, 1956), pp. 610-12.

4. Jean Baudrillard, *Screened Out* (London/New York: Verso, 2002), p. 86. Baudrillard recasts the uncertainty principle as a generally applicable "meteorological" condition where he writes, "This erratic situation, this lack of moorings and generalized uncertainty, is shifting all facts, events and their interpretation into a phase or stage we might term *meteorological*. Yet this is no longer the stage of the natural unpredictability of the elements, of wind and weather, but of a secondary undecidability, arising from the very perfection of calculations and information."

5. John Vidal, "Health risks of shipping pollution have been 'underestimated,'" *theguardian.com*, February 12, 2008.

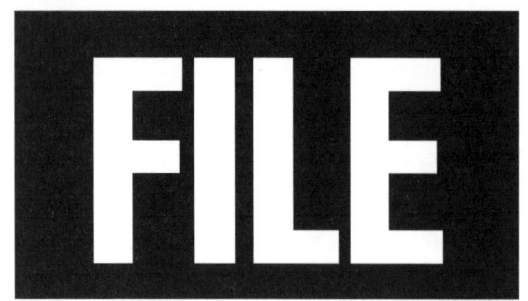

1955

1957

1958

Standing in my living room discussing this project with my friend Itza, she quickly scanned my bookshelves and took down a copy of Nabokov's *Loilita*. She flipped through the book and stopped to read aloud, "I catch myself thinking today that our long journey had only defiled with a sinuous trail of slime the lovely, trustful, dreamy, enormous country that by then, in retrospect, was no more to us than a collection of dog-eared maps, ruined tour books, old tires, and her sobs in the night—every night, every night— the moment I feigned sleep."[1] In a later exchange Itza shares that "the inability to 'fix' Lolita on a plane (literally a map) is frustrating for Professor Humbert Humbert."[2] It is not only the recurring road trips but also the unfixity and slippery adolescence of Lolita herself that propels the text. The, "sinuous trail of slime" ostensibly left upon the road is perhaps viscous residue of what HH later describes as an "eternal alchemy of asphalt and rubber and metal and stone."[3]–the price tag of petroleum based road trip Americana an unretractable jinx.

In her recent *Slime: A Natural History* Susanne Wedlich notes that "snails leave molecular messages for potential mating partners in their trails–which might just as well attract hungry predators."[4] Although HH is the designated driver, Lolita may well be the one leaving the trail of slime. Throughout the novel HH attempts to circumscribe Lolita within his journals, ruminations, locations, beach towels, and photographs—a Cartesian urge to constantly

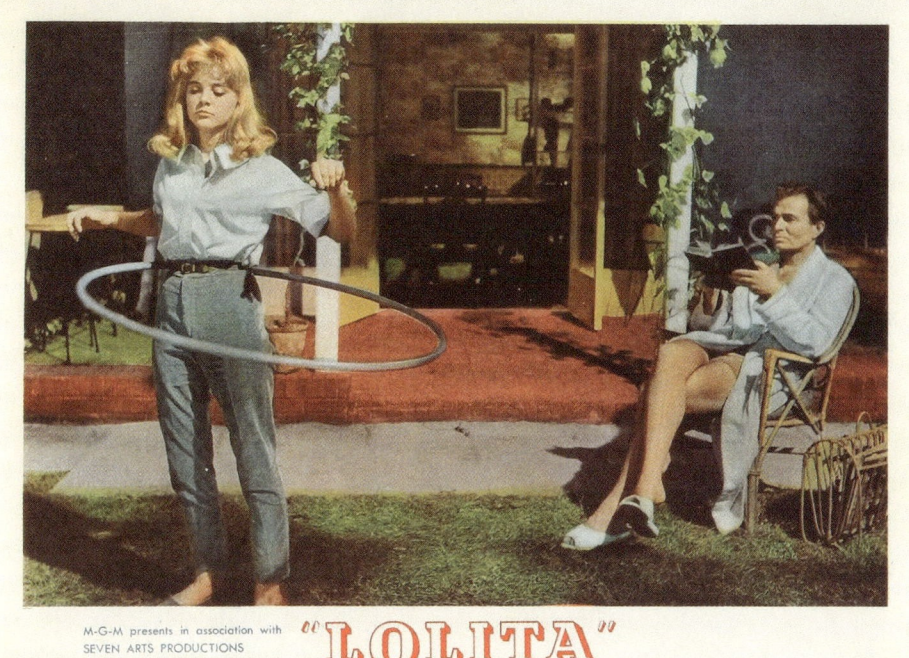

Promotional image for *Lolita*. Directed by Stanley Kubrick. Metro-Goldwyn-Mayer, 1962.

1955

site Lolita. Somewhere else in the book, while watching Lolita play tennis, the professor ruefully exclaims, "Idiot, triple idiot! I could have filmed her! I would have had her now with me, before my eyes, in the projection room of my pain and despair!"[5] While fantasizing a scenario to gain legal guardianship of Lolita, HH imagines drowning her mother - whom he has just recently married - while swimming in the middle of a lake, pressing her into the lake bottom's "inky ooze."[6]

Generationally speaking, Lolita is both bobby soxer and baby boomer, the progenitor of a newly anointed teenage demographic's eclectic and fickle desires.
In the gay town of Lepingville I bought her four books of comics, a box of candy, a box of sanitary pads, two cokes, a manicure set, a travel clock with a luminous dial, a ring with a real topaz, a tennis racket, roller skates with white high shoes, field glasses, a portable radio set, chewing gum, a transparent raincoat, sunglasses, some more garments—swooners, shorts, all kinds of summer frocks.[7]

This advantaged generation is known for their disposable income and abundant opportunity, their resource extraction habits triggering irreversible ecological effects. The popular image of Lolita is a cinematic one.[8] She sucks on a lollipop, wears heart-shaped sunglasses and red lipstick-glossy signifiers of consumer trends with youthful targets and mass production, film itself notwithstanding. Industrial adoption of plastic in particular accelerated and amplified cheaply produced and affordably acquired vestimentary postiche consumer trends. In 1957 Roland Barthes wrote that, "Plastic has climbed down, it is a household material. It is the first magical substance which consents to be prosaic."[9] Ten years later in Mike Nichol's film *The Graduate* plastic is conveyed to still retain a novel speculative status when young Braddock's father's friend offers the unsolicited life advice, "I've got one word for you, Benjamin: plastics."

In *Lolita* we experience a world of symbolic order characterized by fluidity of intratextual memories, movements, and descriptions. HH ruminates, "How vividly I recalled Lolita, just before our departure from Beardsley, prone on the parlor rug, studying tour books and maps, and marking laps and stops with her lipstick!"[10] Here again Lolita leaves her mark on the grid. ¶

NOTES

1. Vladimir Nabakov, *Lolita*, 1955 (New York: Vintage, 1997), p. 231. Itza Vilaboy. Personal Communication. December 9, 2021.
2. Vladimir Nabakov, *Lolita*, 1955 (New York: Vintage, 1997), p. 88.
3. Susanne Wedlich, *Slime: A Natural History*, trans. Ayça Türkoğlu. 2021 (First published in German as *Das Buch vom Schleim* in 2019), (London: Granta, 2021) p. 52.
4. Vladimir Nabakov, *Lolita*, 1955 (New York: Vintage, 1997), pp. 175-176.
5. Ibid., p. 87. "And when some twenty minutes later the two puppets steadily growing arrived in a rowboat, one half newly painted, poor Mrs. Humbert Humbert, the victim of a cramp or coronary occlusion, or both, would be standing on her head in the inky ooze, some thirty feet below the smiling surface of Hourglass Lake."
6. Ibid., pp. 141-142.
7. Lolita is fixed on the plane of the screen in film adaptations of Nabakov's novel by Stanley Kubrick in 1962 and then by Adrian Lyne 1997.
8. Barthes, Roland, "Plastic," *Mythologies*, 1957 (HarperCollins, 2000), p. 98.
9. Vladimir Nabakov, *Lolita*, 1955 (New York: Vintage, 1997), p. 248.

Operation Plumbbob was a series of 29 nuclear tests conducted by the U.S. Military between May 28 and October 7, 1957 at the Nevada Test Site. Midcentury tests such as these evidence the intensification of an international arms race driven by scientific research aligned with militaristic and political goals. Nuclear research is not initially focused on clean energy, sustainability, or ecosystem health. In tests such as these, aside from the speed, power, and reach of fission explosions, "what resulted on the ground below was something never seen before anywhere on Earth. The desert sand melted under the incredible heat, creating a radioactive, green-colored glass known today as trinitite."[1] The result not of blast wave pressure, but of "sand which was drawn up inside the nuclear explosion itself, and then rained down in liquid form... as beautiful, intricate, and interesting as trinitite is, the greatest hope of citizens all over the world is that nothing like it ever gets created again."[2] ¶

NOTES

1.   Ethan Siegel, "This Is How Humanity's First Nuclear Explosion Created A New, Radioactive Mineral," *Forbes*; Starts With A Bang, Nov 22, 2018.
2.   Ibid.

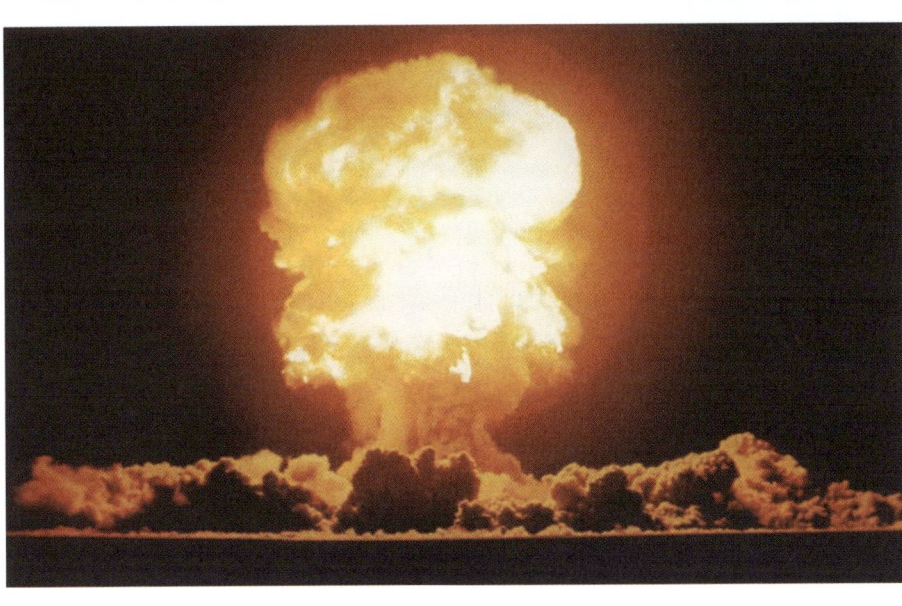

Operation Plumbbob, Fizeau, 1957. The cloud from Fizeau, the 19th nuclear shot of the summer 1957 test series begins its ascent to a height of about 40,000 feet. The shot was fired at 9:45 am from a 500-foot tower in Yucca Flat, Nevada.

1957

The Blob, directed by Irvin Yeaworth and Russell Doughten was released in the fall of 1958 and stars Steve McQueen in his first leading role. The film's absurd title aptly describes its villain, an amorphous mass from outer space that fatally absorbs every living thing it comes into contact with. *The Blob* fulfills the tried-and-true cumulative tension of a three-act horror film structure with a few outstandingly prophetic moments. The blob arrives from outer space, as though whatever is happening globally at the time the film was released was not frightening enough, and then begins its ambling terror.

Yeaworth and Doughten's blob is Sartre-esque aesthetically and existentially, reddish in this incarnation, and inaugurates an extraterrestrial origin that sets a lasting precedent for later representations of the slimy in popular culture. The meteor is a figurative missile, deflecting public cold war paranoia into the realm of science fiction. The blob consumes the farmer who discovers it, a mechanic, a janitor, a group of inebriated bar patrons, and then continues on through the town eventually oozing from the projection booth of a movie theatre into a terrified crowd below. "To touch the slimy is to risk being dissolved in sliminess."[1] The moment of red gush through the projection booth windows is a filmic moment that touches on techniques and tropes that are borrowed from and clumsily innovate cinematic lexicon. During the theater scene, the blob transgresses in two important ways, breaking the fourth wall of the cinema patrons as well as threatening to transgress the frame of the film itself in true close-up fashion. As film theorist Philippe Dubois has written, a subject in close-up is "threatening to transgress its frame, to burst the screen in order to invade the space of the spectator."[2] This scene vividly references the blood gushing elevator scene from Stanley Kubrick's 1980 interpretation of Stephen King's *The Shining*. Kubrick's scene is a phantasmagoric hallucination, whereas the blob is neither phantasm nor poltergeist, but pure movie monster. The reddishness of the blob relates it to human viscera, a flesh-hungry organ turned inside out.

The blob finally chases a group of people into a nearby diner, whereupon in desperation, the diner's owner discharges a fire extinguisher at the blob which has an immediate effect. At this reaction Steve shouts, "CO_2, Dave, CO_2!"[3] recognizing instantly that the blob is vulnerable to carbon dioxide emission of all things. The blob is further extinguished to the point of the terror-form literally freezing in its tracks. It takes just one call from local police to the military and the film's closing scene shows the blob being airdropped from a Boeing C-17 Globemaster into the arctic where its terror is halted, "Yeah, as long as the arctic stays cold," says Steve in the film's closing line. "End" appears in cloud like typography superimposed over this final scene—parachute tethered frozen blob. The letters then morph into two horizontal clouds that join, curve, and contour into a large question mark. Aside from its retrospective irony, the confidence that the blob would be permanently sequestered to an indefinitely frozen arctic is a

Lovecraftian final twist, and moreover indicative of the collective blindness to ecosystem instability at the time of the film's release. ¶

NOTES

1. Jean-Paul Sartre, *Being and Nothingness: An Essay on Phenomenological Ontology*, trans. Hazel E. Barnes. 1943 (New York: Washington Square Press, 1956), p. 610
2. Philippe Dubois, "Le gros plan primitive," *Revue Belge du Cinéma*, nr. 10 (1984-85), pp. 11-34.
3. *The Blob*. Directed by Irvin Yeaworth and Russell Doughten. Paramount Pictures, 1958.

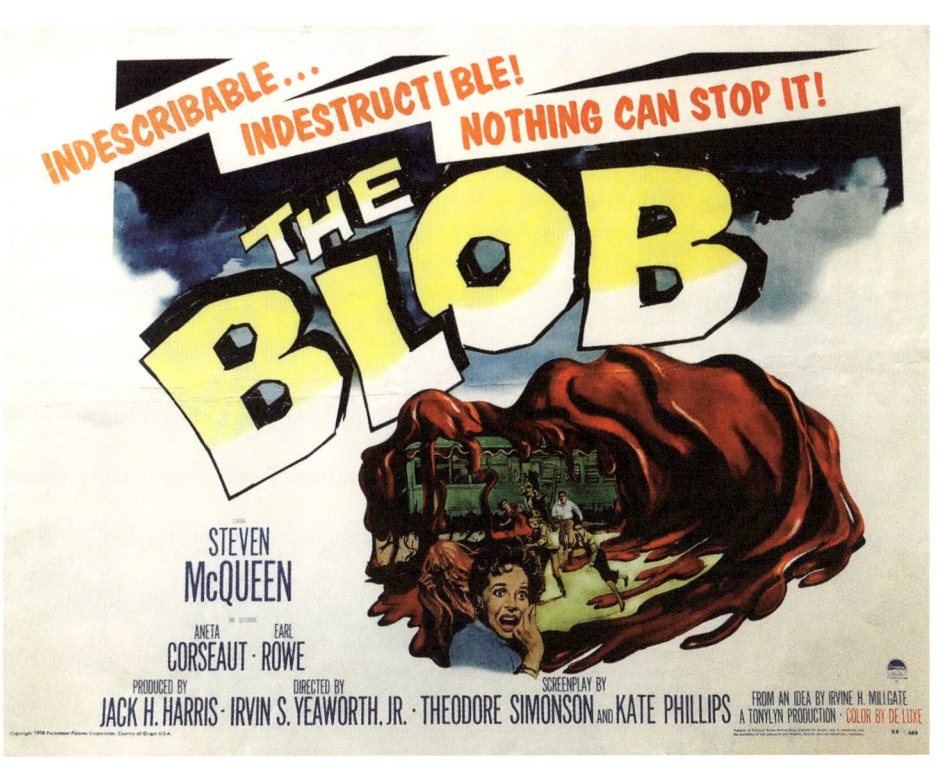

Promotional poster for *The Blob*. Directed by Irvin Yeaworth and Russell Doughten. Paramount Pictures, 1958.

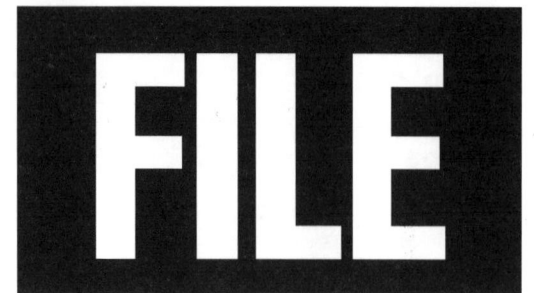

1961

1963

1964

1965

1966

1969

In 1949 the Soviet Union exploded an atomic bomb, kicking off the cold-war era nuclear arms race that extended into the 1990s. Prior to this, the United States had been developing atomic bombs beginning with the Manhattan Project in 1942, two of which were used with unimaginably devastating effect on August 6 and August 9, 1945. Along with the development of this technology grew a particular socio-cultural psychosis laden with fear of nuclear disaster. The 68th episode of the *Twilight Zone*, "The Shelter" succinctly portrayed the paranoia of this cultural moment in the opening narration:

> What you are about to watch is a nightmare. It is not meant to be prophetic. It need not happen. It's the fervent and urgent prayer of all men of good will that it never shall happen. But in this place, in this moment, it does happen. This is the *Twilight Zone*.[1]

The leaden tone-deafness of this episode, seeing as this in fact did happen in 1945 to 200,000 citizens in Hiroshima and Nagasaki at the hands of the U.S. military, highlights the preeminent arrogance of American culture. We are living in the *Twilight Zone* it seems. "The Shelter" highlights middle class differences, and in particular that the significant investment that must be made to prepare for nuclear disaster is a virtue that takes priority over recreation and leisure.

The episode takes place during a dinner party in the home of a doctor who unbeknownst to his guests has scrupulously invested his money in a nuclear bunker in the home's cellar. During the dinner party, a nuclear raid warning is publicly broadcast and pandemonium ensues. It is revealed in the panic that the doctor and his family have a subterranean refuge and when they deny all of their guests entry, but lock themselves securely inside, an ethical turmoil begins to unravel. Door pounding, tears of agony, desperation and uncertainty, pleas for help, accusations and entreaties take place through the barrier of the heavy steel door, a threshold separating the saved and the doomed, the viewer allowed a bilocational vantage point. The episode is an unconvincing infomercial for bomb shelters as the warning is ultimately canceled in the closing minutes of the episode, only after irreparable interpersonal damage has been done to all parties involved through their reactions to the situation. Nuclear disaster may have been averted, but social bonds and contracts have been battered. Rod Serling appears as he does once again at the end to offer that, "No moral, no message, no prophetic tract, just a simple statement of fact: for civilization to survive, the human race has to remain civilized. Tonight's very small exercise in logic from the *Twilight Zone*."[2] ¶

NOTES

1. "The Shelter," Season 3, Episode 68, *The Twilight Zone*, Directed by Lamont Johnson, Created by Rod Serling. CBS, September 29, 1961.
2. Ibid.

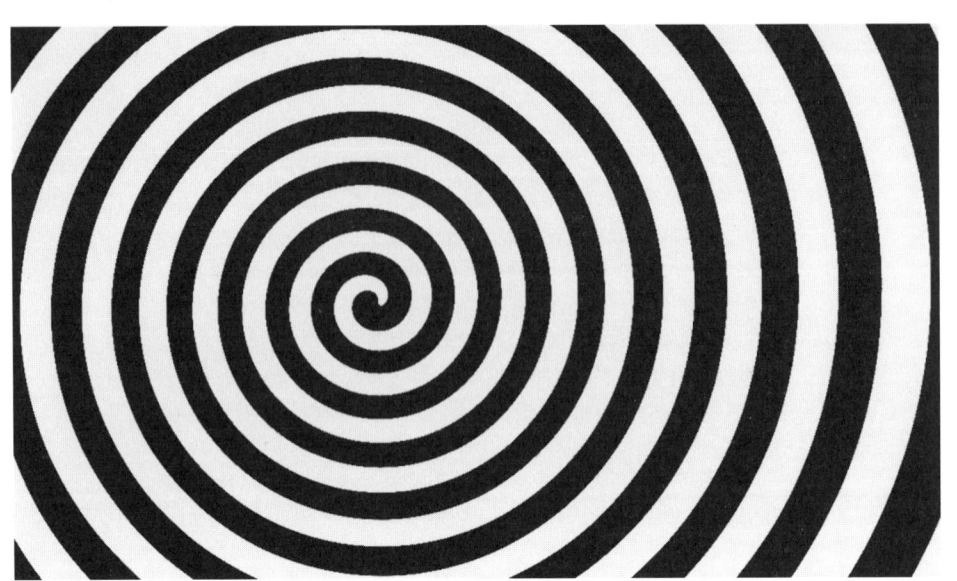

Film still from *The Twilight Zone* opening graphic. Created by Rod Serling. CBS, 1959–1964.

1961

The lava lamp was invented in 1963 by entrepreneur Edward Craven Walker. Political activist and clown Wavy Gravy has said of the iconic lamp, "It causes synapses in your brain to loosen up."[1] Initially marketed as an executive office lighting fixture, the visually lysergic quality of the percolating lamps appealed more to hippie youth culture consumers. The domestic presence of a lava lamp facilitates a visual experience that brushes against the psychedelic without the commitment entailed in ingesting LSD or psilocybin mushrooms. ¶

NOTES

1. Tucker, Abigail, "The History of the Lava Lamp," *Smithsonian Magazine*, March, 2013.

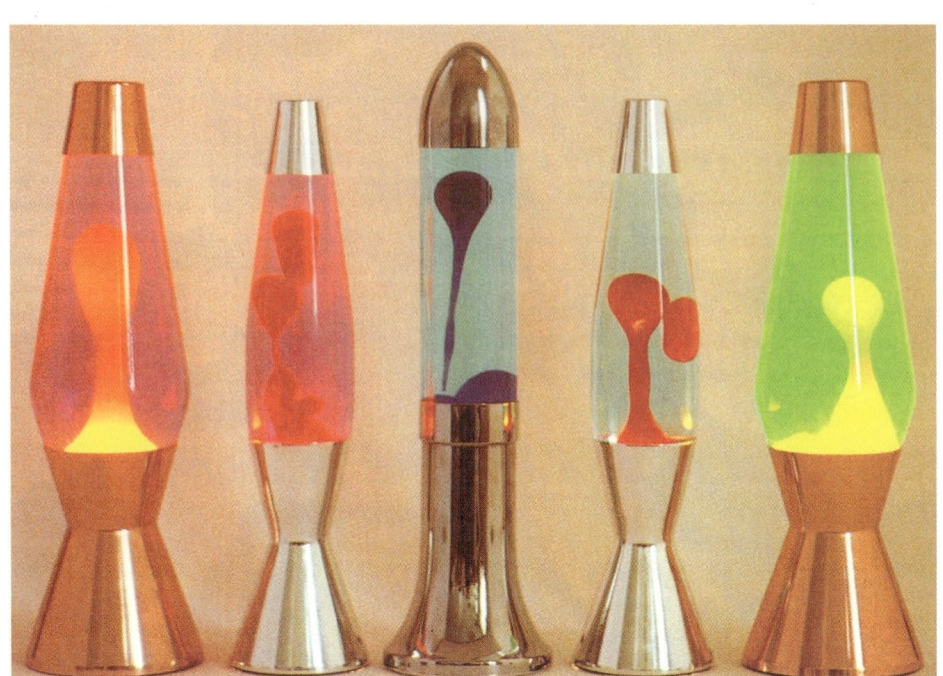

1963

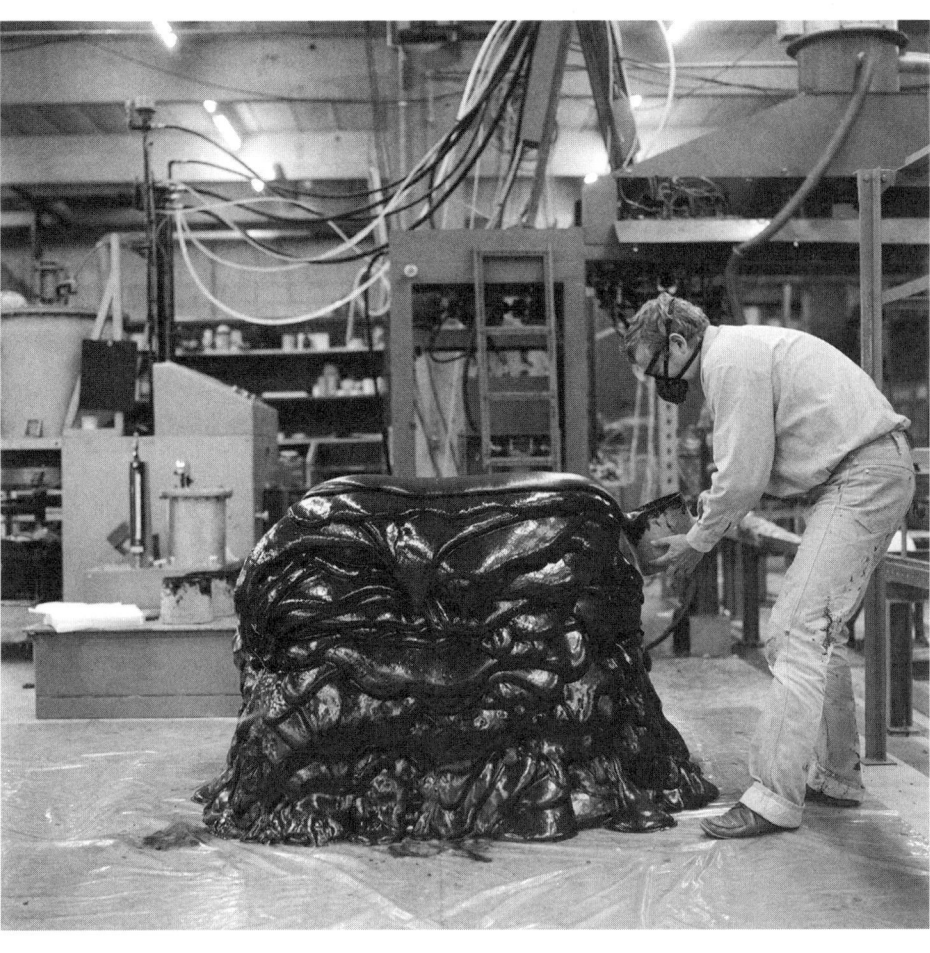

Gunnar Aagaard Andersen, *Portrait of My Mother's Chesterfield*, Dansk Polyether Industri, Denmark, Poured polyurethane, 29 ½ × 44 ¼ × 35 ¼ inches, 1964.

1964

In 1965, Topps Trading Cards released Ugly Stickers designed by Basil Wolverton, Wally Wood, and Norman Saunders. The complete set of 44 stickers, each printed in several name variations, were sold through 1978. The term "gross" generally describes the acerbic visual quality of the stickers. *L.A. Weekly* art critic Doug Harvey has written of Wolverton's work that it "has an exhilarating singularity of focus that comes close to inducing nausea".[1] Wolverton's aesthetic influence can be seen in the works of R. Crumb and the underground comix movement generally, where figures are oozily morphed and slimily rendered, physically and psychologically exaggerated. ¶

NOTES

1.   Doug Harvey, *The Original Art of Basil Wolverton*, Last Gasp & Grand Central Press, 2015.

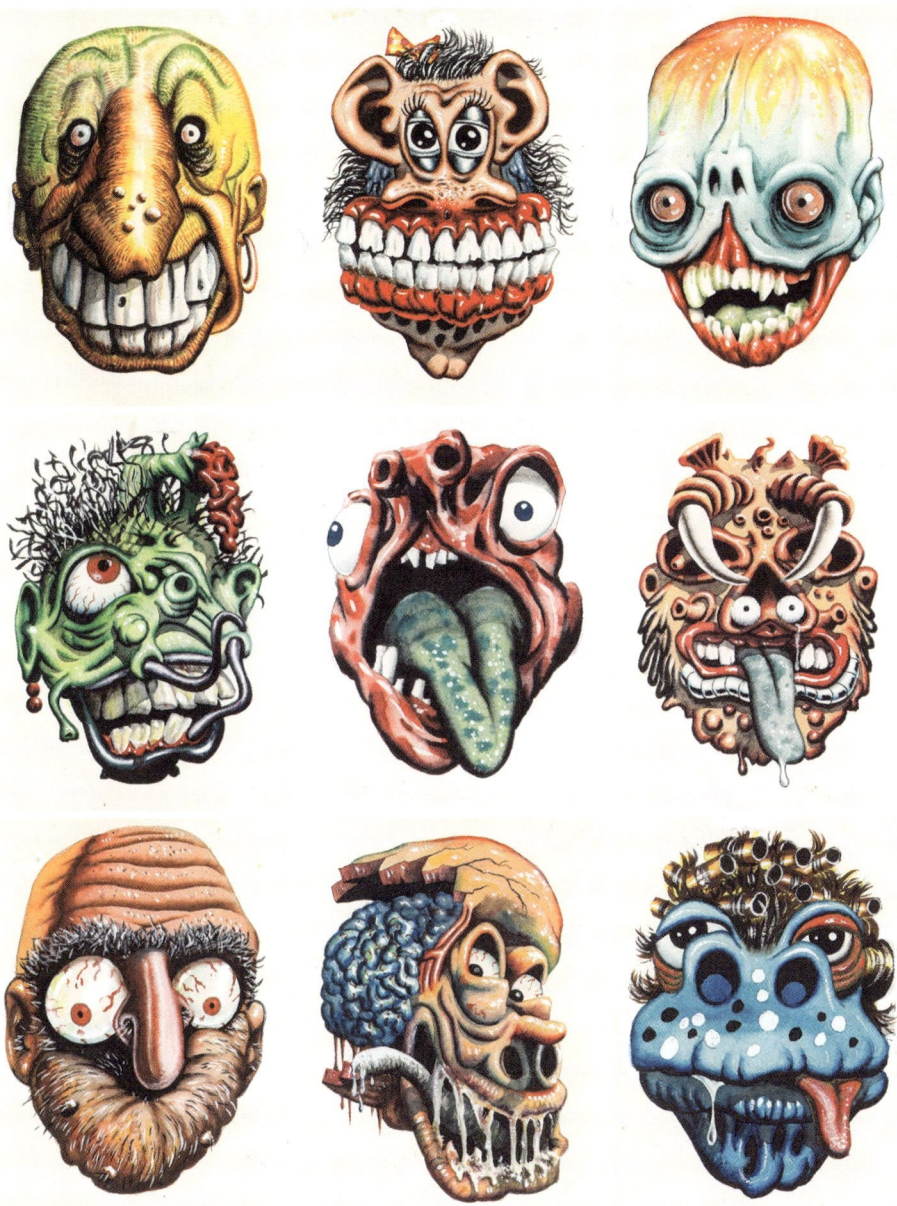

Basil Wolverton and Norman Saunders, Ugly Stickers, 1965, Topps Trading Cards.

1965

Mike Kelley makes a point in his analysis of Jean-Paul Sartre via anthropologist Mary Douglas that slimy byproducts of boundary crossing are ontologically confusing and context specific in their abjection. Moreover, Kelley's characterization of boundary crossing is not strictly corporeal but more broadly a "definition and framework.":

The anthropologist Mary Douglas makes a point somewhat similar to Sartre's, in that she points out that filthiness is not a quality in itself but is a byproduct of a boundary disruption. However, notions of boundary operate here on several levels. She states, "Matter issuing from them [the orifices of the body] is marginal stuff of the most obvious kind. Spittle, blood, milk, urine, feces or tears by simply issuing forth have traversed the boundary of the body."[1] The problematic nature of these materials is not so much their phenomenological qualities (as Sartre would say of the slimy) but that they are confusing materials, being both part of you and separate from you. This is similar to Sartre's slime, that provokes an ontological crisis in its clinging insistence that it is part of you when it obviously is not. But following on her statement regarding materials issued by the body, Douglas makes a second point, "The mistake is to treat bodily margins in isolation from all other margins."[2] This notion of boundary is less specifically ontological and more one of definition and framework—abject qualities are defined by context. A simple example would be—dirt in the house is bad, dirt in the garden is good. This notion of boundary is less all-encompassing than Sartre's phenomenological approach and allows for argument about proper usage and definition of boundaries.[3] ¶

NOTES

1. Mary Douglas, *Purity and Danger: An Analysis of the Concepts of Pollution and Taboo*, (London and New York, Routledge, 1966), p. 122.
2. Ibid., p. 122
3. Mike Kelley, "On the Aesthetics of Ufology," *Blastitude*, #13 (August 1997), blastitude.com. Accessed November 9, 2020.

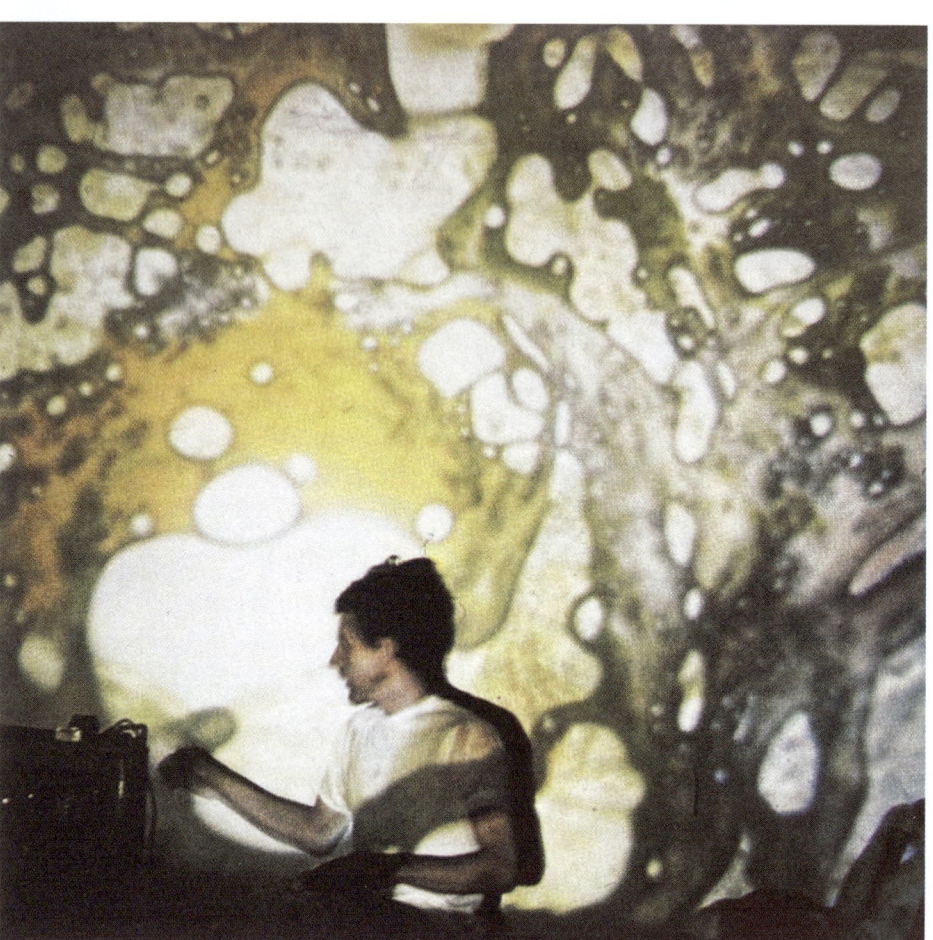

Boyle in the first performance of *Bodily Fluids and Functions* with Aldis projection of stained catarrh, Bluecoats Art Center, Liverpool, 1966.

1966

The liquidy drippy trippy aesthetics of the 1960s are inextricably associated with the use of magic mushrooms and LSD, both of which involve the ingestion of chemicals that bond with serotonin receptors in the brain. The sympathetic nervous system is stimulated by psilocybin and lysergic acid diethylamide, causing a rise in blood-sugar, increased body temperature, and dilated pupils. The body confuses these chemicals for serotonin and sends them to the brain's synaptic cleft with dramatic effect. The barriers between the visual cortex and information carrying regions are broken down, which leads to complex hallucinations.

During the 1960s, artists and musicians in particular established a popularized association of expanded consciousness and uninhibited creative expression with the use of psychedelics, and the visual ephemera that was produced in tandem introduced a psychedelic visual style that soberly represented a lysergic state of mind. Non-Western spiritual practices and their respective aesthetic traditions, especially Hindu yantra and tantra motifs and Tibetan Buddhist mandalas, were simultaneously appropriated by Western popular culture and their distinctive visual characteristics often recast as signifiers of psychedelic experience and expanded, higher consciousness.

Counterculture related graphic design and typography evolved during the 1960s toward fluidity of line and organic interlocking of formal elements to mesmerizing effect. Markedly breaking with the gridded structures underlying crisp and spaciously composed modern typography, psychedelic concert poster designers, such as Wes Wilson, began "to see lettering as a form maker as well as a content of information."[1] Psychedelic posters are distinctively packed with a congestion of letterforms that stretch, slump, and fold like the fluid inside a lava lamp. SFMOMA curator Jennifer Dunlop Fletcher has said that Wilson's posters offer a "slow leak of the information,"[2] reading slowed by the immersion of language in the viscosity of the overall composition. Psychedelic posters make visually pleasing work of discerning legible information. These concert posters became exemplary of psychedelic aesthetics. Notably the distorted and exaggerated typographic anatomy of the 1960s formally references the fluid, winding, undulating formal qualities which came about during the print-media rich period of Art Nouveau.

In his 1908 text *Abstraction and Empathy,* Wilhelm Worringer accounted for the inevitable and complex emerging discourse regarding the psychodynamics of abstraction where he asks, "what are the psychic presuppositions for the urge to abstraction?"[3] Worringer's notion of abstraction connects the individual to an experience of the "dread" and unfathomability of the world, while an empathetic engagement resolves this discord. "Whereas the precondition for the urge to empathy is a happy pantheistic relationship of confidence between man and the phenomena of the external world, the urge to abstraction is the outcome of a great inner unrest inspired in man by the phenomena of the outside world."[4] For Worringer, the advancement of humankind moves further and further away from a pre-technological, transcendental state of the immense spiritual dread of space. Albeit operating within different histories and contexts, a chemically altered state of mind, like the unique phenomenological experience of abstraction, both effect a feeling of immediacy that in some sense circumvents or eclipses reliance on or access to structured, conventional, cognitive mediation of visual experience, giving way to more purely sensorial engagement with oneself and the world.

In *Farewell to an Idea*, T.J. Clark articulates a similar sentiment regarding the revolutionary positionality of abstraction scaffolded by statements made on the subject by Kasimir Malevich. "Let me put it this way,"[5] writes Clark, "Abstract art, right from the moment of its inception in and around 1914, was haunted by a dream of painting at last leaving the realm of convention behind, and attaining immediacy." Clark goes on to characterize instances in the history of abstraction as ranging from technical pursuits to "lunges toward distant reaches of metaphysics: 'unison,' 'presentness,' pure sensation or pure plasticity, 'truth to materials,' final simplicity, 'zero,' 'infinity,' an absolute inwardness or an equally absolute exteriority; being "in" the painting, or escaping from painting altogether, or having painting be the realm of some deep unknown—'paintings the contents of which are not known to the artist' (as Malevich put it in 1915)."[6]

Signaling the desire to escape from the over prescribed conventions of painting, Mark Rothko forcefully articulated the decisive movement away from figuration toward total abstraction in 1947 when he wrote, "with us the disguise must be complete. The familiar identity of things has to be pulverised in order to destroy the finite associations with which our society increasingly enshrouds every aspect of our environment."[7] The multiform nature of abstract painting, its non-representational precondition, its absorption and displacement of the symbolic as substance or essence makes abstract paintings abstract, not about abstraction. Emboldened by the commercialization of the avant-garde by pop art, the state of painting in the 1960s nonetheless succumbed to a wholesale "repressive desublimation"[8] into the marketplace similar to that process which also engulfed the more visually conspicuous facets of global counterculture. Nevertheless, by the end of the 1960s the desire for escape from established reality is visually codified as fluid, formless, and chromatic. The popularization of the lava lamp as a desktop version of psychedelia is repressive desublimation par excellence.

In some ways, a recurrence of Oskar Fischinger's "raumlichtkunst"[9] works from the 1930s and 1940s, an ecstatic intersection of corporeality and visual effect, can be pointed to in Mark Boyle's abstract *Son et Lumiere for Bodily Fluids and Functions* projections from the mid 1960s. Like the association of Boyle's work with psychedelia, Fischinger referred to his own work as a kind of intoxication. Created as live audio-visual performances involving micro-projectors and contact microphones, Mark Boyle's lysergic visual effects were the result of bodily expulsions. "The process of obtaining the fluid was especially awful. Taking an emetic hadn't worked in Liverpool and Bristol, so we had resorted to cruder means."[10] Describing the use of bacon fat to induce onstage vomiting, Boyle went on:

> ...as I started to retch and heave I could hear the sound of my retching and heaving

enormously amplified throughout the theatre. The sound was so awful that it made me retch and heave even more. A number of people left the theater running. At the end we put the fluid in the microprojector, it was so beautiful, silver globes floating in a sea of gold. There was a great ovation.[11]

Boyle's projection performances benefitted from residency at London's *UFO* club, association with influential rock bands, and an avoidance of the mannered superficiality of psychedelic style. "The resulting images, often startling to the audience, and the centrality of the artists' bodies in such performances provided a corporeal counterpart to the disembodied projected imagery associated with light shows that would soon dominate the emerging rock music scene."[12] The notion of the body as a vital site of liberative gesture gained momentum in the 1960s and 1970s through performance art, actions, and happenings, many of which sought new forms and territories for personal liberation, and collective reimagination of increasingly oppressive state structures. By the 1990s, writing about painting had embraced the language of bodily viscerality. Lisa Phillips wrote of Terry Winters' paintings in a 1991 exhibition catalog, "Totally ingratiating and visceral, they are nonetheless tactile and sensual. The paint itself is a psychologically and sexually charged material. Its mucilaginous texture reeks of a sticky sexuality."[13] ¶

1.   Aaron Skirboll, "How a Psychedelic Concert Poster Rocked the World: C'mon baby light my flier," *Smithsonian Magazine*, May, 2016.

2.   Ibid.

3.   Wilhelm Worringer, *Abstraction and Empathy*, 1908, (New York: International Universities Press, 1953), p 15.

4.   Ibid.

5.   T.J. Clark, *Farewell to an Idea: Episodes from a History of Modernism*, (New Haven and London: Yale University Press, 1999), p 253.

6.   Ibid.

7.   Mark Rothko, "The Romantics were prompted", *Possibilities*, no 1, Winter 1947–48, p 84.

8.   Herbert Marcuse, *One-Dimensional Man: Studies in the Ideology of Advanced Industrial Society* (London: Routledge, 2002), p. 60. "Today's novel feature is the flattening out of the antagonism between culture and social reality through the obliteration of the oppositional, alien, and transcendent elements in the higher culture by virtue of which it constituted another dimension of reality. This liquidation of two-dimensional culture takes place not through the denial and rejection of the 'cultural values,' but through their wholesale incorporation into the established order, through their reproduction and display on a massive scale."

9.   Oskar Fischinger, "A Note About R-1" reprinted in William Moritz, *Optical Poetry*, 2004, p. 176. "An intoxication by light from a thousand sources . . . A happening of the soul, of the eyes, of the eye's waves, wave streams, Sun flowing, a level vanishing, a sudden eruption, an awakening, ceremonial, sunrising, effervescent, Star rhythms, star lustre, a singing, surf breaking over chasms, a world of illusions of movements of lights, sound and song tamed, a leaping breath, Atman [soul, ego], a wandering through clouds."

10.   J. L. Locher, "Mark Boyle's Journey to the Surface of the Earth," *Son et Lumiere for Earth, Air, Fire, and Water*, 1978.

11.   Ibid.

12.   Andrew Blauvelt, *Hippie Modernism: The Struggle for Utopia*, Walker Art Center, Cranbrook Art Museum, & Berkeley Art Museum and Pacific Film Archive, (2015). p. 202.

13.   Lisa Phillips, "The Self Similar," in *Terry Winters* (New York: Whitney Museum of American Art, 1991), p. 17.

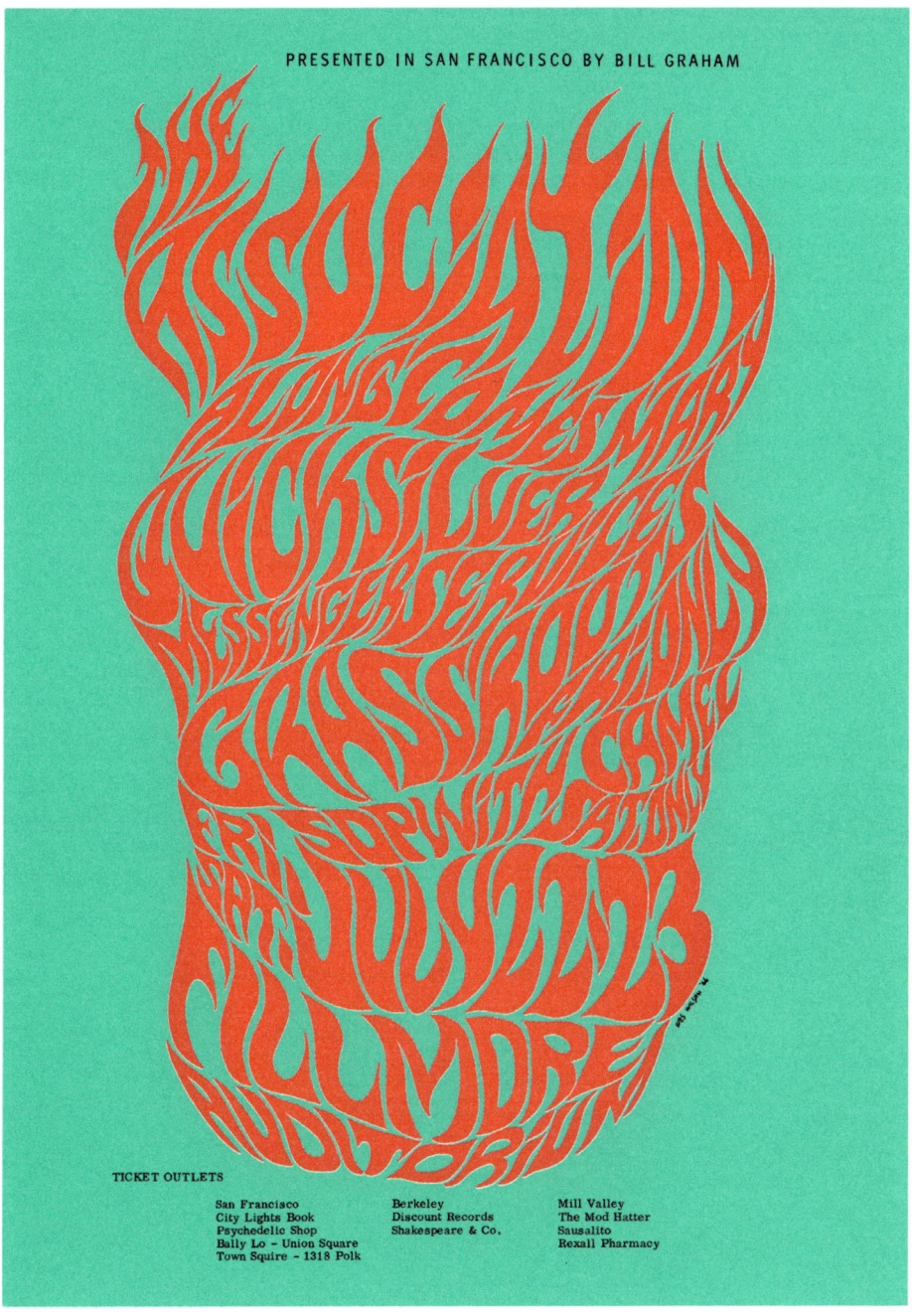

Wes Wilson, The Association, Quicksilver Messenger Service, Grassroots, Sopwith Camel; Fillmore Auditorium, July 22-23, 1966.

1966

In 1969 Robert Smithson created three entropic site-specific "flow pieces"—*Asphalt Rundown* situated in an abandoned and mundane section of a gravel and dirt quarry in Rome in October, *Concrete Pour* at an embankment for unused concrete in Chicago in November, and *Glue Pour* at an eroded dirt site in Vancouver B.C. in December. These three works are particularly illustrative of Smithson's multifaceted obsession with entropy that entangled anecdotes and ideas culled from economics, literature, architecture, engineering, and in the case of these particular works "fluvial" geology. Each of these pieces consist of carefully planned aspects as well as discrepancies in planning and execution that Smithson welcomed as a part of the process and final outcome of the works. Importantly, each of these pieces were also realized on sloped sites already worn and marred by natural and man-made erosion and effluence, sites conditioned by the type of movement Smithson then redoubled with his additional material application. These flow pieces also point to a particular skepticism that Smithson felt regarding the cultural practice of recycling as an expression of environmental consciousness, especially in relation to energy conservation. In an interview from 1973, just two weeks before his death, Smithson said:

> Now, I would like to get into an area of, let's say, the problems of waste. It seems that when one is talking about preserving the environment or conserving energy or recycling one

inevitably gets to the question of waste and I would postulate actually that waste and enjoyment are in a sense coupled. There's a certain kind of pleasure principle that comes out of preoccupation with waste. Like if we want a bigger and better car we are going to have bigger and better waster productions. So there's a kind of equation there between the enjoyment of life and waste. Probably the opposite of waste is luxury. Both waste and luxury tend to be useless. Then other's kind of middle class notion of luxury which is often called "quality." And quality is sort of based on taste and sensibility. Sartre says Genet produces neither spit or diamonds. I guess that's what I'm talking about.[1]

On one hand Smithson's flow pieces are self-reflexive representations of the consumption/waste dialectic within his own practice. The preoccupation with waste, as Smithson puts it, is bookended with the pleasure of consumption, and Smithson cites Freud's pleasure principle as a psychological driver for consumptive behavior that produces waste and is then sublimated and expressed as an impulse to recycle, instigated by Freud's reality principle, which seeks realistic and socially appropriate responses to instinctual gratification.[2]

The entropic flow of Smithson's industrial mediums encoat and appropriate their sites. Unlike Sartre's skier whose "For-Itself" cartesian movement changes the matter and meaning of snow by uniting a point of departure and a point of arrival, the aberrant "In-Itself" movement of Smithson's flow pieces indefinitely defer a point of convergence or fixed destination.

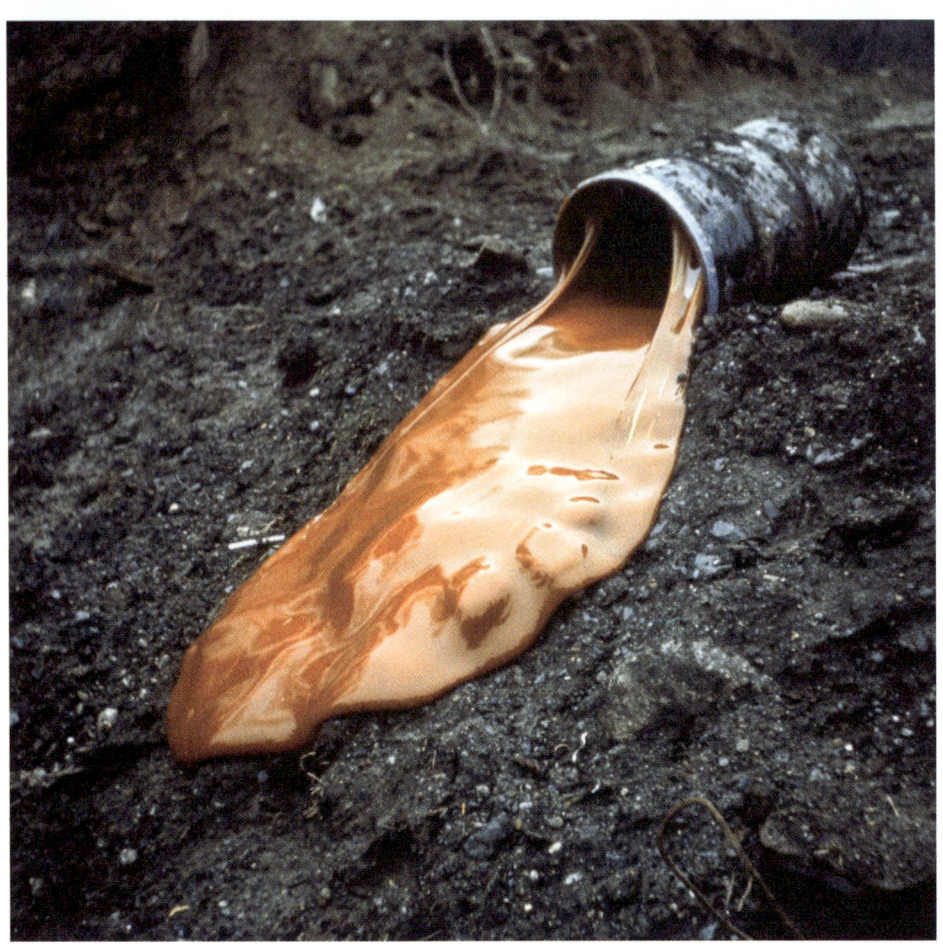

1969

In the case of [Asphalt Rundown] it sort of stops just before it hits the bottom. So in the case of the falls ... it's arrested again ...That's sort of like isolated like a petrified river ... so there you have that sense of something very definitely in time, yet the moment gives you that sense of timelessness. The actual visual experience, perception of that. And of course, out of this we just have this whole kind of domino effect of all the permutations of the notion of the flow, the fall, the downpour, and in a sense it goes a little like some of the receding nonsites. They all converge, and they're converging on a point, but the point is no longer there. The point of convergence is always being lost ... In the case of all these perspectives, you can walk around and they just destroy themselves as perspectives. The gestalt loses itself.[3]

Asphalt, concrete, and urethane glue are all at their peak state of viscosity when Smithson pours them—respectively hot, wet, and exposed to air—whereupon they simultaneously flow and begin to cure, their loss of viscosity capitulating to the incline down which they flow with decreasing speed. The gestalt loses itself, vantage points and perspective are destroyed, and the result is a kinesthetic empathy for an arrested state of flow. ¶

NOTES

1. "Entropy Made Visible" (1973) Interview with Alison Sky, *Robert Smithson: The Collected Writings*, Edited by Jack Flam, 1996, pp. 301–309.

2. Herbert Marcuse, *Eros and Civilization*: A *Philosophical Inquiry into Freud*, 1955 (Boston: Beacon Press, 1966), p. 13. "However, the psychoanalytic interpretation reveals that the reality principle enforces a change not only in the form and timing of pleasure but in its very substance. The adjustment of pleasure to the reality principle implies the subjugation and diversion of the destructive force of instinctual gratification, of its incompatibility with the established societal norms and relations, and, by that token, implies the transubstantiation of pleasure itself."

3. "Entropy Made Visible" (1973) Interview with Alison Sky, *Robert Smithson: The Collected Writings*, Edited by Jack Flam, 1996, pp. 301-309.

1969

Now permanently on display following SFMOMA's 2016 expansion, Richard Serra's *Gutter Corner Splash* had been preserved behind a false wall in one of the museum's fourth floor galleries for nearly 50 years, intermittently revealed for exhibition. Consisting of nine lengths of lead splashed into the corner where the gallery's wall meets the floor, one casting remaining in the corner, *Gutter Corner Splash* evidences the performative origin of its making in relationship to this particular space. In a 2016 *X-TRA* article, Rob Marks wrote, "*Gutter Corner Splash*, in collaboration with its wall, had been an object lesson in seeing, a disruption of the apparently smooth space-time continuum of 'history.'"[1] Marks characterizes the recurrent ontological condition of this work and its peculiar location within the museum as a "shell game" and eventually goes on to say,

> ...prior to its permanent display, *Gutter Corner Splash*, with its wall, had narrated an alternative art history ... the sculpture appeared as both past and present, vanquished and victorious, hidden and manifest, and the museum uncovered its narrative and curatorial process, exposing it not to ridicule but to inquiry.[2]

The history of séances is flush with accounts of false walls, spirit rapping, manifestation cabinets and other parlor tricks and sleights of hand all meant to shrink the communicable gap between the dead and the living, the past and the present. Spiritual sites and mystery houses decouple physical space to delay and augment immediate comprehension. The preservation of the fidelity of *Gutter Corner Splash* to its corner recasts its site in the museum as a spiritual vortex where viewers might experience more acutely a conflation of the past and the present. ¶

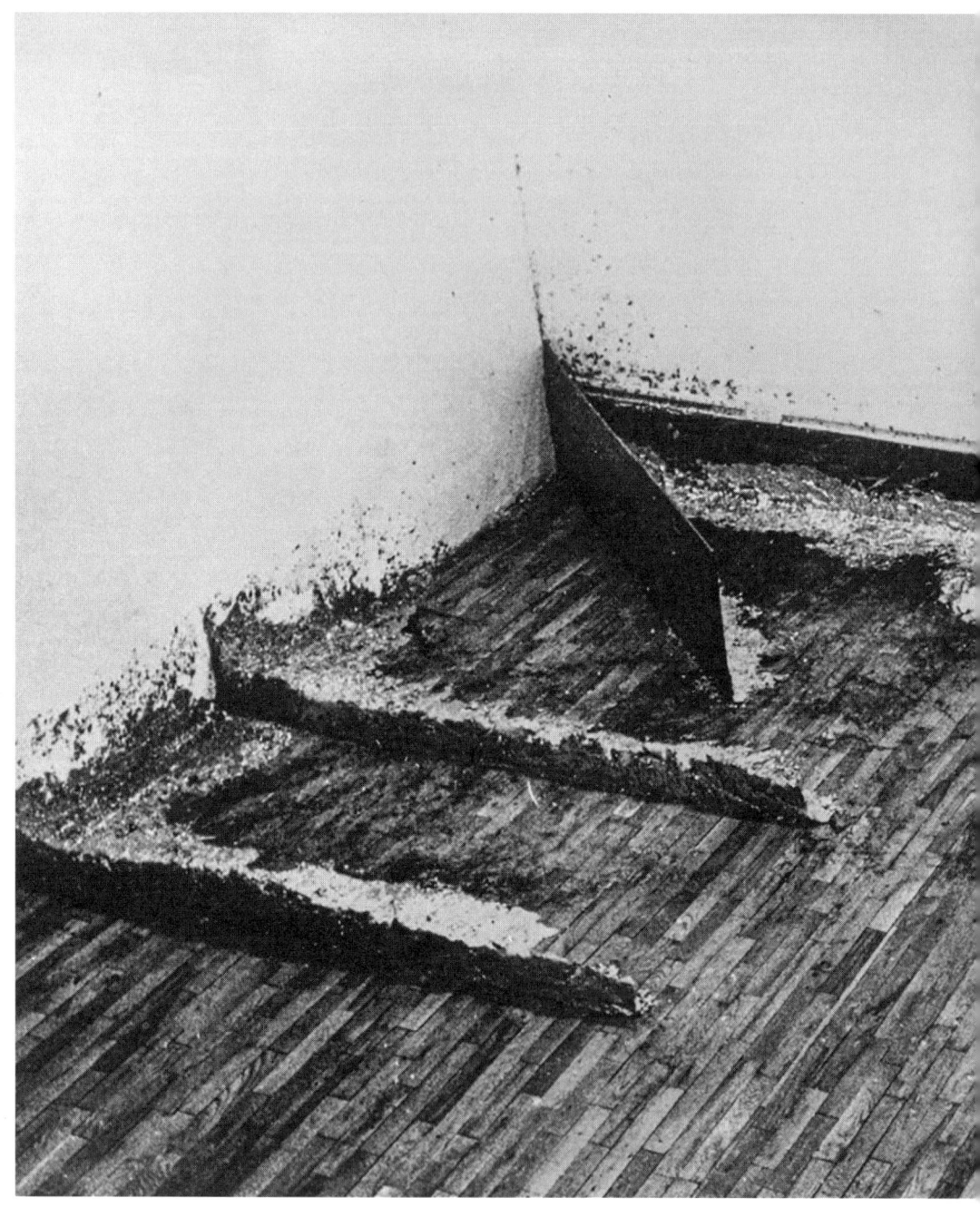

1969

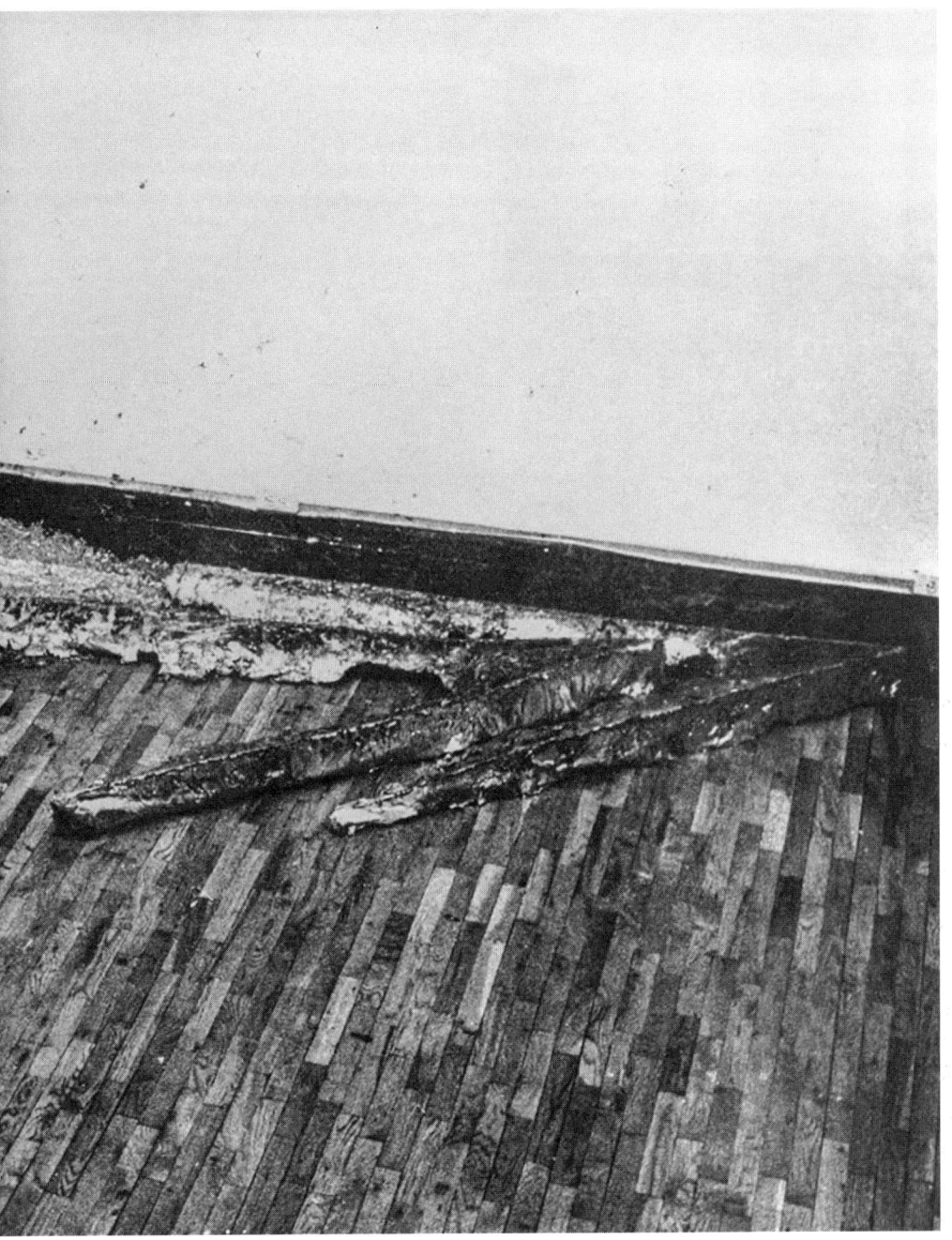

1969

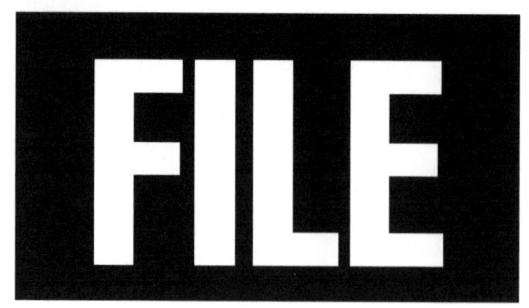

1971

1972

1974

1975

1977

1978

1979

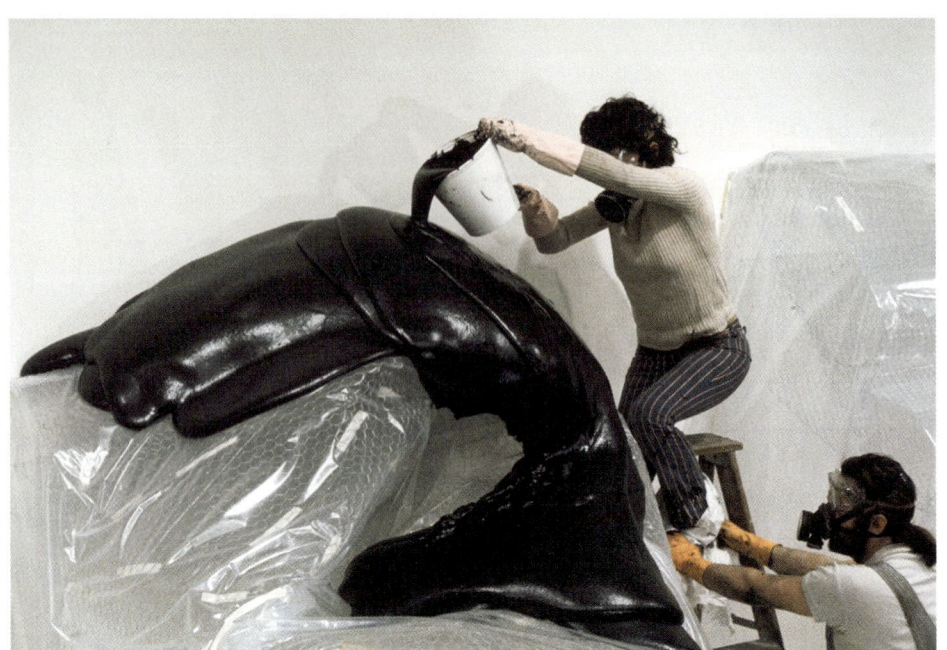

1971

Imbricated with the recalibration of material and
critical parameters of the art world of the 1970s,
Lynda Benglis' poured, multi-colored urethane floor
paintings exemplify a post-minimalist redirection
and initiated a brusque interruption of an overindul-
gence of attention to male artists. Benglis embraced
a theatricality of gesture and an approach to painting's materiality as free from the restrained tenets
of Greenbergian modernism, myths of authenticity,
and machismo in particular. Benglis' *Fallen Painting*
works from 1968 and her later *Adhesive Products*
works from 1971 pursued potential visual and symbolic dynamics beyond what had been previously
dictated by male artists at the time. Benglis' *Fallen
Painting* works explicitly play on Pollock's drip paintings in their reliance on the fluid dynamics of their
chosen materials, however, where Pollock's drips are
reducibly legible as resulting from gestural action,
Benglis' poured works obliterate their originary act,
the aberrant flow declarative of the "in-itself" agency
of urethane. In a review of a 1974 exhibition of her
knot works, Jeremy Gilbert-Rolfe wrote of Benglis'
material sensibility, "She uses materials that—as
did the plastic foam she employed in her earlier
work—suggest gesture by virtue of their own material condition. This reminds us that the art that has
sought to replace Abstract Expressionism has relo-
cated, rather than eliminated, gestural emphasis."[1]

Benglis' *Fallen Painting* pieces are amorphous and
open in their formal presence. Importantly these

works—part painting, part sculpture, part performance—were made directly on the floor without a substrate or fixed location. Multiple colors of urethane poured from five-gallon buckets were roughly choreographed along the length of the works, often in irregular stripes, sometimes pooled or mottled, like liquefied rainbows or melted sherbet. Extremely thick, noxious, viscous and relatively slow drying, Benglis' use of urethane rather than paint draws out the artist's process, and forefronts the difficult nature, irreverence, and material autonomy of this sticky medium.

Suggestive and evocative, Benglis' brightly chromatic, amorphous floor pieces interrupted the uncompromisingly male-dominated conversation surrounding minimalism and responded heavy handedly to the Pollock mythology via a pop lens. The unwieldy and distinctly industrial, unforgiving nature of urethane adhesives, whose virulent ingredients are also in pesticides and fungicides, further amplified the material discourse of Benglis' pieces to recapitulate the action of the artist and the resulting mess as polysemous. ¶

NOTES

1. Jeremy Gilbert-Rolfe, "The Clocktower," *Artforum,* March, 1974. p. 69. Gilbert-Rolfe bears down further on this point later in his review where he writes, "Benglis, in going some way toward implying that we inevitably read certain kinds of material configuration as gestural even when in fact—literally—they aren't, obliges us to reflect upon that complexity."
2. Herman W. Land, "Childrens' Television Workshop: How and Why It Works. Final Report." Nassau County Board of Cooperative Educational Services, Jericho, N.Y., National Center for Educational Technology, Washington, D.C., 1973

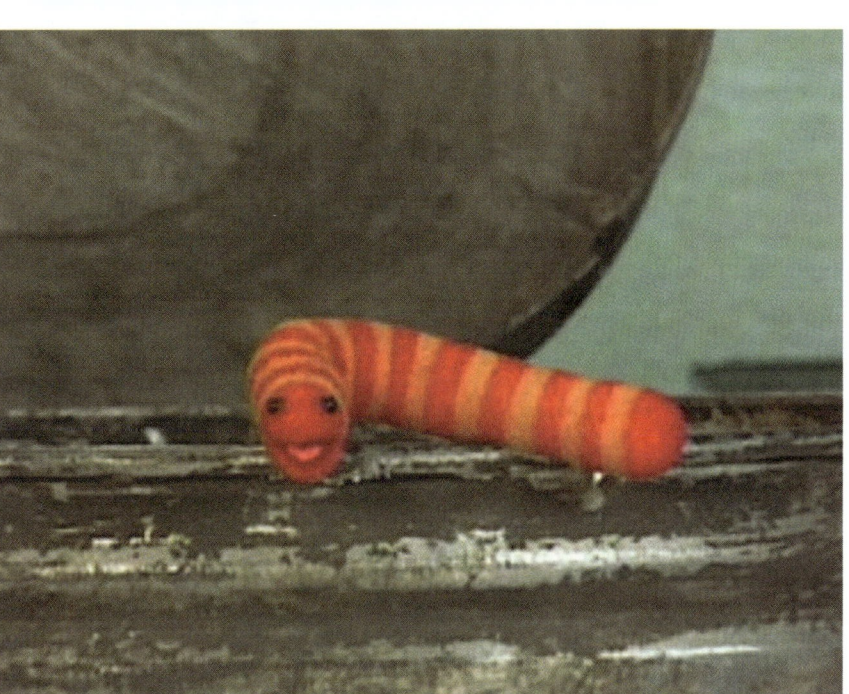

Still from *Sesame Street*, Episode 262: "Pet Show". Slimey, the worm, was introduced during a pet show skit in 1971. An educational research initiative focused on childrens' reactions to *Sesame Street* episodes from this season observed, "The children were very interested in this theme at the beginning. They were attentive, responsive, and loved Slimey, the worm. But, by the time first prize was awarded, the children were restless and inattentive."[2] Slimey was initially a silent character who communicated through movement alone, though in later episodes he speaks and eventually forms the band Earth, Rain and Mud with other worms.

1971

97

Deep Throat starring Linda Lovelace as herself, and *Behind the Green Door,* starring Marilyn Chambers as Gloria, were both released in 1972. These films made headway in establishing "porn chic" culture as well as a general audience for pornography. Both films are of the first in the genre to feature plots and character development, though the similarities don't go much farther.

Behind the Green Door was released in Cannes and is often described as having cinematic, artful pretensions, despite the regrettable abduction premise that puts the film into motion. Most notably Marilyn Chambers' cultural capital as the face of Ivory Snow detergent created a public stir, the confluence of her starring role in a pornographic film irresistibly irreconcilable with her public image as the baby-holding woman on Ivory Snow packaging and advertisements.

Deep Throat on the other hand has been described as slavish. *New Yorker* contributor Anthony Lane described *Deep Throat* as, "...numbly, grindingly, trouser-saggingly dull. If you want arousal, get in your car and drive very slowly over a speed bump."[1] Roger Ebert, in his 1973 review of *Deep Throat* wrote, "It is all very well and good for Linda Lovelace, the star of the movie, to advocate sexual freedom; but the energy she brings to her role is less awesome than discouraging. If you have to work this hard at sexual freedom, maybe it isn't worth the effort."[2]

What these two films along with others that followed do have in common is a formalization of the trope of the "money shot," "cum shot" and "facial," male climax externalized on, not in, the body of another as visual evidence for the audience of the exact moment of maximum male pleasure. Mike Kelley's tentacular[3] historiography points to early ectoplasm photography as an origin for this kind of shot in pornography[4] and one might look even further back to painted and sculpted depictions of religious ecstasy in which spirit-filled altered states of consciousness are rendered with highly mannered and expressive modes of representation. Ectoplasm photography is a specifically useful precedent however as these images depict expressions of ecstasy accompanied by the presence of a mysterious substance, evidencing contact with another, albeit phantasmic.

The climactic final scene of *Deep Throat* borrows heavily from Soviet montage theory and editing techniques developed in Russian avant-garde experimental cinema of the 1920s and 1930s. Specifically, Sergei Eisenstein's technique of "intellectual montage"[5] is applied in a rather heavy-handed fashion. Eisenstein wrote of his technique: "What then characterizes montage and, consequently, its embryo, the shot? Collision. Conflict between two neighboring fragments. Conflict. Collision."[6] *Deep Throat's* final close-up blowjob scene is rhythmically intercut with footage of a rocket launching in an increasing tempo, the cum shot itself finally montaged with clips of fireworks bursting in the night sky, establishing metaphorical association so obvious that the scene has been cited in at least one cinema studies textbook.

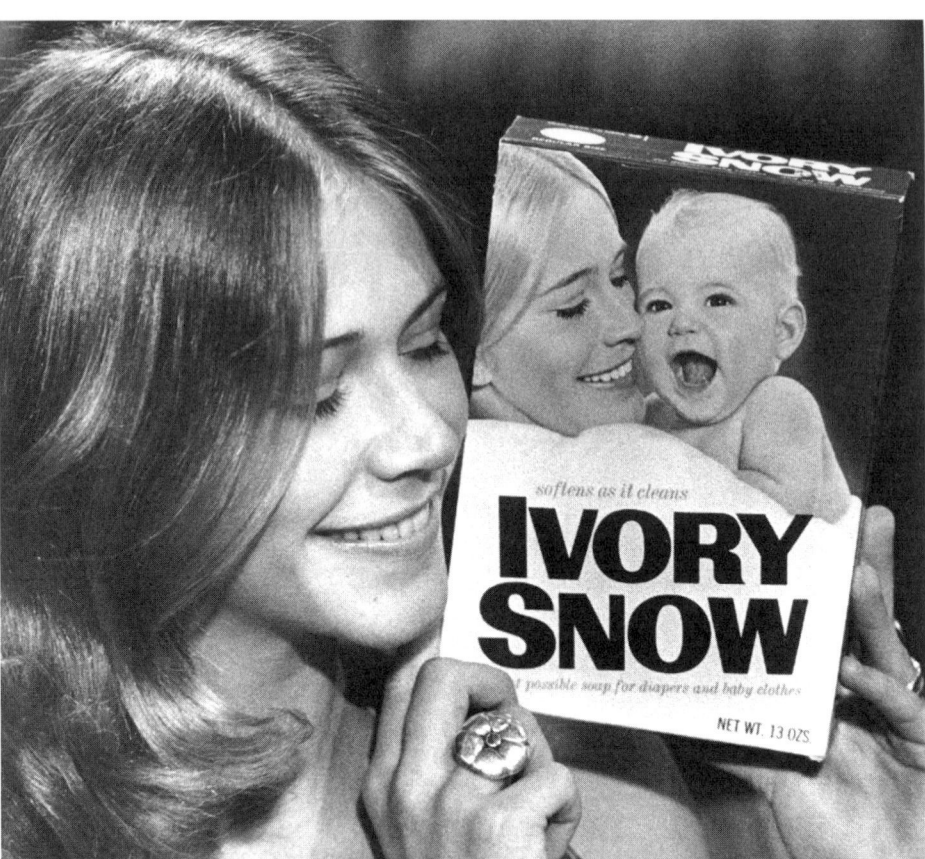

Marilyn Chambers posing with an Ivory Snow detergent box featuring an image of her holding a baby. Procter & Gamble, 1970.

1972

Likewise, the final scene in *Behind the Green Door* relies on experimental cinematics, albeit more contemporary, to capture, mirror, slow down, extend, repeat, and color saturate the money shot. In this sequence, we see Marilyn Chambers' face mirrored like a Rorschach emerging from the bottom of the screen as though in water. The color saturation is psychedelic in chromatic greens and blues, the cum shot a seemingly never-ending, slow motion spurt. Notably the money shot is visually deferred, Chambers' silhouetted face floating in the foreground uninterrupted, suggesting that two pieces of footage were superimposed using an animation technique. In her seminal work *Hard Core*, Linda Williams describes this scene with aesthetic emphasis as:

> ...a series of slow-motion money shots in extreme close-up follow one another in exaggerated heroic spurts. Gloria's face and mouth are there to welcome each. Optical printing adds stylized orange-green and red-green color effects. At the end, particles of slow-motion, optically printed ejaculate fly about the frame as if in an animated Jackson Pollock painting.[7]

Ultimately the aestheticized, misogynistic utopia of *Behind the Green Door* as well as other pornographic films of this era "fail to deal with a problem that, in the 1970s, was emerging but had not yet been articulated: namely, the unspecified desires of females who might not wish to be consumed objects and who certainly did not wish to be ravished or raped."[8]

Jacques Lacan scholar Owen Hewitson analyzes the relationship between pornography and desire

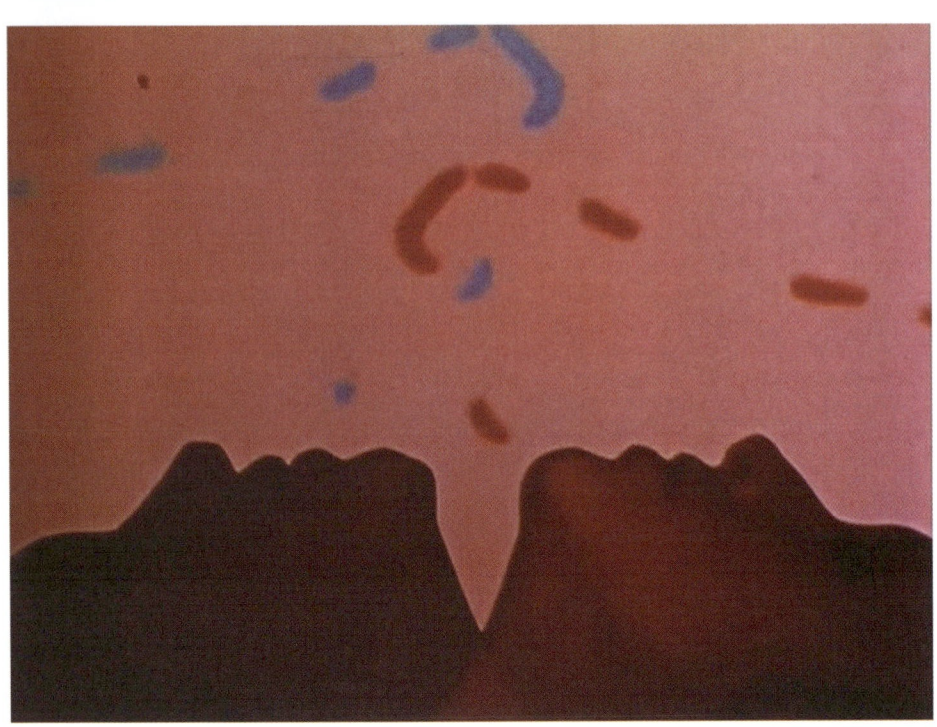

Film still from *Behind the Green Door,* directed by Artie Mitchell and Jim Mitchell, starring Marilyn Chambers, Mitchell Brothers Film Group, 1972.

1972

beginning with the rhetorical question, "When we look at a sunset, or into the eyes of our partner, or at pornography, what do we see? More precisely, what are we looking for in what we see?"[9] According to Lacan, desire is ultimately a desire for recognition as well as a desire for what we believe the Other desires.[10] Pornography like any object constellates networks of representation where we seek substitutions for our exact requirements of arousal. Williams' mention of the "unspecified desires of females" references both the nescience of desire in general, as well as the narrow scope of representation in pornographic films of the early 1970s which would quickly give way to multivalent, polysemous production, proliferation, and consumption of pornographic media. ¶

1. Anthony Lane, "Oral Values: 'Inside Deep Throat,'" *The Current Cinema*, *The New Yorker*, February 21, 2005.

2. Roger Ebert, (March 6, 1973), "Deep Throat". Rogerebert.com. Retrieved April 7, 2015.

3. Donna Haraway; "Anthropocene, Capitalocene, Plantationocene, Chthulucene: Making Kin." *Environmental Humanities*, May 1, 2015; 6 (1): 159– 165. Donna Haraway employs "tentacular" as an open taxonomy as well as a reference to networks of multiplicitous identities.

4. Mike Kelley, "On the Aesthetics of Ufology," *Blastitude,* #13 (August 1997), blastitude.com. Accessed November 9, 2020.

5. Dana B. Polan, "Eisenstein as Theorist," *Cinema Journal*, Vol. 17 No. 1, (Autumn, 1977), University of Texas Press on behalf of the Society for Cinema & Media Studies, pp. 14-29. "Eisenstein had come across the possibilities of a conceptual montage through his research into hieroglyphic and ideogrammatic language which had culminated in his belief in the possibilities of a non-diegetic metaphor which yet could comment on the diegesis. In intellectual montage the juxtaposition of two concrete images leads to an abstract concept not full contained in either of the two images. For example, the massacre of worker juxtaposed with the butchering of a cow suggested that workers were being butchered."

6. Sergei Eisenstein, "Beyond the Shot [The Cinematographic Principle and the Ideogram]," *Film Theory and Criticism*, eds. Leo Braudy and Marshall Cohen (Oxford: Oxford University Press, 2009), 19.

7. Linda Williams, *Hard Core: Power, Pleasure, and the "Frenzy of the Visible",* (University of California Press, 1999), p. 158.

8. Ibid.

9. Owen Hewitson, "Pornography and the Paradoxes of Pleasure – On the 'Identity of Perception'. *LacanOnline.com*, October 28, 2016.

10. Jacques Lacan, *Ecrits: A Selection,* trans. Bruce Fink (New York: W.W. Norton & Co, 2004.) p. 300. "For it is clear here that man's continued nescience of his desire is not so much nescience of what he demands, which may after all be isolated, as *nescience of whence he desires.*"

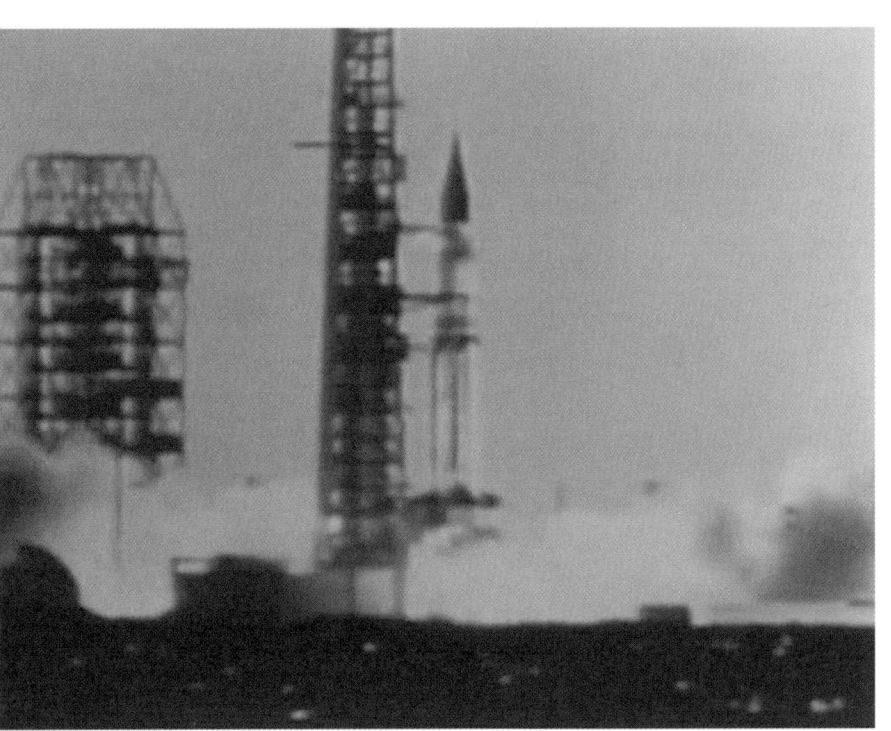

Film still from the launch of the Saturn I SA-5 during NASA's Apollo program on January 26, 1964. Clips from this footage are used in *Deep Throat* during the final montage sequence. There is no specific connection between the significance of this particular launch footage and the film in which it was used nearly a decade later. The generally phallocentric connotation of a rocket launch and the likely inexpensive availability of this footage dictated its inclusion in the *Deep Throat* montage sequence.

1972

I was studying pornography. I was really studying pornography and I really wanted something that alluded to it and mocked both sexes... I wanted it to be ambiguous enough that it couldn't be said what it was. And, so that's what I strove for–what I really tried to do.[1]

–Lynda Benglis

NOTES

1.   Richard Meyer, "Bone of Contention: Richard Meyer on Lynda Benglis' Controversial Advertisement," *Artforum*, November, 2004. Lynda Benglis speaking about her controversial 1974 *Artforum* advertisement in conversation with Richard Meyer.

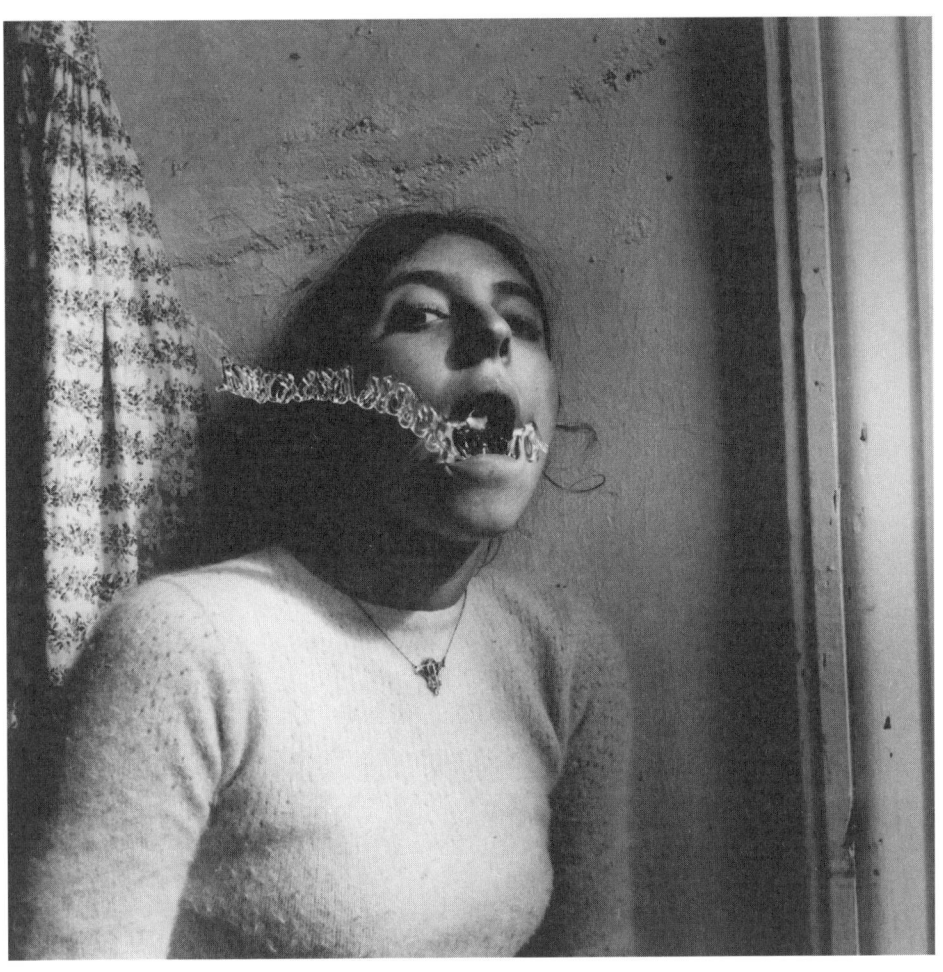

Francesca Woodman, *Self-portrait talking to Vince*, Gelatin silver print, Sheet: 8 × 10 in. (20.3 × 25.4 cm), 1975/78.

1975

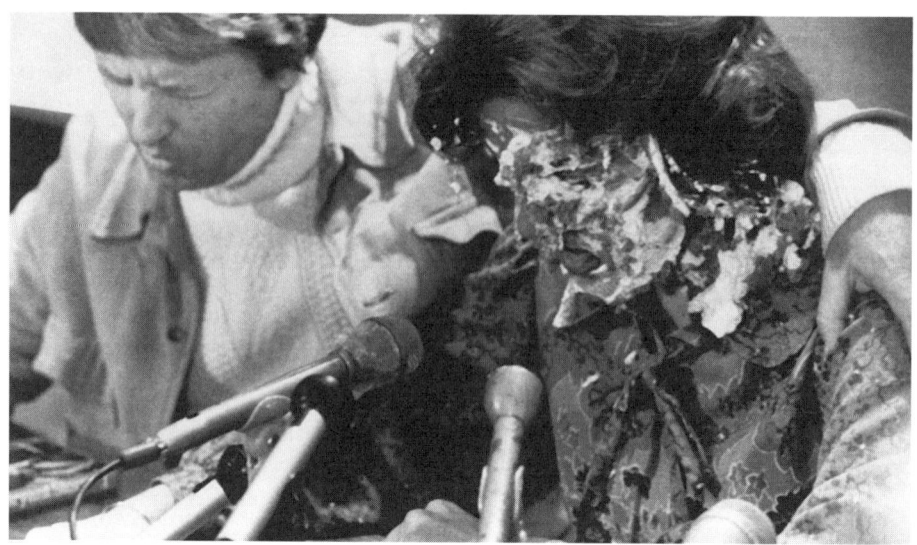

During an October 14, 1977 press conference in Des Moines, Iowa, while reporters are questioning Anita Bryant about her national crusade against homosexuals, gay rights activist Tom Higgins throws a pie in Bryant's face prompting her to pray for Higgins' salvation.

1977

The Ectoplasm series is linked to a project made in association with artist David Askevold in 1978, titled *The Poltergeist*. David and I shared an interest in the aesthetics of the occult which led us to make a series of photographic works that addressed that history. My portion of the project includes faux spiritualist photographs of a "medium" (myself) exuding the mysterious ethereal substance ectoplasm. The photos mimic the look of period spiritualist photography from the early part of the 20th century.[1]

–Mike Kelley

NOTES

1. Mike Kelley: Photographs/Sculptures, published on the occasion of the exhibition at Wako Works of Art, Tokyo, October 16 - November 28, 2009.

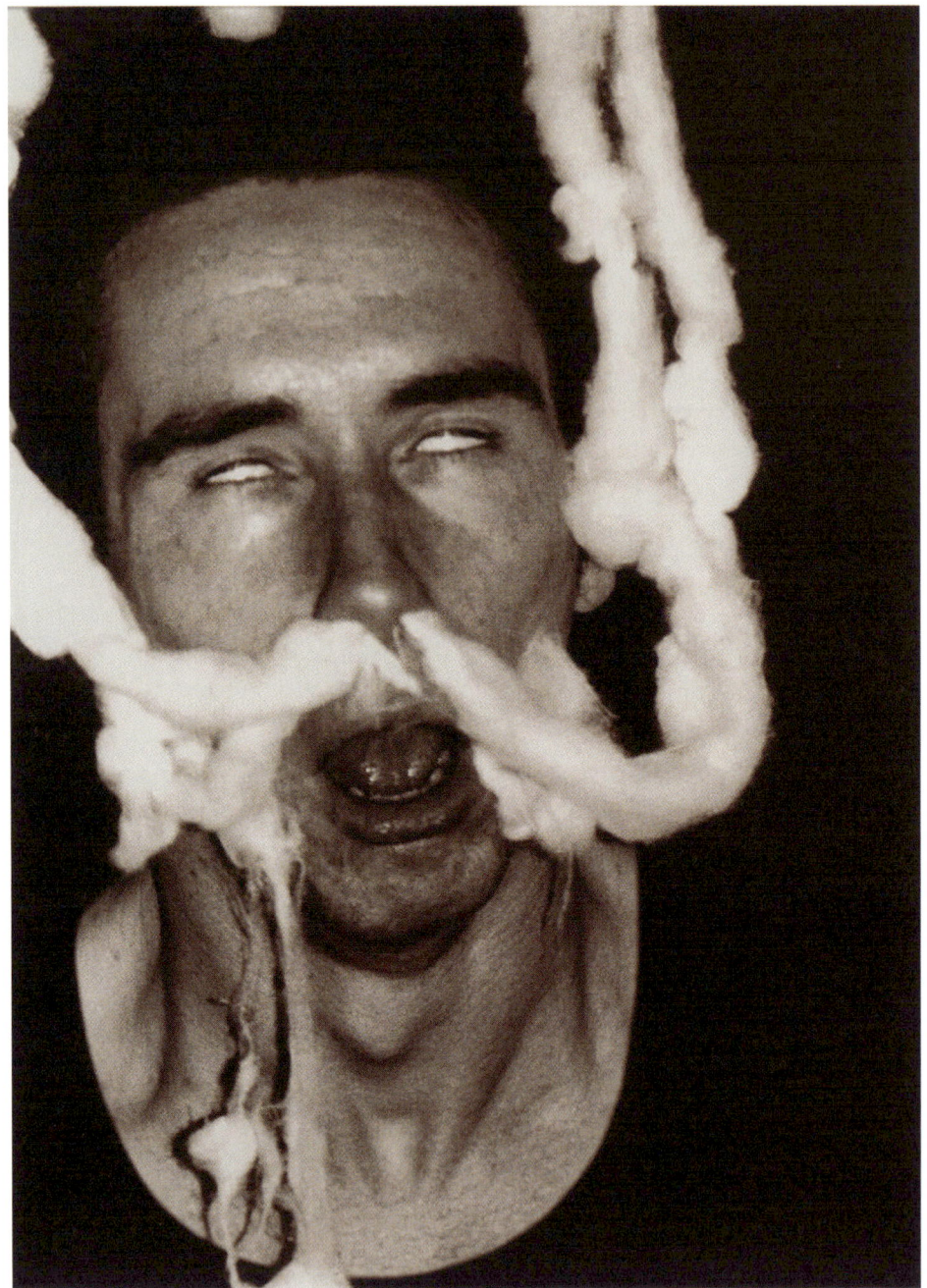

1978

You Can't Do That On Television was a Canadian program that first aired locally in 1979, eventually airing internationally in 1980. Featuring pre-teen and teen actors in interview-show style sketch comedy scenes, being slimed was the hallmark of the program and occurred copiously whenever a guest said, "I don't know," which would cue the producers to dump slime on their head, audience laughter ensuing. *YCDTOT* was eventually picked up by Nickelodeon and green slime became synonymous with the network. More than any other visual representation of slime, *YCDTOT* indelibly introduced slime as a green, viscous material. Secondarily, *YCDTOT* introduced slime as a verb, something that happens to guests, involuntarily, and from above. Whereas the trope of the pie-in-the-face is a reasonable possibility within the narrative vernacular of slapstick comedy, being slimed was a foregone conclusion, hardwired into the comedic mechanizations of *YCDTOT*. Triggered by a guest's inability to answer a question slime violently disrupts the scene as an excessive sign for what George Bataille refers to as "nonknowledge," the limit of thought. Ironically, the dumping of slime and the resulting laughter immediately bring the experience of nonknowledge to a close:

> Laughter is the exposition of play, that is, of sovereignty, of violence. But the total affirmation of violence is its very negation. Eroticism communicates what language refuses to communicate. This is a question of two different kinds of communication. This is the foundation. This is also the profound meaning of nonknowledge. One must cease knowing (speaking) in order to experience. Likewise to laugh.[1]

Nickelodeon used slime as a featured element in other programs such as *Double Dare*,[2] and explored the scalability of being slimed, eventually putting on live "Slime Fests" and other events involving industrial size containers of slime dumping onto swimsuit-clad participants below. Nickelodeon also instigated the merchandising of slime as a product that could be bought as a stand-alone item in toy aisles as well as a featured element in a range of other slime extruding toys.

The naturalization of slime as a product and its simple ingredients eventually gave way to the massively popular DIY slime phenomenon of the 2010s where communities of slime enthusiasts share slime recipes; make, touch, and record themselves making and touching; and sell small-batch slime. The DIY slime trend also commingles slime as a cathartic subject-substance within ASMR (autonomous sensory meridian response) videos, where the grasping, poking, and stretching of slime is recorded with highly sensitive cardioid microphones and captured on video, resulting in a viewing sensation characterized as low-grade euphoria, a slimy eroticism. ¶

NOTES

1.   Georges Bataille, "Nonknowledge, Laughter, and Tears," in *Unfinished System of Nonknowledge*, (University of Minnesota Press, 2001), pp. 238-239.

2.   Ada Calhoun, *Why We Can't Sleep: Women's New Midlife Crisis* (New York: Grove Press 2020), p. 216. "I keep thinking about the 1980s-90s TV show *Double Dare*, in which child contestants had to find orange flags among obstacles such as mountains of slime. That, I think, is an excellent analogy for our generation in mid-life: we've been glopped with slime, but somewhere in the mess there's that little orange flag."

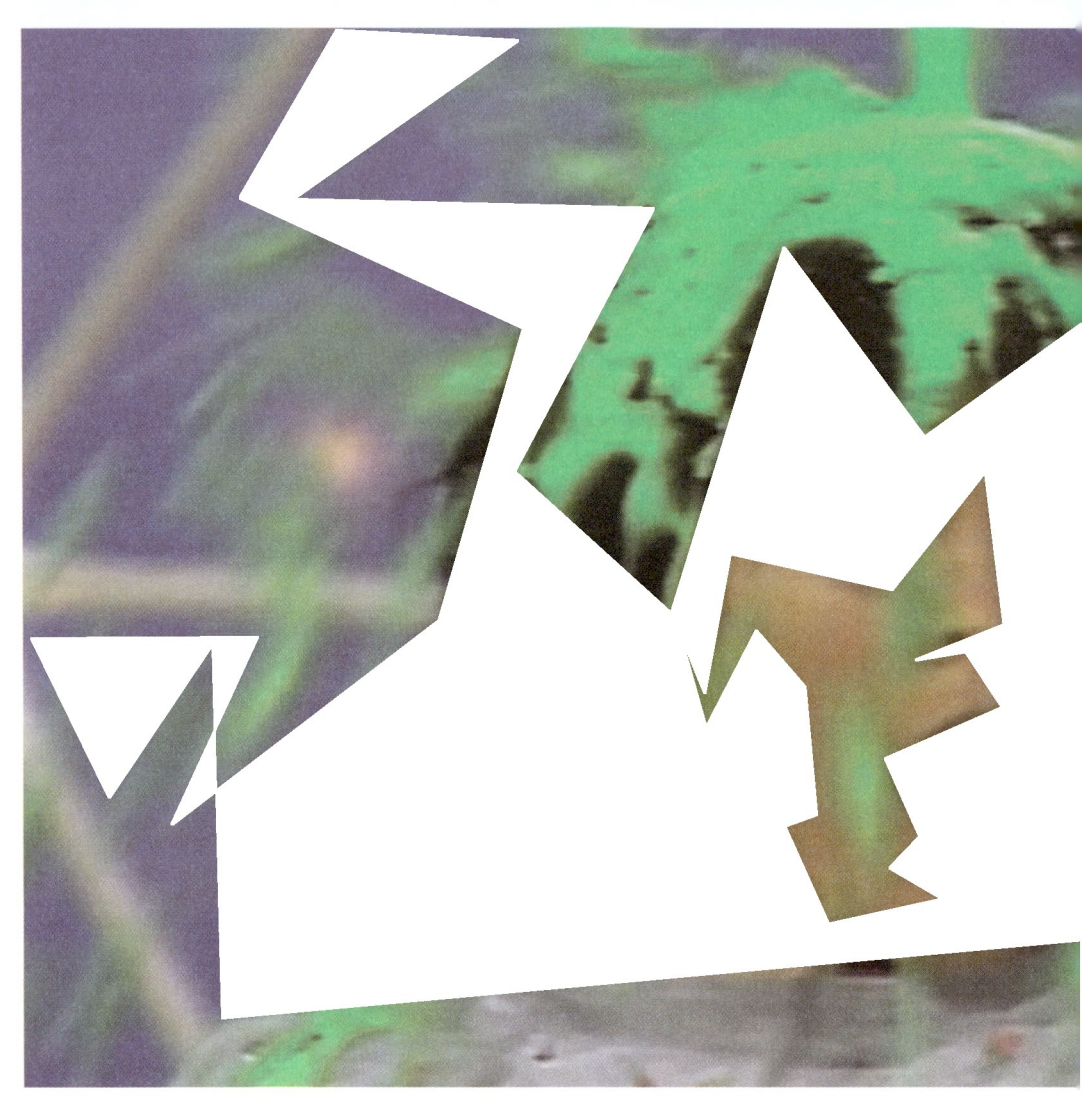

1979

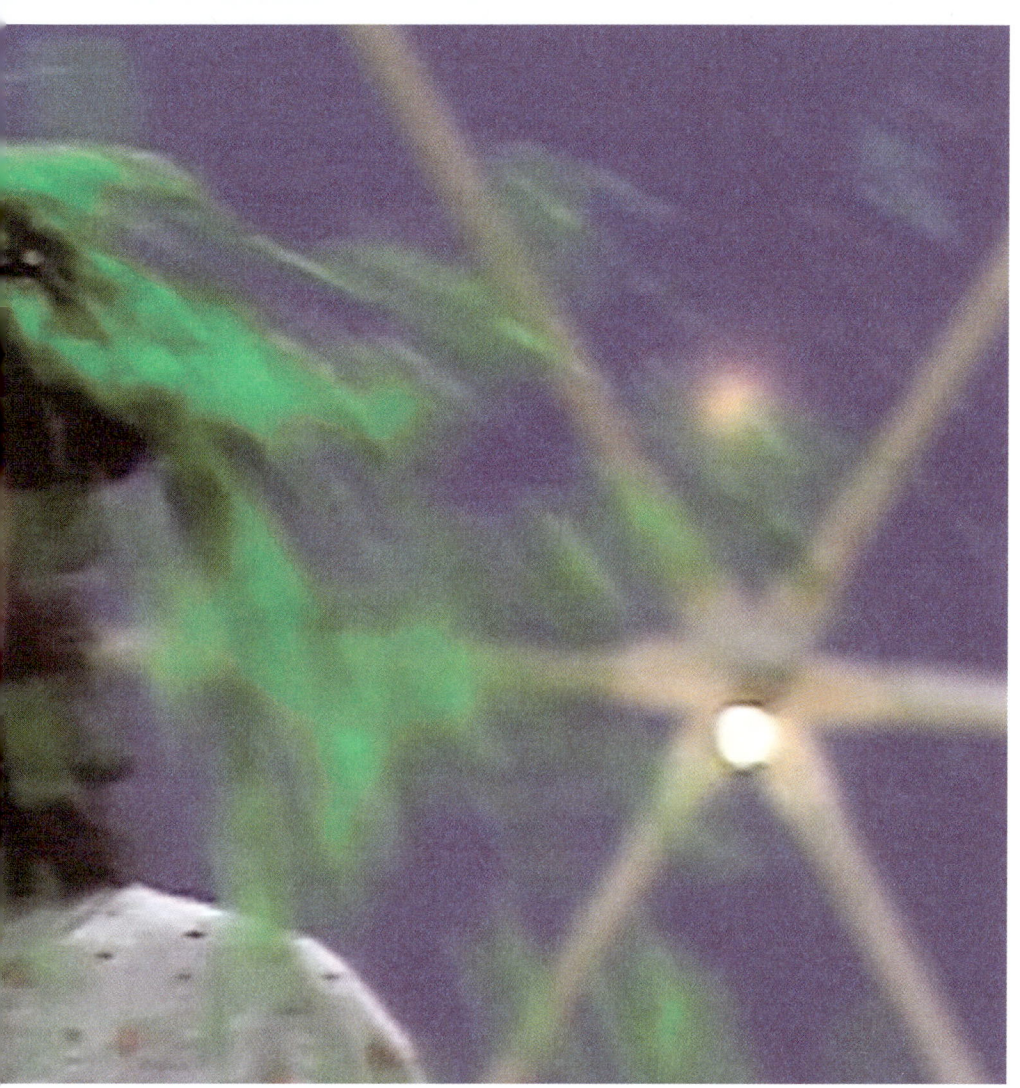

Production still from *You Can't Do That On Television*. Nickelodeon, 1979.

The xenomorph "feature creature" in Ridley Scott's 1979 film *Alien* embodies all of the accumulated ontological characteristics of slime and its blood is additionally corrosive. With nightmarishly bio-mechanical art direction by H.R. Giger, the *Alien* costume had a tube plumbed into the armature through which liquid was pumped so that the creature's jaws could drip profusely with saliva on command. Saliva plays an important role in the film as instances of the xenomorph's excessive drooling often precurses the realization by the film's characters that the creature is somewhere directly above or overhead.

The xenomorph, however, is not the only preternatural creature on the USCSS Nostromo. There is a trackable trend of cats performing a kind of quasi-mediumship within horror cinema, a canary in the coalmine-like, diegetic/non-diegetic fright early warning system. *Alien* notoriously features Jones the cat, whose appearance and movement throughout the film somewhat suspiciously cris-crosses the escalating, chaotic movement of the xenomorph.

Ripley, the heroine of *Alien* played by Sigourney Weaver, memorably searches for Jones before her attempted escape. Eventually found and then left unattended in his crate, Jones is approached but left undisturbed by the alien while locked inside his cage. Slimy saliva plus Toxoplasmosis[1] is perhaps the explanation for the alien's deferential[2] attitude toward Jones, as well as Ripley's oft cited "irrational" decision to save the cat. The last stand between Ripley and the xenomorph comes to a close as the creature is effectively ejected from the ship with a

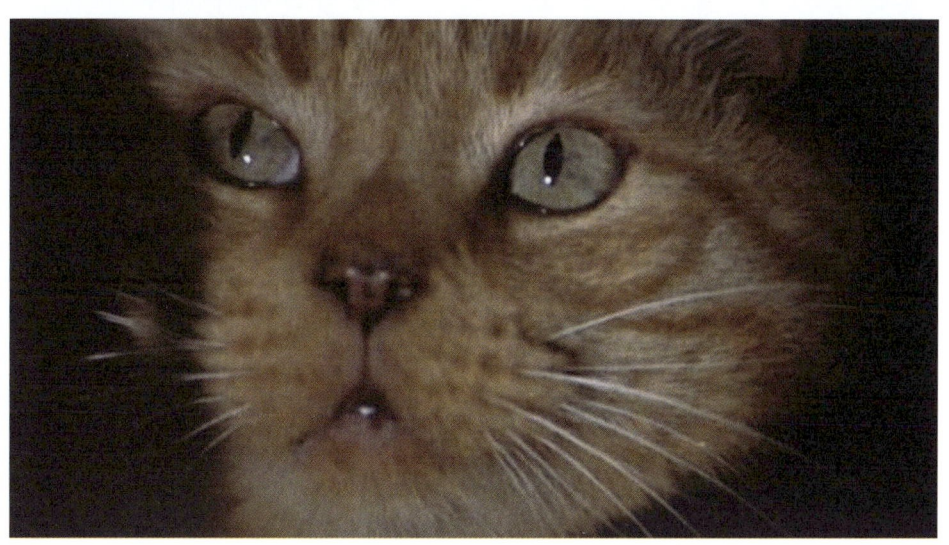

Film still from *Alien*. Directed by Ridley Scott. 20th Century Fox, 1979.

1979

grappling hook whose cord accidentally becomes an umbilical-like[3] tether. The alien climbs the cord into one of the ship's engines, and Ripley unceremoniously pushes a button igniting the engine bringing the film, as well as the alien, to a conclusion. ¶

NOTES

1. Pat Bailey, "How slime can take parasite from cats to sea otters," futurity.org, UC Davis, October 9, 2014, Original Study DOI: 10.1098/rspb.2014.1287. In recent laboratory tests, researchers have discovered that slimy, gelatinous polymers are a highly conducive environment for the transmission of *Toxoplasma gondii* egg cells, amplifying the intricate chain of disease transmission from cats. Toxoplasmosis infection usually occurs by eating undercooked contaminated meat, exposure from infected cat feces, or mother-to-child transmission during pregnancy. Some of the common effects of Toxoplasmosis are seizures, eye infections, headaches, dizziness, confusion, poor coordination, blurred vision, as well as increased risk of schizophrenia and obsessive-compulsive disorder.

2. Sarah Zielinski, "The Parasite That Makes a Rat Love a Cat: Toxoplasma gondii alters activity in a rat's brain," smithsonianmag.com, September 22, 2011. Recent studies have also shown that rats infected with *Toxoplasma* lose their natural response to cat urine and no longer fear the smell, in some cases even resulting in attraction to cats.

3. Birth/reproduction and motherhood figure heavily in the narrative universe of *Alien*. In the 1979 film, the infant xenomorph violently exits the abdomen of a Nostromo crew member "host" in the notorious "chestburster" scene, setting the onboard terror in motion. In the 1986 sequel *Aliens*, Ripley and the xenomorph confront each other mother-against-mother, each defending their children. Subsequent sequels further expand on the psychodynamics of maternity.

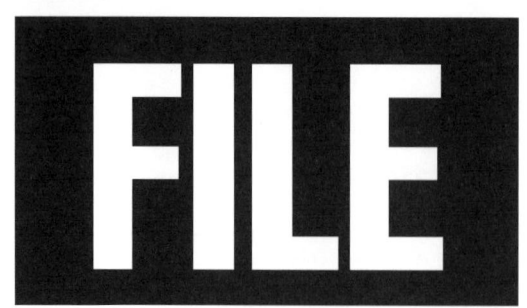

1980 **1981**

1982 **1983**

1984 **1985**

1986 **1987**

1989

Formally if not also hauntologicallyl connected to
the scene from *The Blob*, in which the amorphous
mass squeezes itself through a theater's projection
booth aperture onto the panicked audience below,
director Stanley Kubrick's *The Shining* famously
includes an elevator scene in which the camera fixes
on an elevator that opens and floods its entryway
with a deluge of blood. Consideration of these scenes
in relation to one another highlights their striking
formal similarities, conjuring a hypothetical scenario wherein Kubrick, having perhaps seen *The
Blob* in the theater in 1958 later folds this transgressive trick into his production. The proscenium
plays prominently in both scenes in multiple dimen-
sions and points of view. Whereas the panic-stricken
audience in *The Blob* screams and flees the theater,
their suspension of disbelief interrupted, the *actual*
audience ostensibly watches on, though their critical examination of the scene might momentarily
elicit some self-reflection. In the elevator scene from
The Shining on the other hand, the audience is the
audience, and the visual depth of the scene is made
shallow, drawing the focus in through pure cinematics, the proscenium replaced with the elevator door
which opens to horrifying effect. In both scenes, the
cinematic threshold-crossing of formless substances
provides the psychological charge, the retrospective
interpretation of this intergenerational referencing
a critical manifestation of the haunting of creative
influence, intentioned or not.

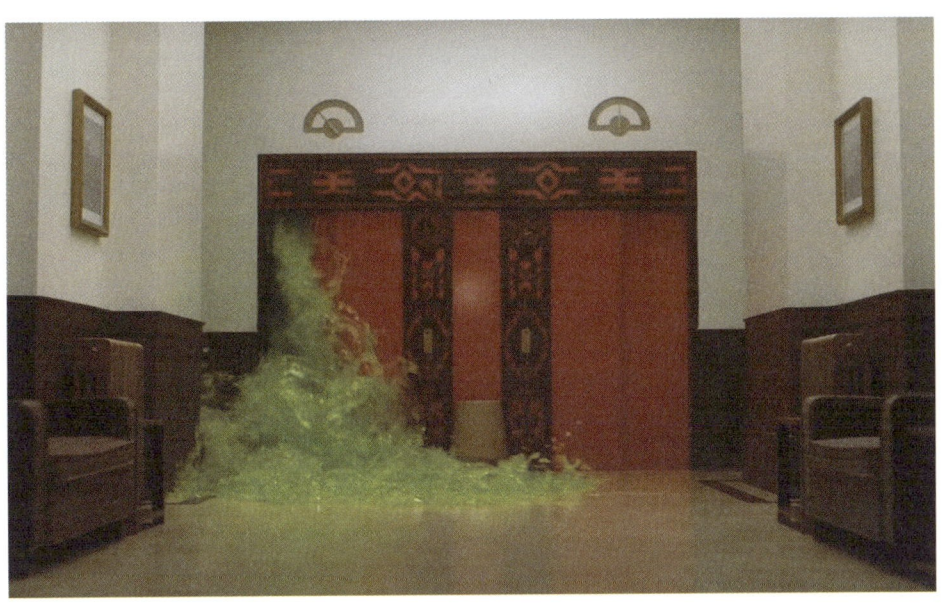

Video still from Mountain Dew's *The Shining* inspired 2020 Super Bowl commercial.

In a 1987 Washington Post op-ed, ABC Correspondent Bill Blakemore shared his analysis of the elevator scene, tethering it to a spectral subtext of Native American genocide that he hypothesizes runs throughout the film.

> The first and most frequently seen of the film's very real American "ghosts" is the flooding river of blood that wells out of the elevator shaft, which presumably sinks into the Indian burial ground itself. The blood squeezes out in spite of the fact the red doors are kept firmly shut within their surrounding Indian artwork-embellished frames. We never hear this rushing blood. It is a mute nightmare. It is the blood upon which this nation, like most nations, was built, as was the Overlook Hotel.[2]

The exterior hotel scenes from *The Shining* were filmed in Oregon at Timberline Lodge, built in 1937 at an elevation of 6,000 feet on the south side of Mt. Hood as a nordic retreat. Although historically referred to by many names, Wy'east is the most often cited *original* name given to the volcanic mountain, allegedly by the Klickitat people—the origin tale of the mountain ensconced in a myth of unresolved love and transmutation.[3] ¶

NOTES

1.   Jacques Derrida, *Specters of Marx*, trans. Peggy Kamuf, (New York/London, Routledge, 2006) pp. 201-202. Beyond the aesthetic appeal or "use-value" (in this case a particular effect of horror) of a cinematic moment wherein a red substance spills through an aperture (commodity form)–projection booth or elevator–this type of shot affects another shot like it which might follow, before it comes to be. "It affects and bereaves it in advance, like the ghost it will become, but this is precisely where haunting begins." Derrida continues, "To haunt does not mean to be present, and it is necessary to introduce haunting into the very construction of a concept. Of every concept, beginning with the concepts of being and time. That is what we would be calling here a hauntology. Ontology opposes it only in a movement of exorcism. Ontology is a conjuration." The spatio-temporal, circulatory dynamics of cinema are especially conducive to hauntological affect and ontological exorcism of concepts.

2.   Bill Blakemore, "Kubrick's Shining Secret," *The Washington Post*, July 12, 1987. Blakemore leans further into his theory where he continues, "The Overlook has Navajo and Apache motifs throughout, as manager Stuart Ullman tells the caretaker's wife Wendy in the only lines in the film in which the American Indians are mentioned. Ullman says, 'The site is supposed to be located on an Indian burial ground and I believe they actually had to repel a few Indian attacks as they were building it.' This bit of dialogue does not appear in Stephen King's novel *The Shining*."

3.   Andy Matarrese, "Anthropologist dispelling myths with plankhouse talk: Lesson on Native American history held at Ridgefield's Cathlapotle Plankhouse," *The Columbian*, June 11, 2017. There is recent doubt cast on the provenance of the name Wy'east by anthropologist David Lewis whose research focuses on the colonization of Native American history by white American culture.

The acronymically palimpsestic frozen yogurt
company TCBY launched in 1981 with the motto,
"This Can't Be Yogurt," which might have begged
the question, "Then what is it?" Rather, TCBY was
promptly sued by their competitor, "I Can't Believe
it's Yogurt!" wherein TCBY rebranded themselves
as The Country's Best Yogurt, while retaining their
acronymic shorthand. TCBY was marketed as a
healthy alternative to ice cream, whereby a sweet
frozen treat could be enjoyed without interfering
with popular sugar-free diet trends and products
such as Slim Fast, Jenny Craig, and Weight Watchers.
TCBY advertisements promised "All of the pleasure
and none of the guilt." The method of delivery and
consistency of frozen yogurt is important in its relationship to the customer in that it is dispensed from
a self-serve levered machine, rather than scooped
by hand like gelato or ice cream. This type of self-
serve extrusion of food locates the consumer in
close proximity to the manufacturing apparatus,
a relationship that parallels the abstracting of
ingredients, labor, and consumption that occurs in
industrialized food production, distancing consumer
consciousness from food sources and ethics of food
production broadly considered, while making food
more conveniently consumable. ¶

TCBY®™ The Country's Best Yogurt logo, 1981–1996.

"TCBY"®

1981

127

Julia Kristeva's 1982 *Powers of Horror* includes a physically and psychologically vivid description of food loathing and the ensuing urge to vomit as an act of defense against an experience of the abject. A thin layer of skin on the surface of milk is used to illustrate a "fascinated" initial resistance to ingestion, the experience of which is furthermore used to illustrate the experience of separation from one's parents, in both cases marked by "clouding dizziness, nausea." Symbolic of parental connection, the ingestion of milk and, in turn, its expulsion can be read as maintaining or breaking this bond. Kristeva characterizes abjection as an experience of threshold crossing wherein one expels oneself in an effort to separate from the Other, of which one is also in some sense a part. This is described as an existentially wretched process of "becoming an other at the expense of my own death." Kristeva cites food, filth, waste, and dung as abjection inducing things, each of which might also be described as having phenomenological qualities of sliminess in their post-use state. The passage of things in the world through bodies and consumptive processes imbues them with slimy qualities that signify their boundary crossing and our encounters with such things threaten convulsion and abreaction:

> Loathing an item of food, a piece of filth, waste, or dung. The spasms and vomiting that protect me. The repugnance, the

retching that thrusts me to the side and turns me away from defilement, sewage, and muck. The shame of compromise, of being in the middle of treachery. The fascinated start that leads me toward and separates me from them. Food loathing is perhaps the most elementary and most archaic form of abjection. When the eyes see or the lips touch that skin on the surface of milk—harmless, thin as a sheet of cigarette paper, pitiful as a nail paring—I experience a gagging sensation and, still farther down, spasms in the stomach, the belly; and all the organs shrivel up the body, provoke tears and bile, increase heartbeat, cause forehead and hands to perspire. Along with sight-clouding dizziness, nausea makes me balk at that milk cream, separates me from the mother and father who proffer it. "I" want none of that element, sign of their desire; "I" do not want to listen, "I" do not assimilate it, "I" expel it. But since the food is not an "other" for "me," who am only in their desire, I expel myself, I spit myself out, I abject myself within the same motion through which "I" claim to establish myself. That detail, perhaps an insignificant one, but one that they ferret out, emphasize, evaluate, that trifle turns me inside out, guts sprawling; it is thus that they see that "I" am in the process of becoming an other at the expense of my own death. During that course in which "I" become, I give birth to myself amid the violence of sobs, of vomit. Mute protest of the symptom, shattering violence of a convulsion that, to be sure, is inscribed in a symbolic system, but in which, without either wanting or being able to become integrated in order to answer to it, it reacts, it abreacts. It abjects.[1] ¶

NOTES

1.   Julia Kristeva, *Powers of Horror: An Essay on Abjection*, (New York: Columbia University Press), 1982. pp. 2–3.

Released in 1982, the experimental film *Koyaanisqatsi: Life Out of Balance,* directed by Godfrey Reggio, draws bold visual parallels in time-lapse footage between the movement of people by various means, manufacturing, and the built and natural world. One hour into the film is a scene in which several food manufacturing workers in lab-like coats and PPE, backs turned and blocking the camera, move aside to reveal that they are tending to a hotdog making machine, a superhighway of hotdogs cascading from a vertical conveyor. This scene cuts brutally to a lengthy sequence of commuters packed onto eight side-by-side up escalators. This technique of montaging particular clips of film to achieve specific conceptual insinuation is used of course in scores of other films. Federico Fellini's 1963 film *8 1/2* sequences the protagonist's moment of post-dream oceanic impact with a clip of his hand shooting into the air upon being startled awake in his bed. Differently in *2001: A Space Odyssey,* Stanley Kubrick captures a slow-motion flung bone cut abruptly to an orbiting space station. Categoric micro-units of conceptual montage, respectively referred to as contrast cuts and graphic match cuts, the hotdog/escalator scene in *Koyaanisqatsi* pulls both of these levers, resulting in an illustration of a consumption dialectic with such vividness that it debases the viewer through spectatorship. The viewer becomes a hot dog. Film scholar James Stephan Boman wrote of this scene:

> The argument to be gleaned from this visual equivalence is embarrassingly banal if spelled out in words. As a propulsive visual-acoustic experience, however, the unity of this mass-production regime compels at the level of the senses. By means of the film's carefully

calibrated time-lapse sequences, we perceive not only the mechanicity and fluidity of several isolated activities, but the systematic analogies that bind habits, institutions, and routines into a "way of life."[1]

Regarding hot dogs, which are situated near the low end of the edible meat quality spectrum, there have long been tolerable suspicions about the exact ingredients in these pre-cooked edible extrusions, their range of ingredients a demonstration in the elasticity of legal and ethical boundaries of food production. To eat a hot dog is an expression of indifference to its production relative to its ingredients. Extrapolating from Karl Marx, when the use-value or enjoyment of a hot dog is used to measure the value of its ingredients then this also means that the concrete labor which creates the use-value of a hot dog serves as an expression of abstract human labor.[2] Insofar as products are consumed as signs and consumption plays a role in class signification, everyone in this equation is a hot dog. "You are what you eat"[3] the old adage goes. In a virtuosic analysis of the "ambiguity surrounding the characteristics of value-constituting labor"[4] cultural theorist Sianne Ngai, in her essay "Visceral Abstractions", interrogates the ambiguity of Marx's use of "Gallerte", which is at once "a gelatinous condiment made from the 'meat, bone, [and] connective tissue' of various animals"[5] as well as a description of undifferentiated human labor, the term performing an instance of visceral abstraction. Beyond the edible, the inedible raw materials of the fat-and-protein economy are processed into re-marketable products for high profit at rendering facilities. In a gruesomely ironic twist, most inedible dead-animal parts including dead pets are rendered into undifferentiated slime which is then used in feed products used to fatten up future generations of their kind. Others are transmogrified into paint, car wax, rubber, and industrial lubricants, and to this day many rendered products are used in soap and cosmetics. ¶

NOTES

1. James Stephan Boman, (2019) *Unstill Life: The Emergence and Evolution of Time-Lapse Photography*, Doctor of Philosophy in Film and Media Studies Dissertation, UC Santa Barbara, UC Santa Barbara Electronic Theses and Dissertations.

2. Karl Marx, "Estranged Labour," *Economic and Philosophic Manuscripts of 1844, trans.* Andy Blunden, 2000, First published by Progress Publishers, Moscow, 1959, marxista.org. p.28. "The worker becomes poorer the more wealth he produces, the more his production increases in power and extent. The worker becomes an ever cheaper commodity the more commodities he produces. The *devaluation* of the human world grows in direct proportion to the *increase in value* of the world of things. Labour not only produces commodities; it also produces itself and the workers as a *commodity* and it does so in the same proportion in which it produces commodities in general."

3. Ludwig Andreas von Feuerbach, "Concerning Spiritualism and Materialism," 1863. "Der Mensch ist, was er ißt."

4. Sianne Ngai, "Visceral Abstractions,*" GLQ: A Journal of Lesbian and Gay Studies*, Volume 21 Issue 1, Duke University Press, 2015.

5. Ibid.

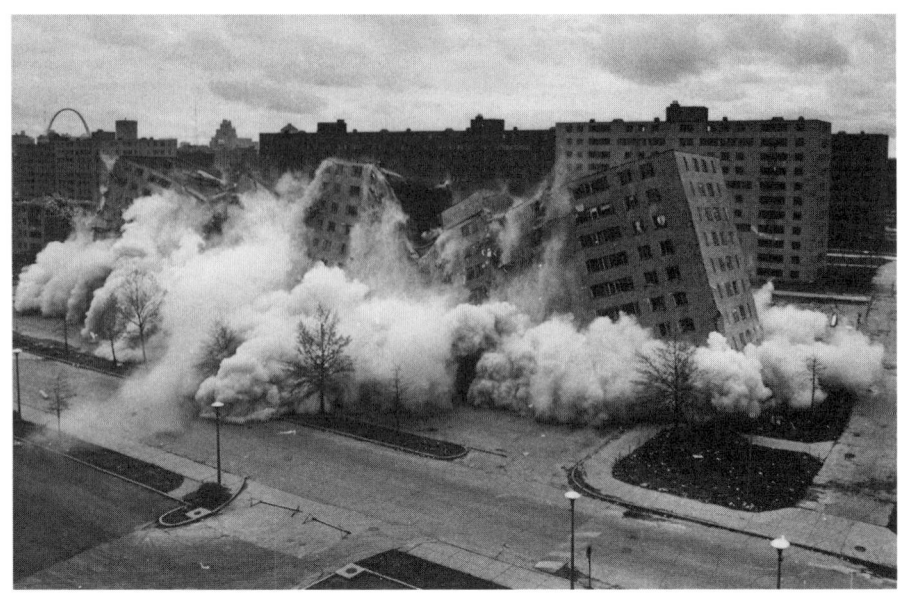

The destruction of Pruitt–Igoe, March 16, 1972. The date of the first demolition has now become mythologized as the point at which modernism gave way to the amorphousness of postmodernism, a theory posited in postmodern theorist Charles Jencks' 1977 book *The Language of Post-Modern Architecture* where the destruction of Pruitt–Igoe is cited as "the day Modern architecture died." *Koyaanisqatsi* cinematographer Ron Fricke shot footage of the demolition of one of the 33 Pruitt–Igoe towers in 1975 that later appeared in the film.

1982

The 1982 supernatural horror film *Poltergeist* is set in the fictional suburban community of Cuesta Verde, California, and the plot centers on the Freeling family whose home has been illegally constructed atop a graveyard. A popular mischaracterization of this plot detail is that the Freeling's home sits on an American Indian burial ground, and while this is somewhat of a horror film trope, it is explicitly not the case within the narrative framework of *Poltergeist*. However, the actual set location of the Freeling home is Simi Valley, historically inhabited by the Native American Chumash people indigenous to the central and southern coastal regions of California. There is real-life precedent for this cinema trivia myth—one well-known incident in 1969 involving the discovery of human remains during the construction of a supermarket in Agoura Hills. Work was stopped and for about six months, while archaeologists and others performed a full excavation of the site and found that it was a Chumash burial ground. Hundreds of bodies were found on the site, which supposedly was used by the Chumash from 1600 to 1785. The expansion of American suburbs into lands previously inhabited by indigenous people is a form of recurrent colonization, archeological in its scope. Regardless of the interior narrative mechanisms of this *Poltergeist* plot detail, the actual, slightly-expanded analysis of the plot and context reframes *Poltergeist* as perhaps an anti-colonial thriller. In this scenario, the hapless and aloof middle-class white family is not only run out of town, but also their home actually implodes and disappears through a bilocational portal in the films' final scene as retribution for grave desecration within and outside of the film.

At the center of the story is the family's youngest daughter Carol Anne, who is abducted through a staticky television set by a poltergeist midway through the film. Carol Anne can be heard through the television set, but to retrieve her from the other dimension requires the assistance of the eccentric medium Tangina who assures the family that the girl is not dead or lost, explaining, "There is no death. There is only a transition to a different sphere of consciousness. Carol Anne is not like those she's with. She is a living presence in their spiritual earthbound plane. They are attracted to the one thing about her that is different from themselves—her life-force."[1]

The penultimate scene from *Poltergeist* unfolds in a step-by-step manner—Tangina directing the Freeling family and her assistant Ryan as though demonstrating how to do something for the first time. "Ryan! Get downstairs and wait by the target! Steven! Give me the tennis ball marked number 1!"[2] she shouts over the gale force howl of the portal through which she plans to enter and retrieve Carol Anne. After successfully passing two tennis balls respectively marked "1 THE" and "2 SPIRIT" into the large portal in Carol Anne's bedroom and out of a smaller portal in the living room downstairs, the group is ready for their rescue attempt. A sturdy manila rope is fed between the two portals and Carol Anne's mother Diane is tethered and lowered into the portal by her husband. Tangina loudly coaches Stephen to wait until the time is right to pull Diane and Carol Anne out of the portal, but Stephen in his impatience pulls the rope too soon. A giant fiery skull suddenly emerges from the portal, Stephen lets go of the rope in a panic, the skull sucks back in, and finally Diane falls through the

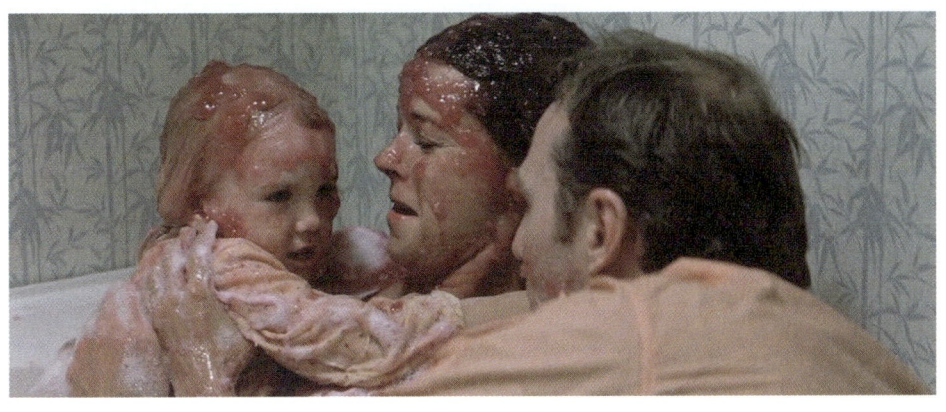

Film still from *Poltergeist*. Directed by Tobe Hooper. Metro-Goldwyn-Mayer, 1982.

small ceiling portal in the downstairs living room, cradling Carol Anne and covered in thick pink ectoplasm, stunned but physically unharmed. Carol Anne's "life-force" is what allows her to pass from her family's home in Cuesta Verde and the "spiritual earthbound plane" of the poltergeist, and her rescue-reemergence plays out like a phantasmic rebirth of both her and her mother. ¶

NOTES

1.   *Poltergeist*. Directed by Tobe Hooper. MGM/UA Entertainment Company, 1982.
2.   Ibid.

Initially labeled with the tagline "so ugly they're cute," Cabbage Patch Kids were first introduced to the consumer market at the American International Toy Fair in New York City's Jacob K. Javits Convention Center in February 1983, generating an unprecedented overnight following that had rarely been seen before. An estimated one million Cabbage Patch dolls were shipped to US and UK retailers in June of that year and by October, manufacturing was at maximum capacity of two million units per month, however even this was not enough to match fanatical demand. Cabbage Patch Kids expanded consumer psychology beyond a purchase mindset. Ownership of a Cabbage Patch Kid was often initialized at point-of-purchase "adoption centers" and finalized through the completion and registration of adoption paperwork, reifying[1] the connection between consumer and object thereby personifying the stuffed dolls as family members.

In his writing about the consumer culture psycho-dynamics of collecting, Jean Baudrillard cites a television show about collectors in which:

> ... every collector who presented his collection to the viewing audience would mention the very special "object" that he did not have, and invite everyone to find it for him. So, even though objects may on occasion lead into the realm of social discourse, it must be acknowledged that *it is usually not an object's presence*

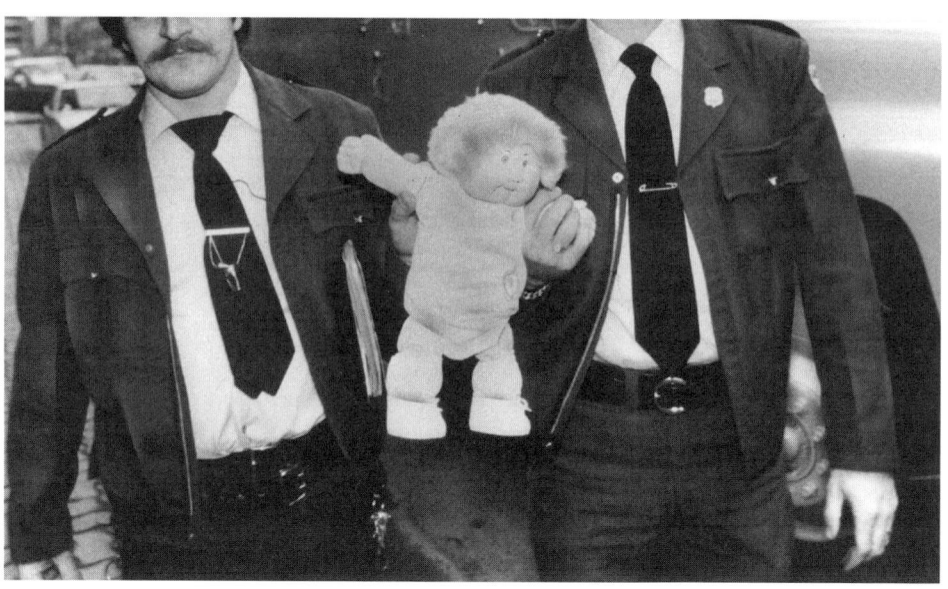

Brinks guards in Toronto escort a Cabbage Patch Kid to its new owners, who paid $5,600 in an auction to help the Hospital for Sick Children, 1983.

but far more often its absence that clears the
way for social intercourse.[2]

The Cabbage Patch Kids phenomenon was notable in its marketing declaration "each one is unique,"[3] encouraging multiple non-redundant purchases.

By 1984 sales for Cabbage Patch Kids branded products, including the dolls themselves, related toys and accessories, children's clothing, and even a full-length album released on vinyl and cassette, *Cabbage Patch Dreams*, came close to a toy brand property record of two billion dollars. *Cabbage Patch Dreams*, which was also released in French as *Les Rêves Des P'tits Bouts De Choux* and in Spanish as *Felices Sueños* was written and produced by noted children's music composer Tom Chapin, released by Parker Brothers' music, and achieved Gold and Platinum sales records.

Cabbage Patch Kids retrospectively encapsulate a facet of the consumer frenzied grotesquerie of the American 1980s, their demand in stores often instigating physical altercations, and their possession often resulting in hoarding-like behavior. Naturalizing orgiastic consumption but not slimy per se, Cabbage Patch Kids are a radical example of consumer product boundary crossing lubricated by an adoption inspired object relationship not achievable through purchase. ¶

1. David Gartman, "Reification of Consumer Products: A General History Illustrated by the Case of the American Automobile." *Sociological Theory*, vol. 4, no. 2, 1986, p. 172. "In reified consumption, just as in reified production, the connection of products to the system of exploitative, class-divided labor that produces them and provides their actual meaning is obscured, and they seem to take on a life of their own."

2. Jean Baudrillard, *The System of Objects*, (London/New York, Verso, 1996), p. 105.

3. Ibid., p.88. Regarding this Cabbage Patch Kids jingle lyric Baudrillard again comes to mind where he writes, "In both cases gratification flows from the fact that possession depends, on the one hand, on the absolute singularity of each item, a singularity which puts that item on a par with an animate being–indeed, fundamentally on a par with the subject himself–and, on the other hand, on the possibility of a series, and hence of an infinite play of substitutions. Collecting is thus qualitative in its essence and quantitative in its practice."

1984's *Ghostbusters* is a film perhaps most notable for reinforcing a horror-larious relationship between slime and food vis-à-vis a phantasmically augmented giant marshmallow. Bill Murray's character famously comes face to face with a slimy apparition in a hotel hallway and the moment of impact fulfills all of slime's cumulative attributes—viscous, sticky, pale green, dripping from the face, evidencing contact with a ghost, signaling boundary crossing, and ultimately leaving its recipient stunned but unharmed. The confrontation leaves Murray rolling lollingly on his back as though suffering from overeating.

The significance of slime is corporeally augmented in *Ghostbusters 2* where the negative energy of New York City manifests itself as a river of pink slime flowing beneath the urban grid. The cinematic focus on the underground channeling of greywater and sewage, subterranean networks dedicated to waste diversion, plays on the horror trope of the bathroom and in particular the toilet/bathtub/shower as the site of terror. Unpacking the psychodynamics of cinema-in-general in his film *The Pervert's Guide To Cinema,* Slavoj Žižek rhetorically inquires, "When we spectators are sitting in a movie theater and looking at the screen, are we not basically staring at a toilet bowl, waiting for things to reappear out of the toilet?"[1] Society's relationship to wastewater is contingent on its management and treatment, the efficiency of its movement away from us, and the prevention of its unwanted, potentially messy or even dangerous return. Aside from domestic wastewater, every industry from raw materials processing to human labor interacts with cycles of wastewater and some of the water expelled during industrial processes is eventually reintroduced for various uses as "recycled water" following treatment.

The role of wastewater management, or lack thereof, can be tracked in relation to a history of pandemics and most recently, COVID-19 researchers have focused on the analysis of wastewater as a predictive tool for detecting elevated presence of viral load in communities. Reporting on the challenges of managing overloaded wastewater systems resulting from homebound Americans during and before the COVID-19 pandemic has relayed grotesque, vivid scenarios. For example, one article reports "removing a 'fatberg' of debris, oils, and grease that was 100 feet long and 11 feet wide"[2] from a pumping station in Michigan's Macomb County. The open aqueduct in *Ghostbusters 2*, albeit underground, is ambiguous as to whether its function is to supply or divert liquid from the city, but this small issue of continuity is eclipsed as a supernatural contamination of drinking water begins to have transversal effects on the water supply. In one scene, Sigourney Weaver's character holds a baby in a bathroom, her back turned to a filling bathtub while the water changes in color from clear to neon fleshy-pink.[3] An amorphous, blobular haunt-figure eventually emerges threateningly from the tub, having arrived via the hot water faucet.

In an altogether different, literary universe, Upton Sinclair's 1906 novel *The Jungle* so vividly registers the visceral realities of the turn-of-the-century American meat packing industry that the public was horrified. *The Jungle* describes diseased, rotten, and contaminated meat, treacherous working conditions, and fetid environmental impacts of slaughterhouses with specificity that led to new federal food safety laws. In a particularly excruciating passage, Sinclair describes an open pit into which runoff from surrounding packing houses collects and stagnantly pools:

"Bubbly Creek" is an arm of the Chicago River, and forms the southern boundary of the yards; all the drainage of the square mile of packing-houses empties into it, so that it is really a great open sewer a hundred or two feet wide. One long arm of it is blind, and the filth stays there forever and a day. The grease and chemicals that are poured into it undergo all sorts of strange transformations, which are the cause of its name; it is constantly in motion, as if huge fish were feeding in it, or great leviathans disporting themselves in its depths. Bubbles of carbonic acid gas will rise to the surface and burst, and make rings two or three feet wide. Here and there the grease and filth have caked solid, and the creek looks like a bed of lava; chickens walk about on it, feeding, and many times an unwary stranger has started to stroll across, and vanished temporarily. The packers used to leave the creek that way, till every now and then the surface would catch on fire and burn furiously, and the fire department would have to come and put it out. Once, however, an ingenious stranger came and started to gather this filth in scows, to make lard out of; then the packers took the cue, and got out an injunction to stop him, and afterwards gathered it themselves. The

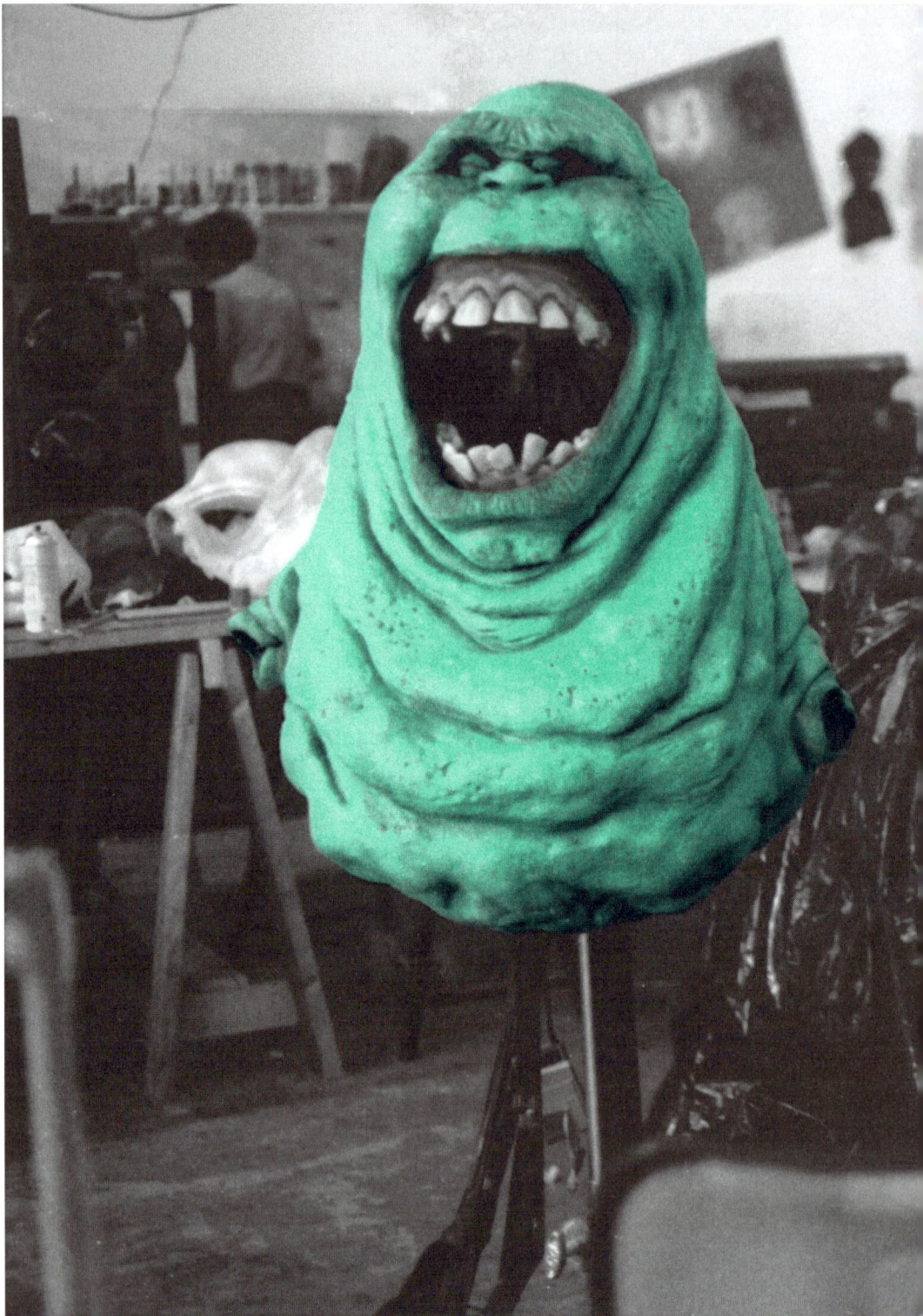

Special effects artist Steve Johnson's "Slimer" models for *Ghostbusters*. Columbia Pictures, 1984.

banks of "Bubbly Creek" are plastered thick with hairs, and this also the packers gather and clean.[4]

But what type of infrastructural networks might result from self-directed complex biological behavior? Left undisturbed what might become of "Bubbly Creek" and the "great leviathans disporting themselves in its depths?" Research into the malleable adaptability of single-celled slime molds such as *Physarum polycephalum*[5] have produced evidence of intelligent networking behaviors able to mimic infrastructure as complex as the Tokyo subway system. Slime molds are efficient at constructing connections between food sources, and slime mold researchers have also speculated that these "Decentralized, adaptable networks would also be important for soldiers in battlefields or swarms of robots exploring hazardous environments."[6] Slime takes us from fantasy to reality and back again. ¶

1. Slavoj Žižek, *The Pervert's Guide to Cinema*, Directed by Sophie Fiennes. P Guide Productions/Zeitgeist Films. 2006.

2. Claudia Lauer and John Flesher. "Epidemic of wipes and masks plagues sewers, storm drains," Associated Press. apnews.com. June 4, 2020.

3. Tobias Menely and Margaret Ronda, "Red," *Prismatic Ecology: Ecotheory Beyond Green*, ed. Jeffrey Jerome Cohen (University of Minnesota Press, 2013), p. 22. Regarding the inundation of local infrastructure with waste from meat processing facilities engaged in globally scaled production, Menely and Ronda write, "Such problems are endemic to areas around horse-slaughter plants, where blood and tissue are a common sight in local streams, even spilling from taps and bubbling up in bathtubs."

4. Upton Sinclair, *The Jungle,* 1906 (New York: Penguin Books, 2006), p. 106.

5. Laura Sanders, "Slime Mold Grows Network Just Like Tokyo Rail System," *Science News*, Wired.com, January 10, 2010. "The yellow slime mold *Physarum polycephalum* grows as a single cell that is big enough to be seen with the naked eye. When it encounters numerous food sources separated in space, the slime mold cell surrounds the food and creates tunnels to distribute the nutrients."

6. Ibid.

"So I pulled out a stack of headshots of John Belushi, poured a gram of cocaine on it and started chopping lines up," Johnson said, completing his wild story by saying that the ghost of Belushi himself appeared to him in the final hours and told him, "Watch that s–t Steve, it'll kill you." That was referring to the cocaine, which was part of the drug injection that killed the comedian.[1] ¶

NOTES

1. Jeremy Fuster, *'Ghostbusters' Origin Story: How John Belushi and Cocaine Helped Inspire Slimer*, Thewrap.com, April 30, 2018. Special effects artist Steve Johnson describing the 24 hours leading up to the deadline to complete his Slimer model, which was to resemble John Belushi. Belushi had been slated to play the ghost prior to his death.

In 1974 graphic artist Jim Phillips, now a legend of the skateboard industry, joined the creative team at Santa Cruz Skateboards to become a central figure in establishing a visual language for Santa Cruz products and in turn, for skateboard culture in general. Following fast-paced material developments related to the design of skateboards in the 1970s—a kind of evolutionary biology of an emergent recreational phenomenon—the popularity of skateboarding surged further in the 1980s driven largely by distribution of skateboard videos released on VHS. These video tapes had an immeasurable impact on subsequent market demand for skateboarding products, clothing, and accessories, all of which proliferated skateboarding's nascent aesthetic.

In 1985 Phillips drew the "Screaming Hand" which became not only an iconic Santa Cruz image, but also an image that would become nearly synonymous with the entire skateboard industry. That same year Phillips also created the graphics for "Slime Balls" wheels and a year later created Santa Cruz's "Slasher" deck graphic. Altogether these three designs articulated a mood of accelerating, grotesque, anthropomorphized disembodiment, the skateboard equipment itself became a horror vision of aggressive movement.

The "Screaming Hand" and "Slasher" lunge forward toward an unseen destination, the former eyeball-less, the latter's eyes bulged and bloodshot, two ghosts. The concentric graphic of the "Slime Balls" wheels quickly becomes an illegible swirl once in motion. Made from cast urethane, "Slime Balls" were originally available in two colors, fluorescent pink and fluorescent green, two colors with which slime is often associated. "Slime Balls" were a coordinated synthesis of nomenclature, materiality, and a phenomenological color experience of a visually implied apparition realized through the blur of actual movement. On the molecular level fluorescence is a flash resulting from a photon absorbing more light than it can emit, shifting wavelengths and appearing as an intense vibration of light. The fluorescent effect is temporary and such pigments are fugitive and unstable. Fluorescence calls attention through an oscillation between the visible and invisible light spectrum, an effect of threshold crossing and, in some sense, ghostly.

Neon, baggy, blobby clothes also became popular in the mid-1980s and the popularization of garments constructed with jersey fabrics became synonymous with the decade. Characterized by its crosswidth stretch and efficient production, jersey fabric is a material that indexes the corporeal closeness of t-shirts and underwear while allowing extreme freedom of movement within largely unstructured items of clothing. Proliferated by the modular fashion lines "Units" and "Multiples" that grew from a fashion/ design school project turned mall store phenomenon by Sandra Garrett, jersey Units became synonymous with stretchy, nondescript cotton pieces that could be reversed, worn in ensemble, and interchanged to create completely new outfits. Rap and hip-hop culture in its preeminent socio-political dynamism radicalized street fashion through synthesized cultural references such as loose fitting sportswear, carceral-issued clothing, recast luxury garments, baggy jeans, billowing M.C. Hammer (harem) pants, bulky parachute pants, and oversized sweaters–all of which played a role in androgynyzing and transcending conservative fashion traditions. Contemporarily we can locate a hyperbolic reemergence of this trend in the styling of Billie Eilish. Aside from the obvious appropriative reference to hip-hop fashion, Eilish has attributed her baggy, puffy style sense to her attempt to prevent the objectification and sexualization of herself as a celebrity with an accompanyingly high public profile. In a recent video campaign for Calvin Klein, Eilish speaks over footage of herself in front of a mirror and in a bathtub, fully clothed:

> I never want the world to know everything about me. I mean that's why I wear big baggy clothes. Nobody can have an opinion because they haven't seen what's underneath. Nobody can be like, "she's slim-thick," "she's not slim-thick," "she's got a flat ass," "she's got a fat ass." No one can say any of that because they don't know.[1]

The absorption of Eilish's body into her clothing is tactfully amorphous, her technicolor green hair and fashion sense slime-like in the way she deploys it to engulf her particular physicality as a foil to her public consumption. ¶

NOTES

1.   Billie Eilish + Calvin Klein, "I Speak My Truth In #MyCalvins." May 9, 2019, #MyCalvins.

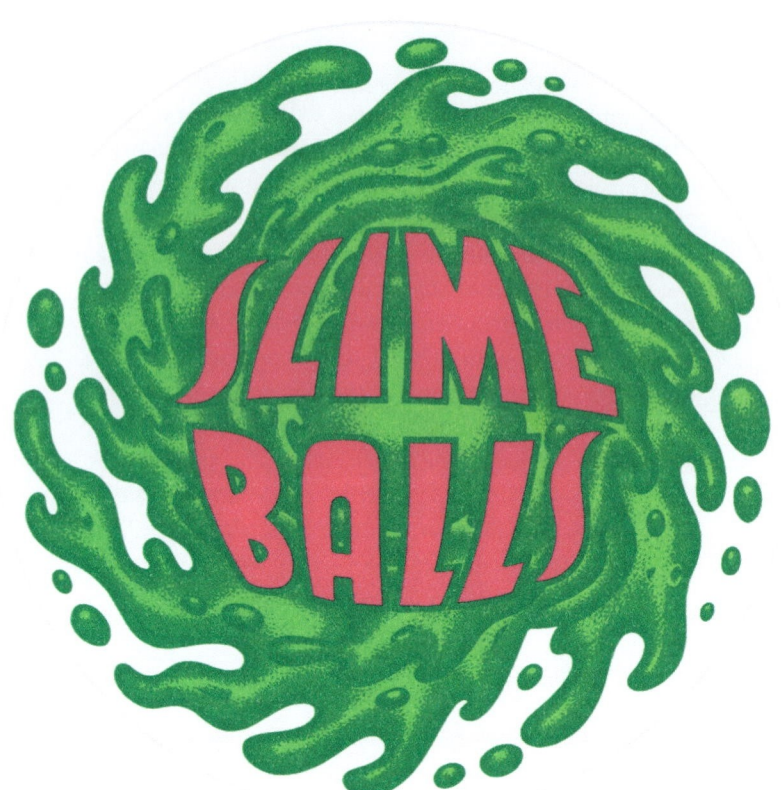

I was in fourth grade during the 1984/85 academic
year, and my school's cafeteria workers[1] would regularly include a single Garbage Pail Kids sticker on
each students' tray as they worked their way through
the lunch line. Occasionally a student would be for-
tunate or unfortunate enough to receive a card
bearing their name, the accompanying illustration
both humorous and embarrassing, though hopefully
not accurate. Garbage Pail Kids were grossed-out
parodic rejoinders to the consumptive grotesquerie
of Cabbage Patch Kids, the popularity of the adhesive backed collectible stickers riding the wake of the
dolls' unprecedented popularity. A losing legal bat-
tle between Cabbage Patch Kids and Garbage Pail
Kids ultimately led to a court order that the stickers deviate from their obvious reference to the dolls.
The fine-tuned, entirely grotesque illustration style
of Garbage Pail Kids originated from a genealogy
of underground commix aesthetics, particularly the
visual language of Basil Wolverton's "Ugly Stickers"
from 1965, which were distinct in their rotten, melting, oozing, dripping, gooey, deformed, sweaty, snotty
aesthetic. A trendy slimy green zeitgeist was in full
force by the mid 1980s, and the connections between
representations and characterizations of slime across
multiple pop culture modes were readily apparent. ¶

NOTES

1.   I retrospectively imagine the cafeteria workers chewing the
      rock-hard stale pink sticks of chewing gum as they opened
      the packages of Garbage Pail Kids to redistribute the cards
      individually.

1985   155

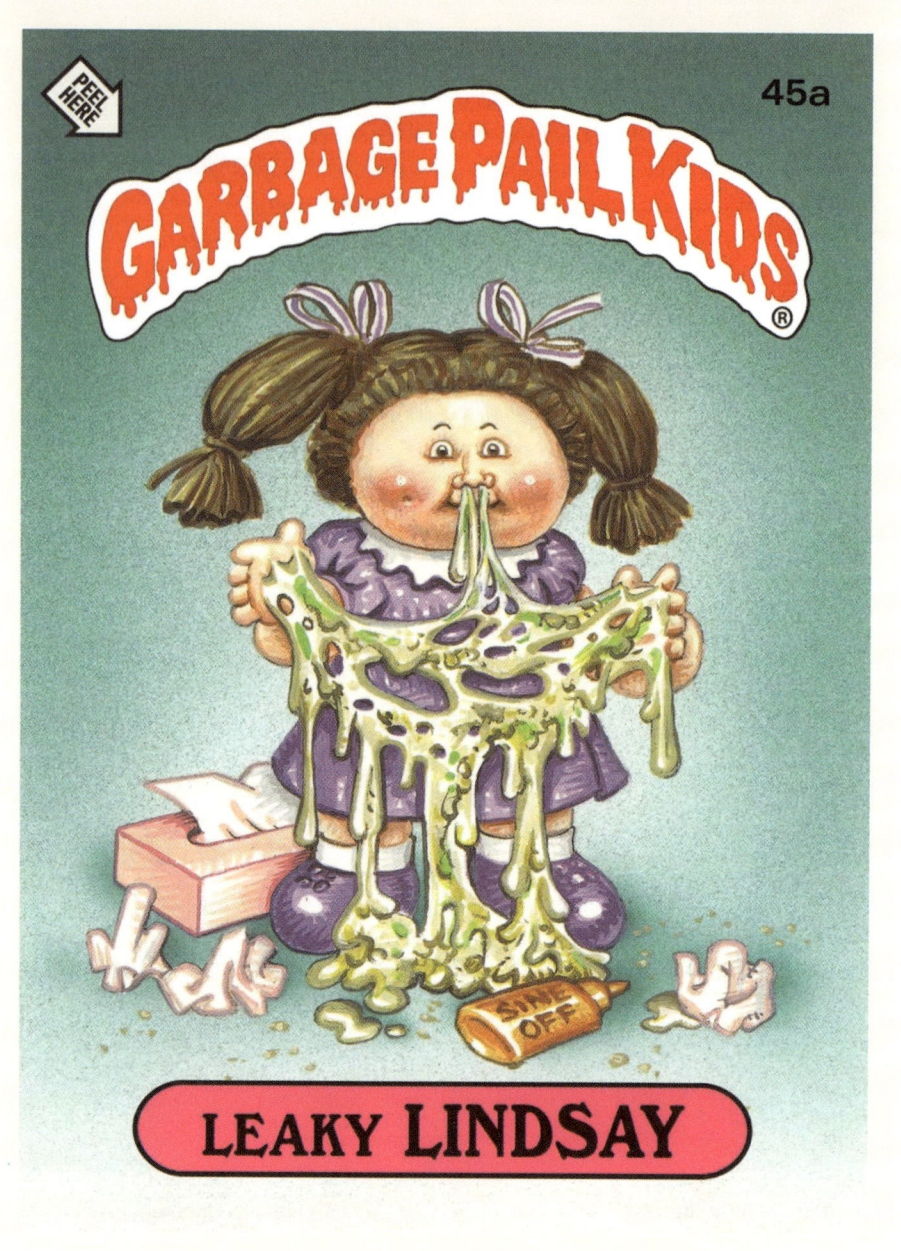

1985

The 1985 film *Better off Dead* is a surreal comedy starring John Cusack whose role subverts and breaks from the dominant rom-com trend of the era for which he is also a central figure. Cusack plays the film's lead, high school student Lane Meyer, whose stalker-like obsession with his girlfriend Beth precurses his mental decline and is conveyed in the early scenes of the film where Lane is shown sleeping with a photograph of Beth, followed by a scene in which we see head and shoulder cardboard cutouts of Beth on every hanger in Lane's closet. Beth breaks up with Lane within the first 15 minutes of the film putting the plot into motion and also triggering Lane's psychological breakdown that is conveyed through repeated suicide attempts and hallucinations.

Possible mental disorders feature prominently and diversely throughout the film—Lane becoming an increasing danger to himself, his closest friend singularly focused on street drugs, his younger brother inhabiting a Leisure Suit Larry persona, to name just a couple of examples. In fact, every primary and secondary character seems to have been developed around a singularly unique fixation. Most notably Lane's mother Jenny seems as though in a trance, unaffected by the ridiculousness unfolding around her, serving improvised 1950s Jell-O recipes, always staring blankly offscreen, and in one scene coaxing her begrudging family onto the sofa for a Christmas photo while she beams into the camera from the guise of an elaborate reindeer costume.

In what is often referred to as "the dessert scene," Jenny serves a thick gummous mucid green dessert, which she admits she improvised upon due to the cookbook pages getting wet. While receiving a lecture from his father, Lane slouches over the table with folded arms prodding the dessert with his fork. The dessert proceeds to slide slowly from his plate and onto the table as Lane watches with an unimpressed or nonplussed expression. Jenny is perhaps a medium conjuring phantasmic food behavior through her culinary improvisations, which might also explain her trance-like state. Alternately, Jenny's aberrant viscoidal cuisine suggests what has been expressed in recent online forums regarding the odd mid-century popularity of Jell-O based recipes, "#maybe 50s jello food actually was a sublimated expression of female rage"[1]

Throughout the film, Lane nearly hangs himself with an extension cord, jumps off of a bridge only to safely land in a passing garbage truck, and talks with invisible personalities throughout the film. In a nod to the final scene in *Poltergeist* in which the camera is firmly fixed upon the family home, the Meyer's home is similarly shown in full view as the credits roll. The home's interior lights begin to flicker erratically, first in the garage, then throughout the second story bedroom windows. Whereas the *Poltergeist* home is spectacularly swallowed into a bilocational vortex, the roof of the Meyer's home suddenly caves and gives way as a small spacecraft launches from within, presumably piloted by Lane's enigmatic younger brother, the real world apparently not having satisfied his increasingly eccentric proclivities. Pushed and pulled between the radically contrasted poles of the film's on-piste and suburbia bi-locales, the characters' behavior in *Better Off Dead* are driven largely by a desire to escape from their current situations. The film's b-grade gimmicks—crawling food, waking

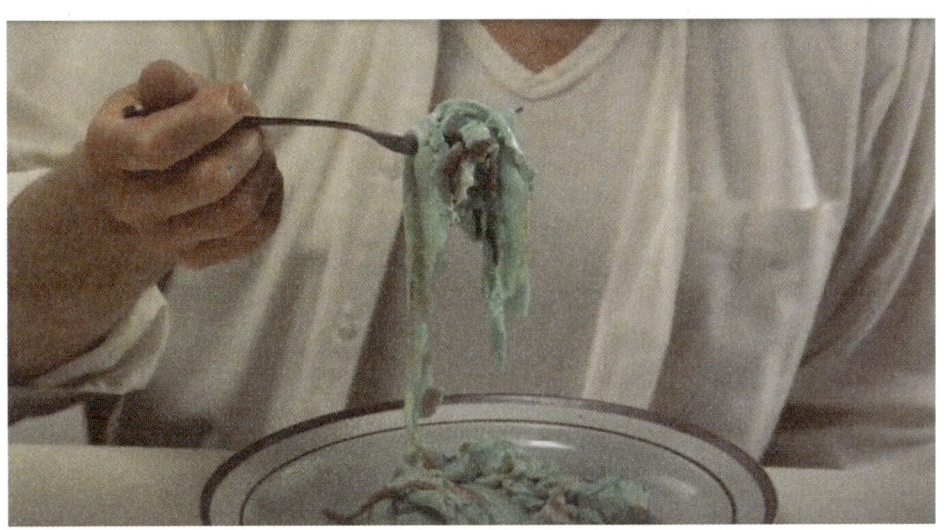

Film still from *Better Off Dead*. Savage Steve Holland. A&M Films/CBS Theatrical Films, 1985.

stop-motion hallucinations, verbose eroticism, drug use, amateur science, street racing, and skiing—are all boundary crossing expressions of a desire for escapism. ¶

NOTES

1. Aimee Levitt, "Were Jell-O salads an act of prefeminist vengeance?," thetakeout.com, November 7, 2019.
2. Jean-Paul Sartre, *Being and Nothingness: An Essay on Phenomenological Ontology*, trans. Hazel E. Barnes. 1943 (New York: Washington Square Press, 1956).pp. 610-12.

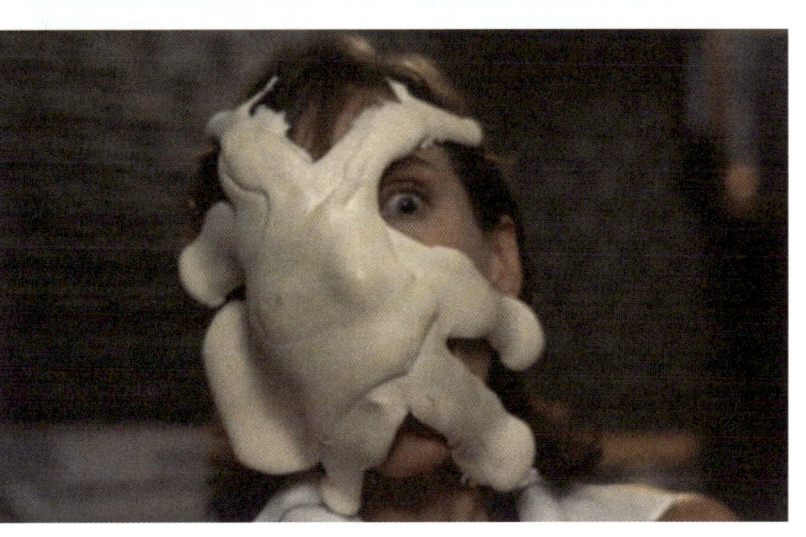

The Stuff. Directed by Larry Cohen. New World Pictures. 1985. In promotions for its release, *The Stuff* was marketed as: "A delicious, mysterious goo that oozes from the earth is marketed as the newest dessert sensation, but the tasty treat rots more than teeth when zombie-like snackers who only want to consume more of the strange substance at any cost begin infesting the world." The source of this peculiar film's horror is the irresistible desire for deadly food, however its truly outstanding feature is that the horror-substance percolates from the earth as a deadly but *natural* substance. In line with the sugary threat of entrapment that Sartre assigns to the slimy, the Stuff is similarly threatening in its irresistibility: 'A sugary-sliminess is the ideal of the slimy; it symbolizes the sugary death of the For-itself (like that of the wasp which sinks into the jam and drowns in it)'⁷² Importantly here, Sartre's wasp drowns in jam, not honey.

Filmed during the summer of 1983 and released on April 11, 1986, *The Toxic Avenger* is prophetic in its pre-Chernobyl visualization of poor toxic waste handling. Melvin 'the mop boy', a 98-pound janitor at a local health club, is persuaded in the locker room by a malicious bombshell to put on a full pink floral unitard and tulle tutu with the promise of a make out session. In full ballet costume Melvin dances excitedly down the hallway, through the gym's lounge and then enters the pool area in complete darkness for the rendezvous, the screen black. Despite what the kissing sounds and sweet talk suggest, the lights are suddenly flipped on and Melvin, to his horror, is embracing and kissing a sheep, also dressed in drag and wearing lipstick. All of the health club patrons are in on the prank and roar in mocking laughter as Melvin, thoroughly humiliated and emasculated, runs from them in embarrassment down a long hallway and smashes through a second story window.

Melvin lands headfirst into an open 50-gallon barrel of bubbling, smoking neon green toxic waste, ostensibly a radioactive fissure byproduct. The barrel itself is one of many loaded onto a flatbed truck coincidentally parked just in front of the health club. The truck's front grill bears the company name, "Tromaville Hi-Tox Chemical Waste Disposal Inc." The slimeball drivers of the truck, faces covered in white powder mid-coke binge, lift their noses out of their plastic bags with surprise. Their dashboard is littered with crushed Budweiser cans and Jack Daniels bottles, the cab's rear window plastered with *Playboy* centerfolds.

Exploded nuclear material threatens to reduce everything to slime, which is not necessarily the point of extinction. In his writing on "queer ecology" Timothy Morton writes, "Nature looks natural because it keeps going, and going, and going, like the undead, and because we keep on looking away, framing it, sizing it up. Acknowledging the zombie-like quality of interconnected lifeforms will aid the transition from an ideological fixation on Nature to a fully queer ecology."[1] Toxic waste contamination and its effects on our relationship to concepts of 'nature' and 'ecosystem' have raised critical conversations about the expansions of these categories to include humans and toxins, versus a sustained vision of undisturbed nature where post-nuclear ecosystems are an exclusionary fantasy.

The effects of his radioactive exposure just beginning, Melvin emerges from the barrel covered in toxic waste and in agony, but alive. His skin begins to melt, he bursts into flames and runs home in broad daylight where he locks himself in the bathroom. Quickly drawing himself a bath, Melvin continues his excruciating transformation emerging from the water in inverted colors and rippling camera effects as a different creature entirely, grotesque and over-muscled, transformation complete. Running into the sunset, the Toxic Avenger crashes through the remaining 60 minutes of the film fulfilling its title's promise. ¶

NOTES

1.   Timothy Morton, "Guest Column: Queer Ecology." *PMLA*, vol. 125, no. 2, 2010, pp. 273–282. *JSTOR*, p.279.

2.   Kyle Hill, "Chernobyl's Hot Mess, 'the Elephant's Foot,' Is Still Lethal," *Nautilus.us*, December 4, 2013.

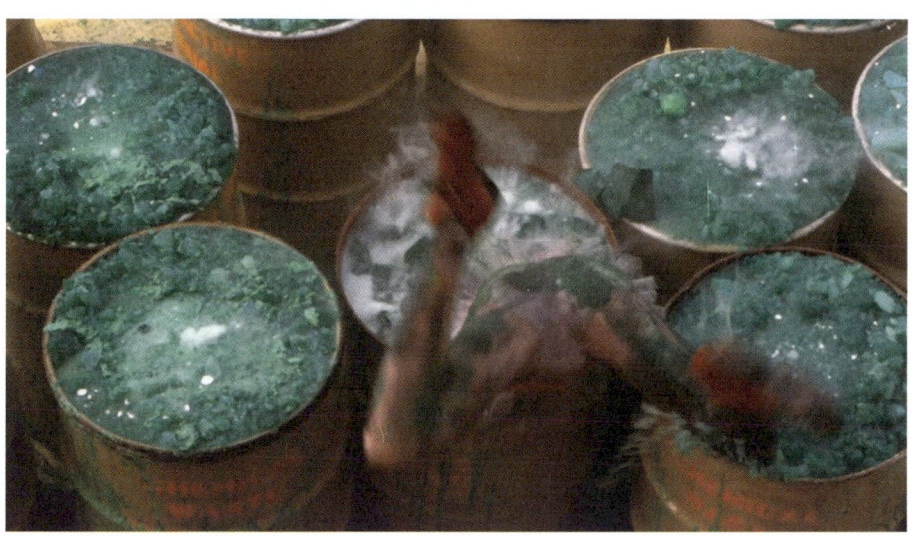

Film still from *The Toxic Avenger*. Troma Entertainment, 1984. Melvin "the mop boy" crashes through a second story window and falls into an open 50-gallon barrel of bubbling green toxic waste.

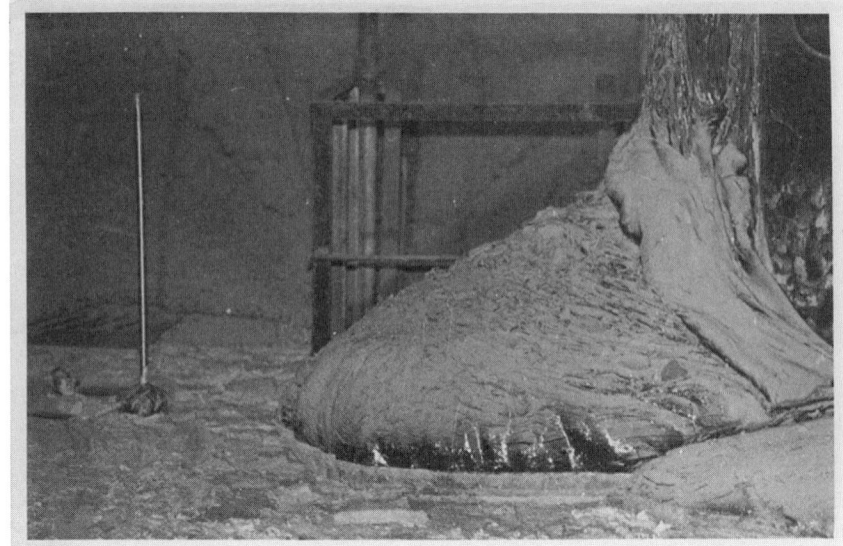

FIG. 11 92.5%
Reduce to 5½" x 8⁵⁄₁₆"

The Elephant Foot, Chernobyl, n.d. As radioactive smoke rose into the air after a failed test of Chernobyl's generator system, the rods within the compromised reactor melted through its container and formed a lava-like material known as Corium which began to collect in a huge mass on the reactor floor. Corium is created during meltdowns when nuclear materials and control rods come into contact with air, water, or steam. "According to readings taken at the time, the still hot portion of molten core put out enough radiation to give a lethal dose in 300 seconds."[1] Chernobyl's radioactive ooze continues to this day to slowly eat through everything in its path.

1986

By the mid-1980s many existing toys were either modified to extrude and dispense slime or were reimagined to have slime dumped upon them. New toys were designed with chests that cracked open so that organs could be excavated from slimy cavities. Slime was also sold on its own, sometimes in clear plastic containers, sometimes in mini green plastic garbage cans. Other toys such as Nerf-esque Madballs prominently featured slimy visual details. In a 2011 *Wall Street Journal* article, actor-director-writer Jordan Peele reflects back on slime where he writes, "It was sold to us as something scatological in nature. A messy substance of mischief. Something snot-like, or worse. A blended concoction of all the grossest things imaginable. Mystical in its grossness."[1] The preternatural qualities of slime as an incorporated feature in toy production broadened the horizon of play and imagination into a territory of abjection and amorphousness. Preceding the popularity of slime, the trend of toys designed to facilitate feigned productivity ranged from the borderline realistic Easy-Bake Oven, to the devolution of play into pure simulation in toys such as Play-Doh kitchen sets where every process involves stamping and extrusion–processes which are mini versions of the very manufacturing gestures used to make the toys themselves, activities which are then reenacted by children as a conflation of play, food preparation, and unskilled labor. Slime by comparison is an unmanageable play substance, distinctly un-moldable and useless, psychodynamics aside. Peele goes on, "We could sense that the thick green liquid meant something important, but we didn't know what."[2] True to its long oozing arc of signification, toy slime was degradable, an un-assimilable accessory to its hard plastic counterparts and containers.

Toy slime, like Play-Doh and Silly Putty, is best experienced fresh, before evaporation sets in, before it gets stuck in the carpet. ¶

NOTES

1. Jordan Peele, "What Ever Happened to Green Slime? Jordan Peele Investigates," *The Wall Street Journal*, February 21, 2012.
2. Ibid.

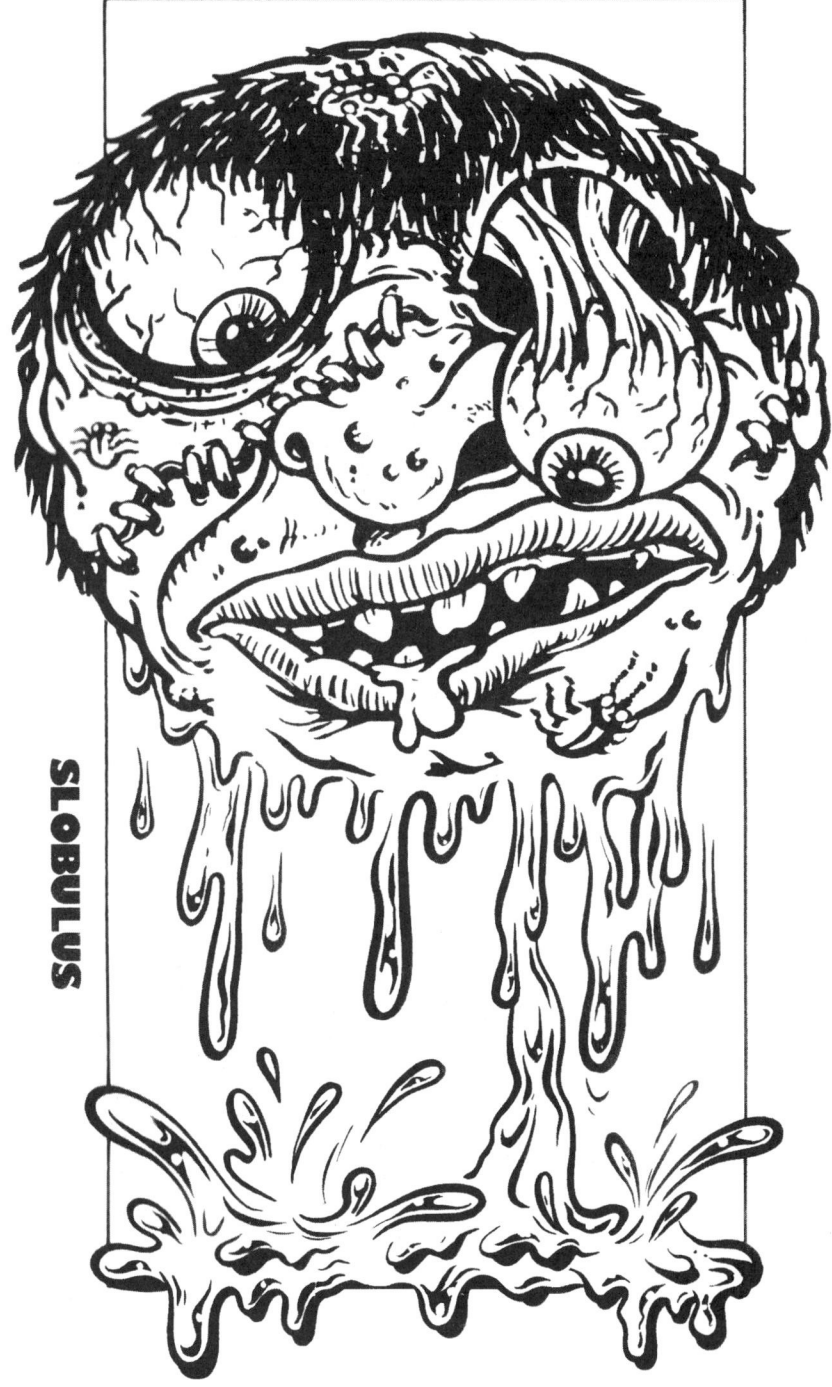

SLOBULUS

James Groman, "Slobulus" illustration from *The Madballs Handbook*, AmToy, 1986.

1986

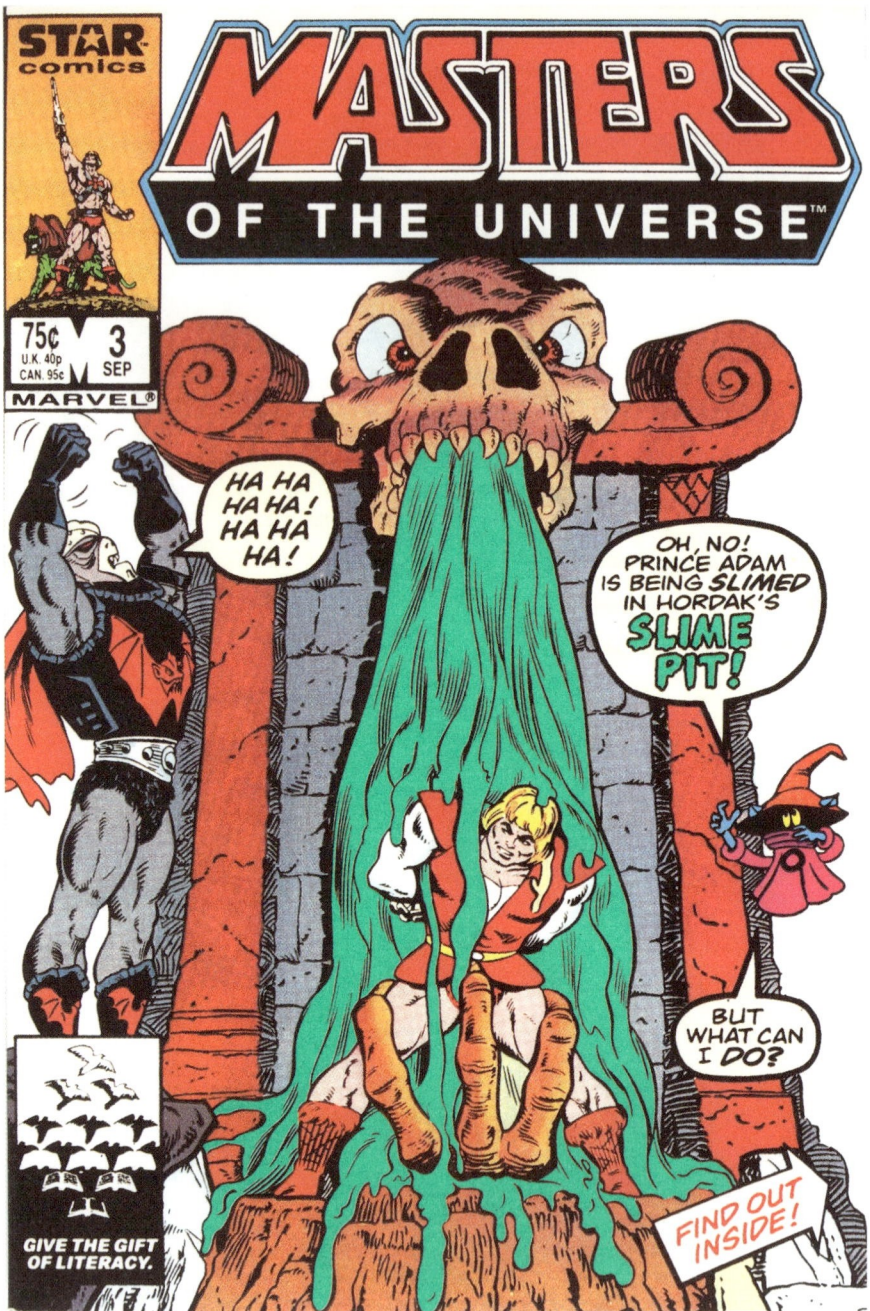

1986

In her 1991 essay "A Phantasmagoria of the Female Body: The work of Cindy Sherman," Laura Mulvey describes the shifted perspective central to Sherman's series of bulimia pictures from 1987 as a transgression of the "delicately painted"[1] veil of femininity. Devoid of any figure at all, along with a ground level point of view in which the entire field is intensely foreshortened, "nothing is left but disgust—the disgust of sexual detritus, decaying food, vomit, slime, menstrual blood, hair."[2] Mulvey describes with precision that, "With the disintegration of the body, the photographs lose any homogenous and cohesive formal organization."[3]

The threshold crossing dynamics of Sherman's photographs from this series, such as *Untitled #175* from 1987, immerse the viewer in a visual experience that Rosalind Krauss later refers to as "a kind of feminine sublime, albeit composed of infinite unspeakableness of bodily disgust: of blood, of excreta, of mucous membranes."[4] Krauss seems particularly interested in Mulvey's analysis of Sherman's figureless photographs in which an inside/outside topography of femininity is established and then "exhausted"[5]. These works undermine the semiotics of fetishism (and their abject counterparts) in their absence of any figure, a disastrous spatial metaphor taking its place. The photographs from this period are large in scale—boundaryless—their compositions not constricted by the picture frame, but alluding to a larger field of debris.

Notably in *Untitled #175,* a jettisoned pair of sunglasses lay upside down in the upper right corner of the frame, facing forward, partially obscured. Reflected in the one unobstructed lens is a face expressing horror or agony looking back out at the viewer, acting as a phantasmic index to the cathartic pathos of these photographs. Krauss' articulation of formlessness in this instance has to do with dispersal as a refusal of the gestalt as well as a fragmentation of point of view. Krauss succinctly describes the experience of these pictures where she writes, "It is in this sense that to be 'in the picture' within this alternative model is not to feel interpellated by society's meaning, is not to feel, that is, whole; it is to feel dispersed, subject to a picture not organized by form but by formlessness."[6] Here, Krauss articulates a liberative function of formlessness as a formalized foil to the objectification and fetishization of a photograph's subject. ¶

NOTES

1. Laura Mulvey, "A Phantasmagoria of the Female Body: The work of Cindy Sherman," *New Left Review*, Volume: 188, 1991.
2. Ibid.
3. Ibid.
4. Rosalind Krauss, "'Informe' without Conclusion," *October*, Vol. 78, (Autumn, 1996), pp. 89-105 Published by: The MIT Press.
5. Ibid.
6. Ibid.

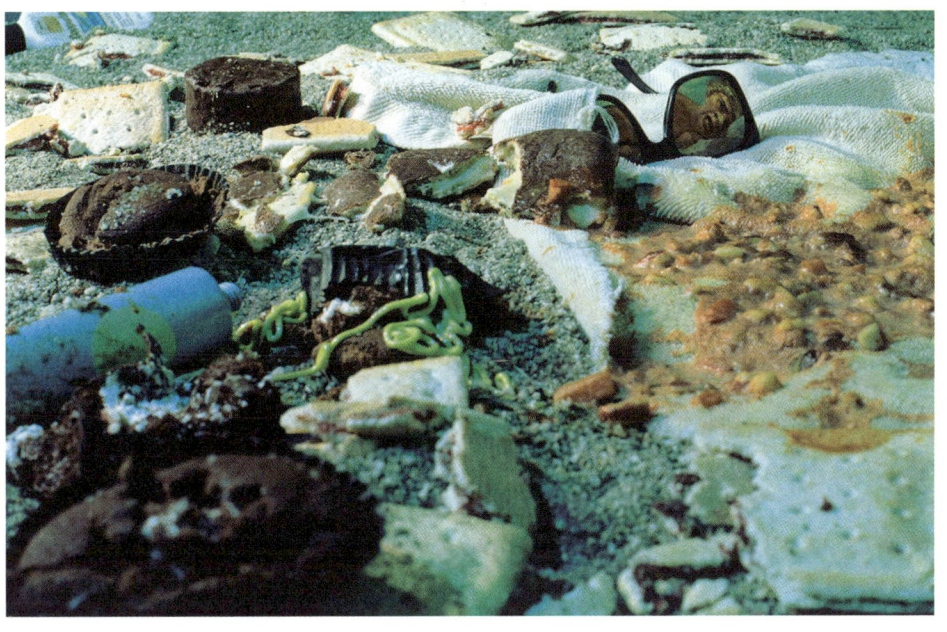

Cindy Sherman. *Untitled #175*, Chromogenic color print, 46 ⅝ × 71 ½, 1987.

1987

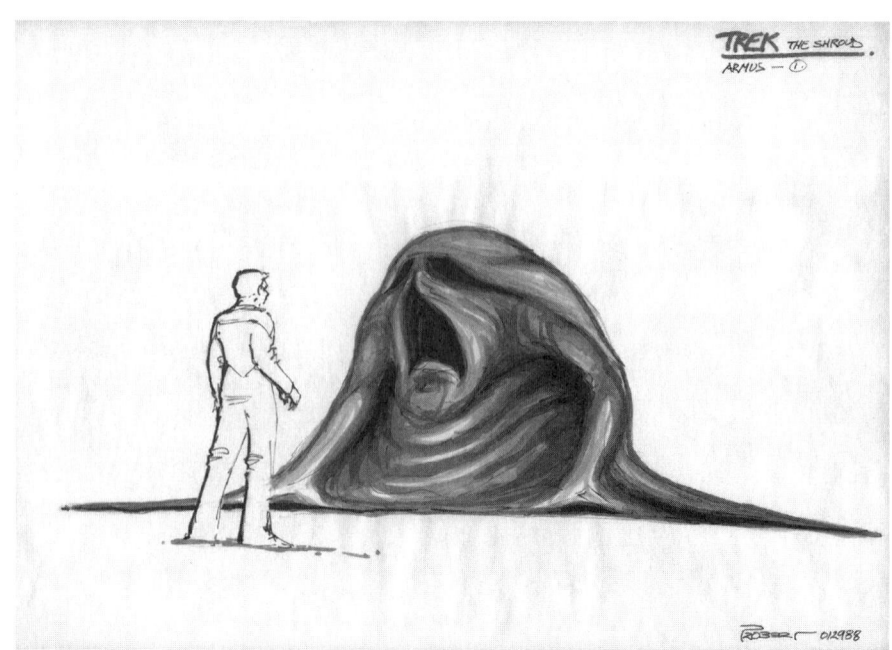

Andrew Probert, Armus concept art, *Skin of Evil, Season 1, Episode 23, Star Trek: The Next Generation*, Paramount Domestic Television, 1988. Part costume, part special effect, Armus was created using a concoction of Metamucil and printing ink and the armature itself was in a constant state of degradation due to a mysterious chemical reaction. Claustrophobic, heavy, and without an oxygen supply, the Armus costume was worn by actor Mart McChesney and takes were limited to 30 seconds each to prevent suffocation.

1988

COUNSELOR DEANNA TROI:
Who deserted you?

VOICE OF ARMUS:
Creatures whose beauty now dazzles
all who see them. They would not
exist without me.

COUNSELOR DEANNA TROI:
You were together?

VOICE OF ARMUS:
They perfected a means of bringing
to the surface all that was evil and
negative within, erupting, spreading,
connecting. In time, it formed a
second skin, dank and vile.

COUNSELOR DEANNA TROI:
You.

VOICE OF ARMUS:
Yes.

Joseph Stefano, Armus dialogue excerpt, *Skin of Evil, Season 1, Episode 23, Star Trek: The Next Generation*, Paramount Domestic Television, 1988.

Released in June 1989 on vinyl and cassette, *Margin Walker* is an EP by American post-hardcore band Fugazi. The cover art features an up-close photograph of the face of the band's front man Ian MacKaye, eyes rolled back and looking upward, an unidentifiable creamy-ish substance on his face. The details of this peculiar album cover are unaccounted for in the album's musical content and liner notes and is not precisely identifiable for lack of context. The overall formal qualities of the photograph are consistent with the trope of ecstasy paintings and the mystery substance ricochets off references to ectoplasm photography, silent film pie-in-the-face slapstick, and pornographic money shots, though the image is not specifically reduceable to any of these things.

Although somewhat notoriously inexplicable, *Margin Walker's* cover photograph recalls images as specific as Caravaggio's 1606 painting *Mary Magdalen in Ecstasy,* where the depiction of supernatural communication is an entirely interior, albeit subtly evident experience. An important aspect of the Fugazi album cover photo is MacKaye's open eyes, a detail that connects to even later ecstasy representations by painters such as Guido Reni and Artemisia Gentileschi. Close-up scenes of Renèe Jeanne Falconetti's face in her notoriously embodied portrayal of Joan in Carl Theodors Dreyer's 1928 silent film *The Passion of Joan of Arc* also come to mind. During a telephone conversation with MacKaye, he recounted that the photograph was one in a series taken during a photoshoot with his friend and fellow musician Tomas Squip.[1] Squip was a student at the Corcoran School of the Arts and Design at the time and enlisted MacKaye as his subject for a photography class color-balance assignment, which MacKaye agreed to do on the condition that the photos be interestingly fucked up. During the backyard photo shoot MacKaye's face and head were wrapped and defaced with packing tape, rubber bands, and shaving cream. Once completely enshrouded, MacKaye and Squip began the painful yet hysterically funny process of removing these things while documenting the process along the way. Tears and laughter ensued. The photo which appears on the album cover was the last in this session, a final piece of packing tape having just been ripped from MacKaye's face. The negatives from the photo shoot are lost, and the only image printed image from the sequence is the one that appears on the *Margin Walker* cover.

In an online forum regarding controversial and banned album cover art, one post reads, "What about the fugazi margin walker EP that has the guy with cum all over his face? No one ever complains about that one." To which another commenter replies, "hmm... that guy is ian mackaye and I don't think that's what you think it is."[2] While there is not a lyricgenius.com equivalent of crowd sourced album cover interpretation, the suggestiveness of *Margin Walker's* cover image has occasionally been discussed, the upshot being that it is confounding. Importantly, the image was not created with the intent of it being on the album cover, but was selected years after as an appropriately provocative image choice.

The EP's title, *Margin Walker,* suggests a potential boundary crossing, a back-and-forth movement consistent with paranormal contact often resulting in traces of ectoplasm. An EP is itself often a transitional release, its format consisting of 1-6 songs in 30 minutes or less. In fact *Margin Walker* was released between Fugazi's eponymously titled debut EP and *13 Songs* which combined both EPs into one full-length release capitalizing on the prodigious novelty of the emergent CD format. There was something specific at stake in *Margin Walker*'s cover, implicating the viewer in an interpretation of a peculiar photograph that variably accepted, deferred, or rejected the referential elasticity of the religious-supernatural-comedic-pornographic-esque image. A consumer/fan of the hardcore music scene of the late 1980s would have experienced an intersection of their desire for ownership of this EP with its dynamic and complex cover image at the moment of purchase, and *Margin Walker's* cover continues to sustain an idiosyncratic reverberation with the album's musical content. ¶

NOTES

1.   Ian MacKaye, Telephone conversation. March 30, 2021. The day after our telephone conversation, MacKaye sent a follow up email regarding the date the photograph was taken where he wrote, "I never was able to find any specific mention of the photo session in my journals, but I did come across a mention of giving a friend a photocopy of the 'crazy photo' that Tomas had taken of me. this was dated 11/23/85. On 10/22/85 I mention that Tomas and I took photos, but didn't offer any details. All of this leads me to think that the *Margin Walker* photo may well have been taken in 1985."

2.   "Banned/Controversial Album Covers," j fail (cenotaph), Friday, 30 January 2004 19:31, ilxor.com

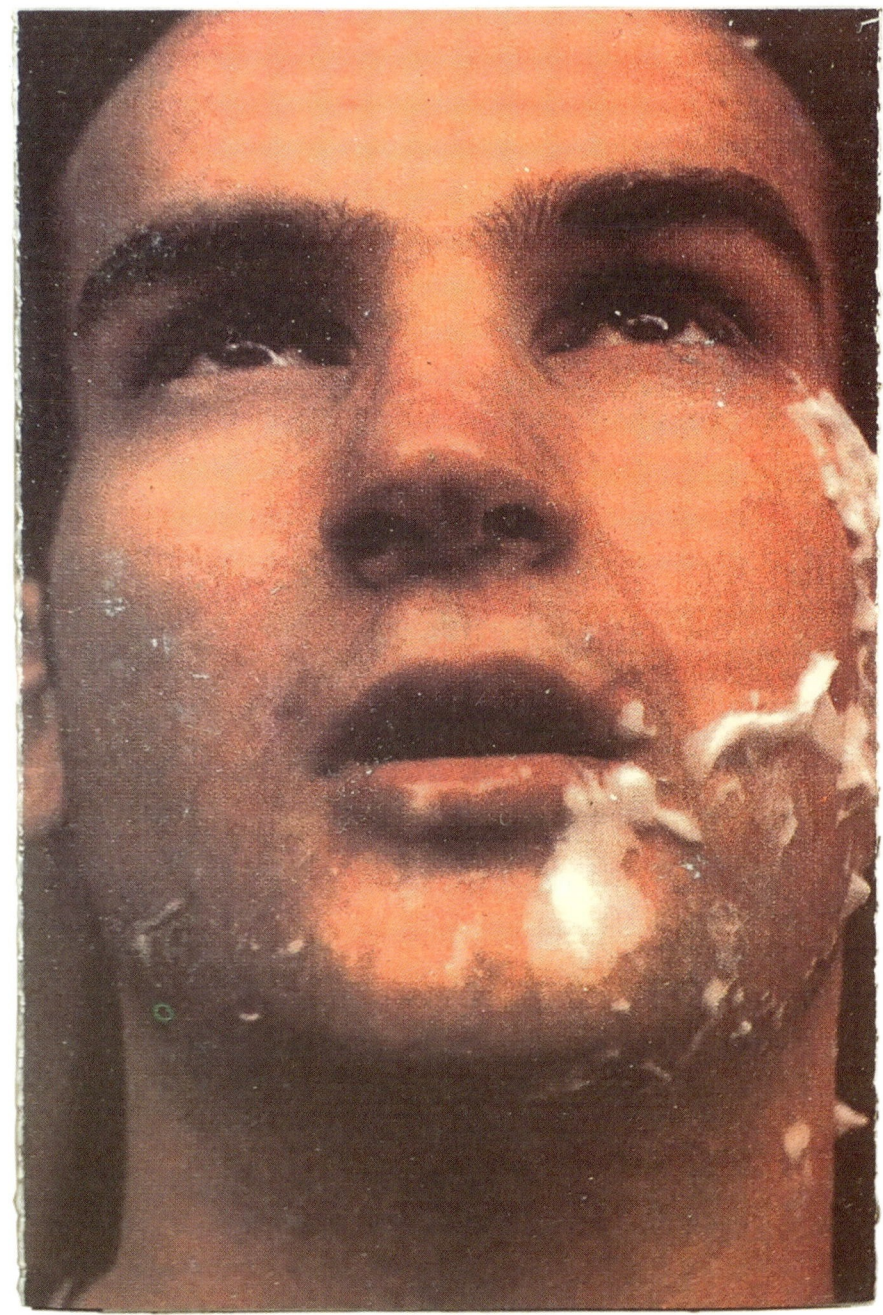

Fugazi, *Margin Walker*, EP cover photograph by Tomas Squip, 1988.

1989

Just after midnight on March 24, 1989, 43-year-old Captain Joseph Hazelwood ran the oil tanker Exxon Valdez into Bligh Reef, a well-documented navigational hazard in Alaska's Prince William Sound, spilling between 11 and 38 million gallons of crude oil. The results were devastating. I was 13 years old and living in Alaska when the accident occurred and much of the news coverage related to the incident featured images and video of sea animals, birds especially, floundering on the shore miserably due to being coated in oil. An estimated 250,000 seabirds, 2,800 sea otters, 300 harbor seals, 250 bald eagles, 22 killer whales, and billions of salmon and herring eggs were killed as a result. In a frantic and ultimately futile effort to minimize the damage to wildlife, hundreds of citizens were hired temporarily by Exxon to hand wash birds on the effected shores with charcoal solutions, antibiotics, and dish soap. Less than one percent of the birds "cleaned" in this fashion survived in the long term, characterizing the effort as more theatrical than effective.[1] Naturally occurring and composed of hydrocarbon deposits and other organic materials, crude oil is the product of the bacterial decomposition of animals and plants from millions of years ago. Crude oil extraction bridges geochronic epochs—it is non-renewable, it is unsustainable, and in the case of the Exxon Valdez oil spill, it expedited the unavoidably negative effect of dependence on fossil fuel, a Capitalcenic catastrophe.[2] Death by direct exposure, not via carbon dioxide emission resulting from use after refinement and as a result of combustion, the inundation of Prince William Sound with crude oil was more akin to animals stepping directly into an inescapably viscous tarpit, the past consuming the present.

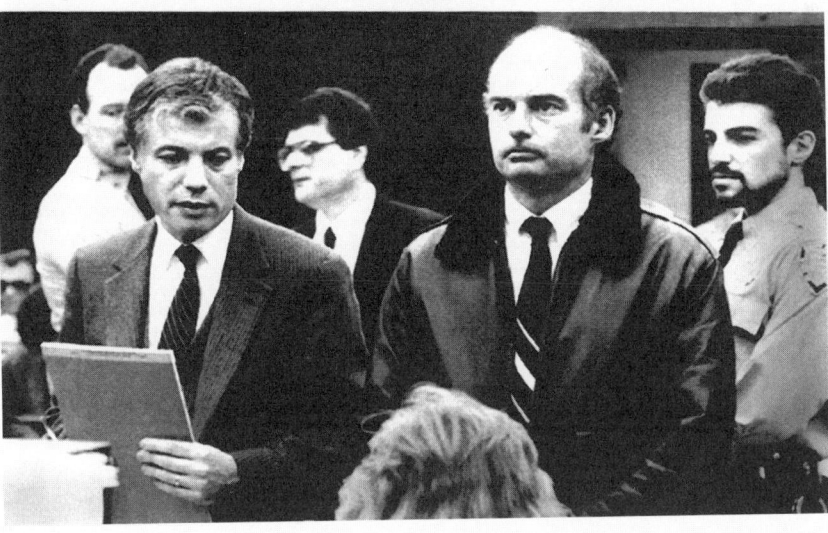

Fugitive Exxon Captain Joseph Hazelwood (R) listens as his attorney Thomas Russo addresses the court on April 5 after Hazelwood surrendered to the Suffolk County District Attorney. Hazelwood was arraigned in state Supreme Court where he was taken to the County Jail in Riverhead, New York, 1989.

In addition to scathing public condemnation and a landslide of legal after-effects, Hazelwood was joked about prolifically. The very idea of a single person being responsible for such a disaster was so abstract and unfathomable that the "glissement" of the event resulted in the circulation of jokes as dumb as "I said give me another Bud Light, not turn right!" Hazelwood himself seemed to internalize and embody the incomprehensible singularity of his responsibility, even making jokes at his own expense. In an *Outside Magazine* article from 1997 Hazelwood jokingly recalls a different tanker run through Prince William Sound, "We left Valdez fully loaded..." He pulls up short. "The ship, I mean—not me."[3] The *Outside Magazine* writer of the same article goes on to say that:

> To be Joe Hazelwood is to be preternaturally alert to double entendres, puns, one-liners, coincidences, any flashing link between this moment and that dark night in March 1989 when he was transfigured from an anonymous but skilled professional into a lasting national symbol of rank incompetence and drunken idiocy. When the opportunity for a joke presents itself, he is coiled and ready, anticipating its arrival, deflecting it with topspin, and then laughing his ersatz laugh at the joke, to be sure, but also at the irony of his telling the joke. To be Joe Hazelwood is to be a connoisseur of irony, a seeker of veiled meanings.[4]

The "transfiguration" of Hazelwood was also a transfiguration of the public imagination to more acute optics on the understanding of the severity and scope of impact resulting from a resource extraction relationship to the environment, conflating notions of immediate and cumulative impact.

In book 10 of John Milton's epic blank verse poem *Paradise Lost* from 1667, "Asphaltic slime" is hauntingly used in the description of the bridge connecting hell to earth by way of a passage through a realm of chaos that is compared with the Arctic:

> And with Asphaltic slime; broad as the Gate,
> Deep to the Roots of Hell the gather'd beach
> They fasten'd, and the Mole immense wraught on
> Over the foaming deep high Archt, a Bridge
> Of length prodigious joyning to the Wall
> Immovable of this now fenceless world
> Forfeit to Death; from hence a passage broad,
> Smooth, easie, inoffensive down to Hell.

Satan's bridge is being constructed as he and his interlocutors travel along it. Conveyed in this scene is the unfolding of an idea, the articulation of a thought, and the writing or reading of verse. Milton's bridge is an apt metaphor for the crude spill of the Exxon Valdez and its consequential trail of asphaltic slime. English painter and illustrator John Martin was commissioned in 1824 by Septimus Prowett to produce mezzotint illustrations for the highly regarded Washbourne Publication of *Paradise Lost*. Martin's mezzotint prints are recognizably romantic in their emotive exuberance—the mountainous clouds, enfolding foliage, and wrinkled ridges of rock—beautiful, but nonetheless familiar.

What makes these illustrations of Milton's poem enduringly fascinating are their traces of early industrial architecture such as in *The Bridge Over Chaos*,

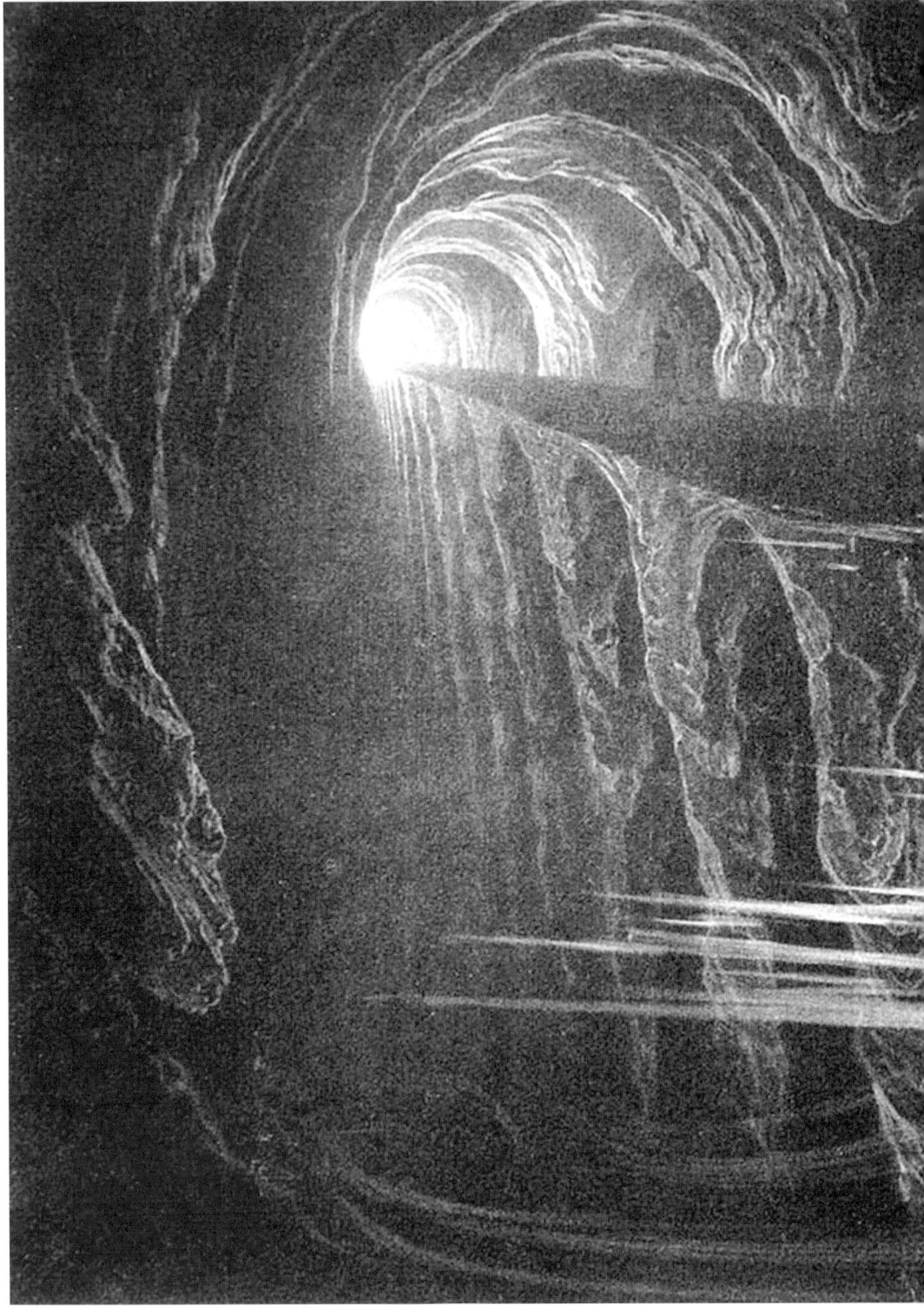

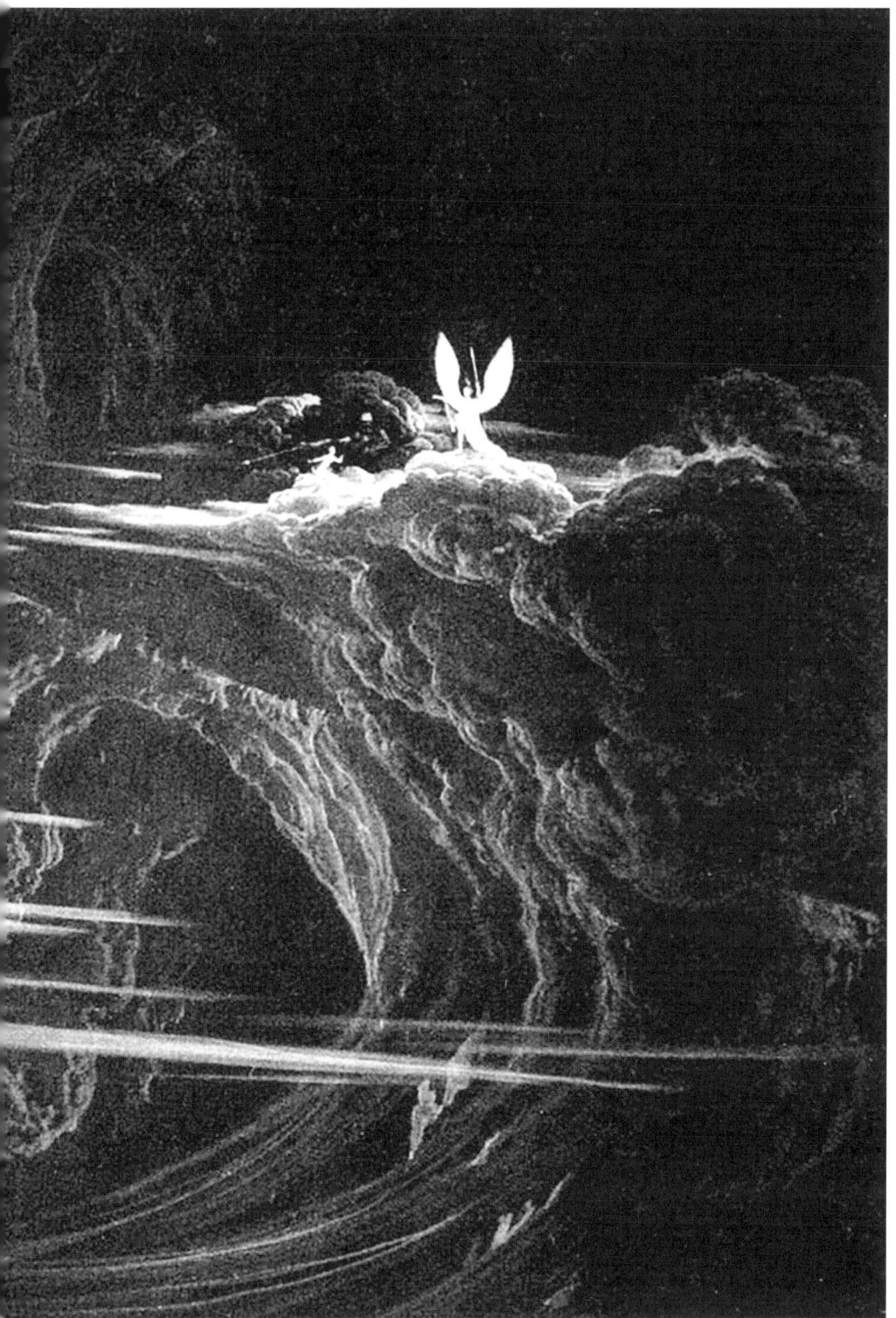

which the British Library catalog describes as "almost like a sewer tunnel or mine-shaft,"[5] perhaps reflecting "the fact that Martin was, at this time, designing schemes for improving towns with embankments and sewers, underground railways and glass shopping complexes."[6]

In an intaglio printmaking process, a prepared yet untouched surface of a mezzotint plate if inked would print a solid black. To create the image, the artist draws by scraping and scratching the surface of the plate using tools such as burnishers and scrapers. The smoother an area, the less ink it will hold and the lighter the plate will print. "The copper-plate [the mezzotint] is done upon, when the artist first takes it into hand, is wrought all over with an edg'd tool, so as to make the print one even black, like night: and his whole work after this, is merely introducing the lights into it; which he does by scraping off the rough grain according to his design, artfully smoothing it most where light is most required ..."[7] An exacting description of the mezzotint process in this case is also an apt description of Martin's illustration of *The Bridge Over Chaos*, the entire scene travelling upward toward illumination. ¶

1. Andrew Nikiforuk, "Why We Pretend to Clean Up Oil Spills," *Smithsonian Magazine*, 2016. "In many respects, society's theatrical response to catastrophic oil spills resembles the way medical professionals respond to aggressive cancer in an elderly patient. Because surgery is available, it is often used. Surgery also creates the impression that the health care system is doing something even though it can't change or reverse the patient's ultimate condition. In an oil-based society, the cleanup delusion is also irresistible. Just as it is difficult for us to acknowledge the limits of medical intervention, society struggles to acknowledge the limits of technologies or the consequences of energy habits."

2. Jason W. Moore, Raj Patel, "Unearthing the Capitalocene: Towards a Reparations Ecology," roarmag.org, Issue #7, January 4, 2018. "Some humans are currently killing everything, from megafauna to microbiota, at speeds one hundred times higher than the background rate. We argue that what changed is capitalism, that modern history has, since the 1400s, unfolded in what is better termed the Capitalocene. Using this name means taking capitalism seriously, understanding it not just as an economic system but as a way of organizing the relations between humans and the rest of nature."

3. Daniel Coyle, "The Captain Went Down with the Ship," *Outside Magazine*, October 1997.

4. Ibid.

5. British Library, "John Martin's illustrations for *Paradise Lost*, 1827," bl.uk., retrieved October 2020.

6. Ibid.

7. William Hogarth, *The Analysis of Beauty*, (1753).

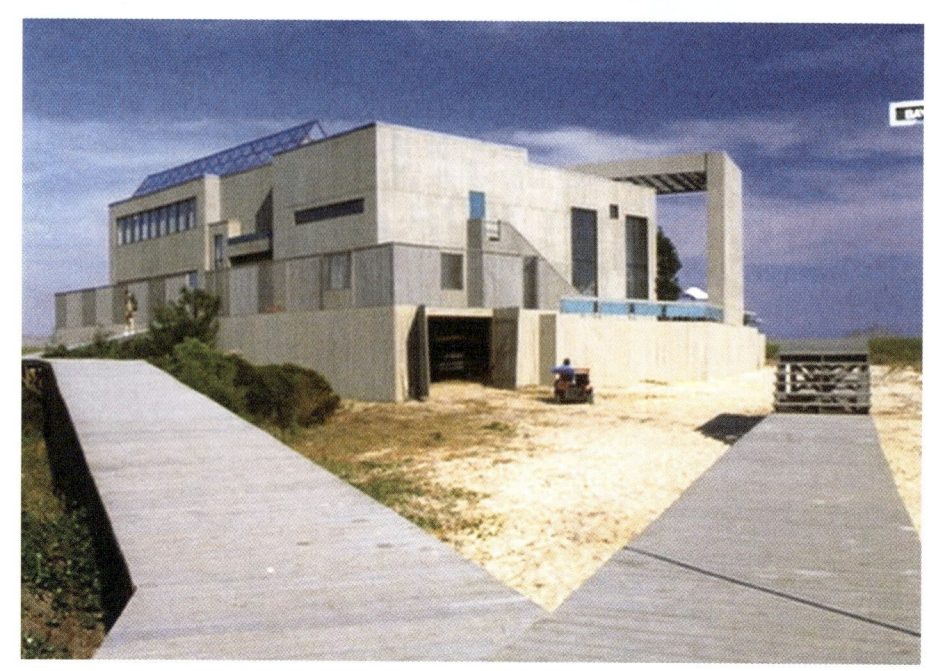

Film still from *Weekend at Bernie's*, Directed by Ted Kotcheff. 20th Century Fox, 1989. A ghost house that can only be experienced through the phantasmagoria of film. Bernie Lomax's House, 1610 Fort Fisher Blvd, Kure Beach, NC, Fort Fisher State Recreation Area. Built specifically for the film and torn down immediately after production.

1989

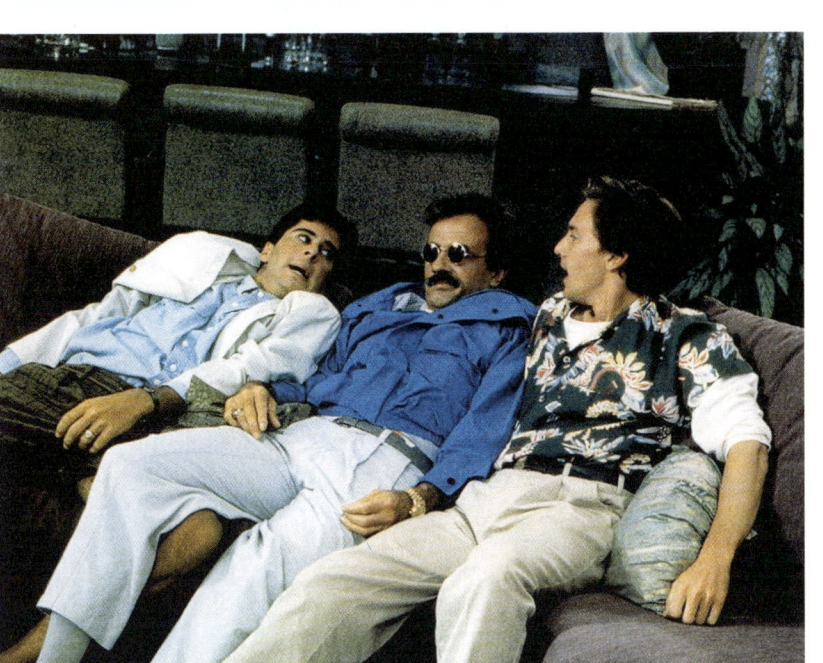

Film still from *Weekend at Bernie's* is a 1989 zombie buddy film in which the deceased main character Bernie Lomax successfully navigates the complexities of social stratification, drug use, sexual relationships, criminal activity, work, and leisure. Whereas most zombie films employ representations of zombies through the use of special effects and highly contrived acting, *Weekend at Bernie's*'s innovatively reanimates its slimy central character through the medium of cinema itself. The commodification of experience, of the everyday, and of "leisure time," has progressed farther than any cultural theorist ever imagined. In *Weekend at Bernie's* we are shown the liberative potential of having it all while being completely dead.

1990

1991

1992

1997

There is also a legend of a place called the Black Lodge: the shadow self of the White Lodge, a place of dark forces that pull on this world. A world of nightmares. Shamans reduced to crying children, angry spirits pouring from the woods, graves opening like flowers.[1]

–Deputy Hawk

NOTES

1. Deputy Hawk dialogue excerpt, *Twin Peaks*, Season 2, Episode 11, "Masked Ball," 1990.

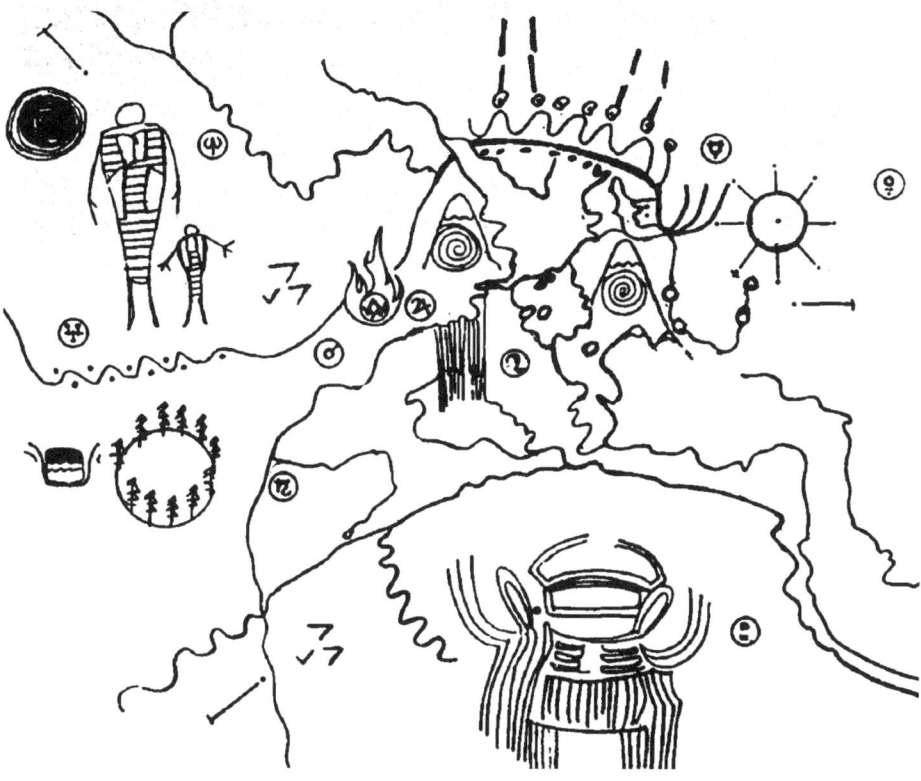

Black Lodge map, *Twin Peaks*, Mark Frost, David Lynch, American Broadcasting Company, 1990. Black Lodge entrance, Glastonberry Grove, Episode 27, "The Path to the Black Lodge," 1991.

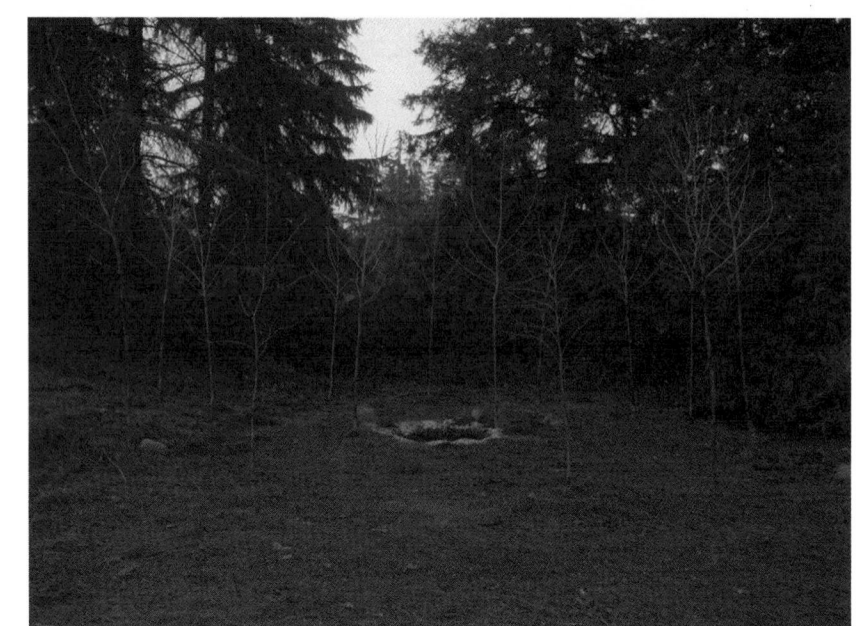

Film still from *Twin Peaks*, Mark Frost, David Lynch, American Broadcasting Company, 1990. Black Lodge entrance, Glastonberry Grove. Episode 27, "The Path to the Black Lodge," 1991. Within the cinematic imagination of *Twin Peaks*, Glastonbury Grove was a circular stand of twelve sycamore trees located in Washington's Ghostwood National Forest, close to Pearl Lakes and the town of Twin Peaks. In the center of the grove flanked by two more sycamores was a rocky pool containing a thick, black substance resembling scorched oil. Under certain conditions, a translucent set of curtains would appear across the grove's center allowing passage into a red-curtained labyrinth believed to be the mythical Black Lodge.

1990

In 2018 the U.S. Department of Nuclear Energy published a post on their blog titled, "7 Things The Simpsons Got Wrong About Nuclear,"[1] that aimed to debunk nuclear power myths with semi-cheeky facts such as "Fuel rods are not used as paper weights," and "Nuclear waste is safely stored." An investigative Vice article regarding the blog post by Aaron Gordon revealed via Freedom of Information Act documents that the post was the project of an at-the-time intern with the Office of Nuclear Energy who must also have been a Simpsons fan. While Gordon's interest in the blog post has more to do with its redacted records than the wider nuclear-cultural dynamics at play in this type of DEA edu-comedic content, Gorgon does corroborate the somewhat-popular association of nuclear power with employee ineptitude and supervisorial malpractice cultivated within the satirical universe of The Simpsons:

> "...when someone mentions "nuclear power," a solid chunk of the American populace hears that phrase in their own heads in Mr. Burns's voice. The show's casting of Homer as an incompetent and lazy safety inspector, along with Mr. Burns as its corrupt, plutocratic owner more interested in winning softball games than running a safe facility is, to Americans of a certain age, the sum total of things they know about nuclear power plants."[2]

In an early first season episode of The Simpsons, Bart catches a three-eyed fish from a pond and declares, "Alright! We eat tonight!"[3] — the scene then pans to show the Springfield Nuclear Power Plan looming in the not-so-distant distance. In another episode Homer is made to eat neon green pudding-like toxic

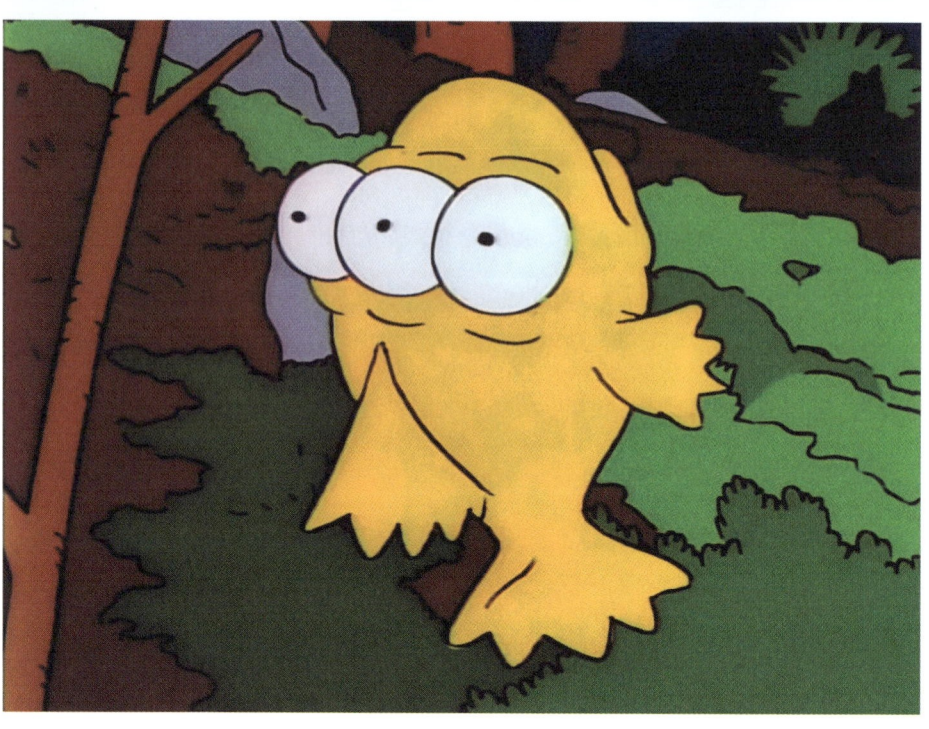

Blinky the fish from "Two Cars in Every Garage and Three Eyes on Every Fish," The Simpsons. Season 2, Episode 4. November 1, 1990.

waste with a spoon from a 55-gallon drum as a form of disciplinary action imposed by the power plant's misanthropic owner Mr. Burns. "That's rough. There must be two ... three hundred gallons in here."[4] commiserates a colleague before inviting Homer to go bowling. I counted and there are over thirty 55-gallon drums visible in the scene. Proximity to nuclear power and casual mismanagement of nuclear waste are prominent features of The Simpsons. Springfield's energy grid is nuclear powered, which might explain the show's longevity?

In their 1983 book *Pure War,* Paul Virilio and Sylvère Lotringer remark on the way in which technocratic administration of nuclear power tends to overshadow its apocalyptic dimension, "When I talk with a general or an admiral, I'm always struck by his lack of knowledge about nuclear destruction, his ignorance of the experience of this destruction."[5] Because of the nuclear casualness within The Simpsons we occasionally get to revel in the visual pleasure of high-chroma radioactive goo, guffaw at the silliness of toxic barrel running, and smack our heads as Mr. Burns colludes to dispose of spent plutonium waste in plain sight all over Springfield. Despite intra-program speculation that the power plant's toxic waste is either dumped in an abandoned chalk mine and covered with cement or sent to a southern state with a corrupt governor, the ooze sticks around, so to speak.

The sardonic nuclear humor in The Simpsons coyly acknowledges cautionary correlations to real world contamination. We experience a weird kind of reverse NIMBYism in the show — Springfield Toxic Waste Dump is located somewhere between the elementary school and the powerplant and we get a glimpse of it only once.

In actuality, minority and low-income neighborhoods and communities in transition are disproportionately targeted by industries whose waste flows toward them in a regulatory path of least resistance. A recent environmental justice paper corroborates decades of studies that have established, "clear patterns of racial and socioeconomic disparities in the distribution of a large variety of environmental hazards."[6] The Simpsons sublimates atomic fear into belly laughs and in doing so naturalizes a shared sense of proximity to nuclear power where we might otherwise dissociate. ¶

NOTES

1. Office of Nuclear Energy, "7 Things The Simpsons Got Wrong About Nuclear," April 4, 2018. energy.gov

2. Aaron Gordon, "Department of Energy Heavily Redacts Documents on Homer Simpson Blog; What did Homer know and when did he know it?," Motherboard; Tech by Vice, July 29, 2021.

3. "Two Cars in Every Garage and Three Eyes on Every Fish," The Simpsons. Season 2, Episode 4. November 1, 1990.

4. "Hello Gutter, Hello Fadder," The Simpsons. Season 11, Episode 6. November 14, 1999.

5. Sylvère Lotringer and Paul Virilio, Pure War, Semiotext(e), 1983. p. 35

6. Paul Mohai and Robin Saha, "Which came first, people or pollution? Assessing the disparate siting and post-siting demographic change hypotheses of environmental injustice." 2015, Environmental Research Letters, Volume 10, Number 11.

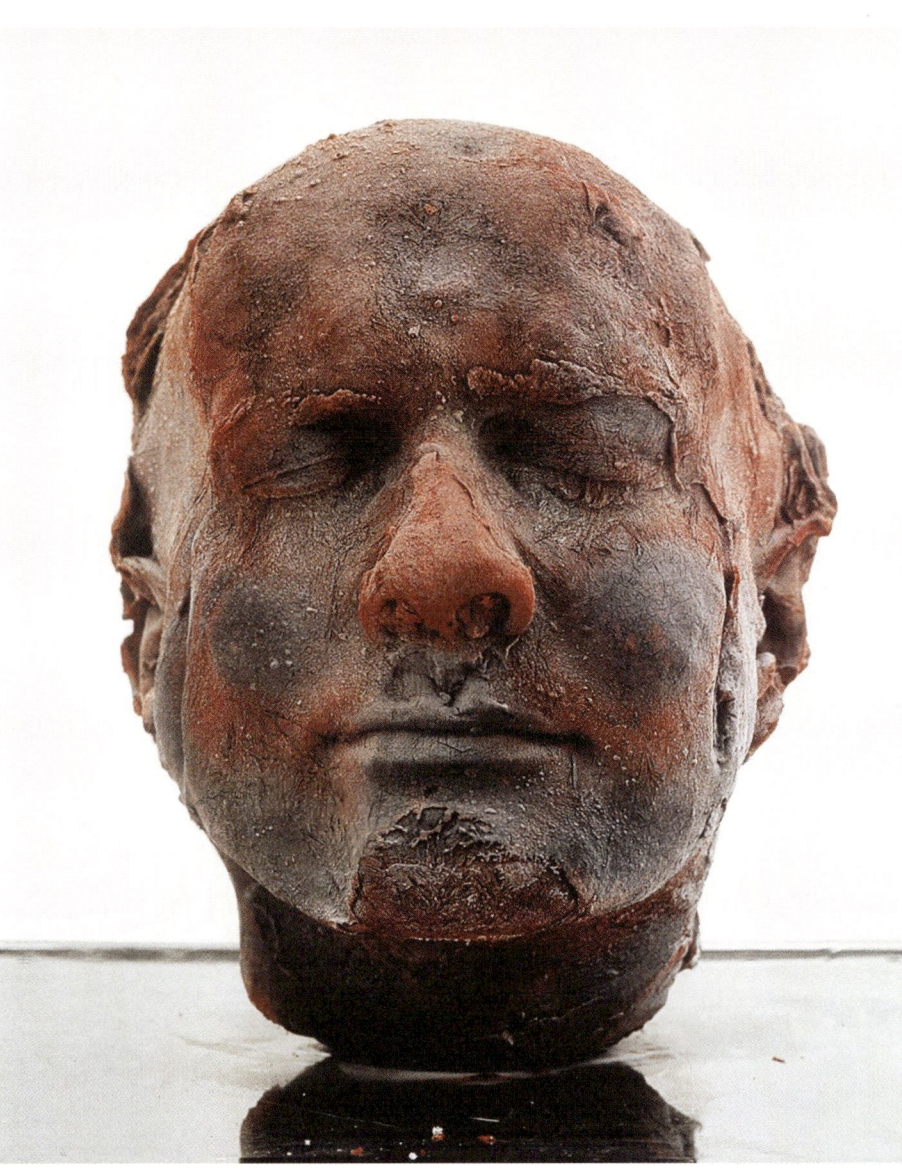

Mark Quinn, *Self*, Blood (artist's), stainless steel, Perspex and refrigeration equipment, 208h x 63w x 63d cm, 1991. Purchased for a rumored £13,000 in 1991, the kitchen refrigerator in which collector Charles Saatchi kept Quinn's *Self* was accidentally unplugged by construction workers in 2002 and the nine pints of melted blood spilled onto the floor.

1991

Thawing permafrost has resulted in intermit-
tent, newsworthy discoveries of preserved "ice
age" megafauna: an extinct cave lion cub in 2017,
an 18,000-year-old prehistoric puppy in 2018, a
42,000-year-old foal, and 32,000-year-old wolf head
in 2019, to name just a few. Climate change research
focused on increased nitrogen concentrations in
Arctic streams has revealed that, "As permafrost
thaws, microbes in the formerly frozen soil become
more active, breaking down organic matter and
releasing more nutrients into the environment, which
can be carried away in seasonal meltwater."[1] Results
of such research show an increase in "Arctic Stream
Slime"–a kind of re-primordial biofilm teeming
with fungal and bacterial communities. The effects
of climate change are dynamic and complex, but
thawing permafrost alone releases vast amounts of
methane and carbon dioxide. The premise of Encino
Man is the accidental discovery of prehistoric man
Linkavitch Chomofsky while excavating a backyard
in Encino, California, in preparation for the instal-
lation of a swimming pool. Preserved in a block of
ice, Linkavitch is thawed free and comes back to
life, putting the plot into motion. Like Poltergeist,
Encino Man makes use of the swimming pool pit as
a cinematic site of trauma. Linkavitch's awakening
is part time-travel part re-animation, and his "ice
age" persona enthralls and repels as he attempts to
integrate into contemporary California. ¶

NOTES

1. Kate Wheeling, "How Will Climate Change Affect Arctic Stream Slime?" *Journal of Geophysical Research: Biogeosciences.* April 15, 2020.

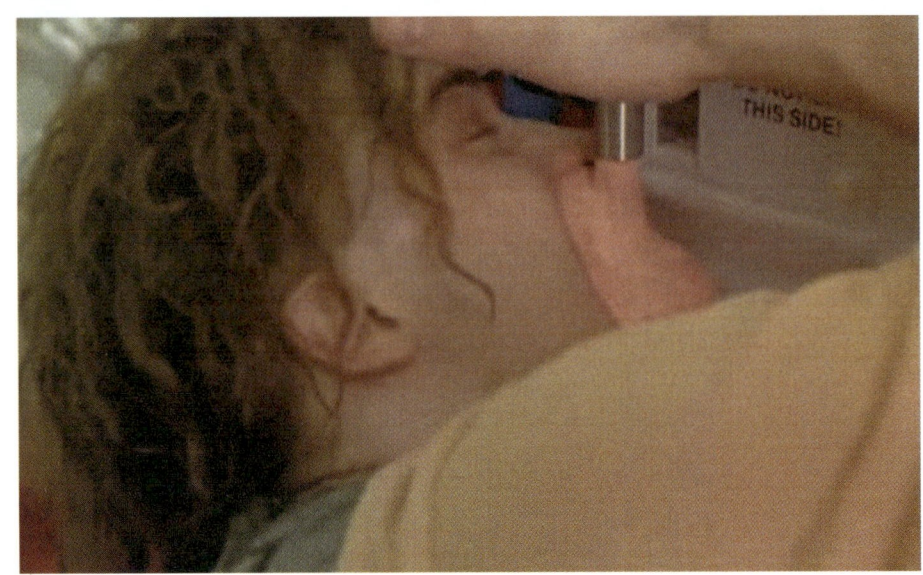

Film still from *Encino Man*. Directed by Les Mayfield. Hollywood Pictures/Touchwood Pacific Partners I, 1992. Linkavitch Chomofsky (portrayed by Brendan Fraser) "wheezing the juice." "Wheezing the juice" is the act of consuming an extruded frozen beverage directly from the machine.

1992

A Nike-outfitted millennial suicide cult in an existential exodus from a planet whose "inhabitants are refusing to evolve,"[1] Heaven's Gate failed to recruit new members between their "final offer" for membership in 1993 and their 1997 mass suicide/consciousness upload to a UFO traveling incognito in comet Halle Bop's trail. In the years leading up to their phenobarbital-facilitated suicides, the cult fortified themselves against Earthly threats constructing "a concrete and earth fortress in the mountains south of Albuquerque,"[2] amassing "a cache of weapons in an Escondido storage locker,"[3] and eventually settling into a 9,000 square foot rental property in Rancho Santa Fe, California. The mass suicides themselves took place in three shifts over three days, the groups' adherents split into "home" teams and "away" teams.

Heaven's Gate was a messy pastiche of theosophy, pop sci-fi, and religious ideology with cult leader Marshall Applewhite evolving his ideas over a 25-year period. Objects entering and exiting Earth's atmosphere are a through line in the collection of precedents in this project, making Heaven's Gate unignorable—spiritualists seek to communicate with the deceased through mediumship, the Blob arrived from outer space, the risks and benefits of nuclear energy are internalized and externalized through power plants and ballistics, *Better Off Dead's* Badger launches himself into space in a homemade rocket. Threshold crossing is central to these examples and

Heaven's Gate collages an accumulation of threshold crossing phantasmic allusions.

Most notably, the world was left with two online videos of Applewhite addressing Earth's remaining inhabitants post-mortem, announcing the group's imminent departure, inviting others to join, and sharing that the world is about to be recycled. In the verbose yet urgent videos Applewhite sits in front of a purple velvet curtain backdrop, close-up and speaking into the camera. Midway through the second video Applewhite shares:

> We have a website now, you know, it's the popular thing–everybody has to have a website. Our website on the Internet is called Heavensgate. Heavensgate–oh, of course, .com. Everything is .com. We're not .org, we're .com. So if you want to, you can learn more about who we are, what we have to say, what I have to say, what my Older Members can share with you through what we have said, and know of our history.[4]

Still in existence, Applewhite's website posthumously catches its visitors in the slime of his parting words. ¶

NOTES

1. Lawrence K. Altman, "Death in a Cult: The Drugs. One Thing Is No Mystery: Lethal Nature Of a Mix," *New York Times*, March 28, 1997.
2. Don Lattin, "The Gospel According to Applewhite / A bit of Theosophy, a bit of X-Files, a bit from the Book of Revelation–the mix-and-match theology of the Heaven's Gate cult had antecedents everywhere," sfgate.com, Sunday, April 6, 1997.
3. Ibid.
4. Marshall Applewhite, *Last Chance to Evacuate Earth Before It's Recycled–Your Only Chance To Survive–Leave With Us*, Edited transcript of videotape, October 5, 1996, heavensgate.com

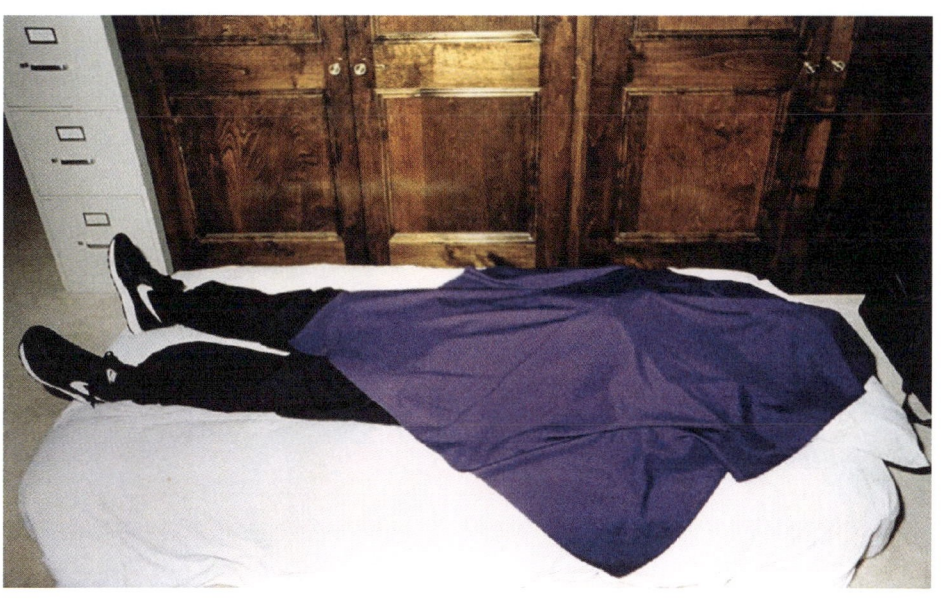

1997

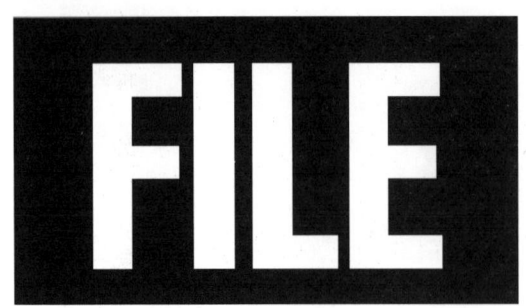

2001

2003

2004

2007

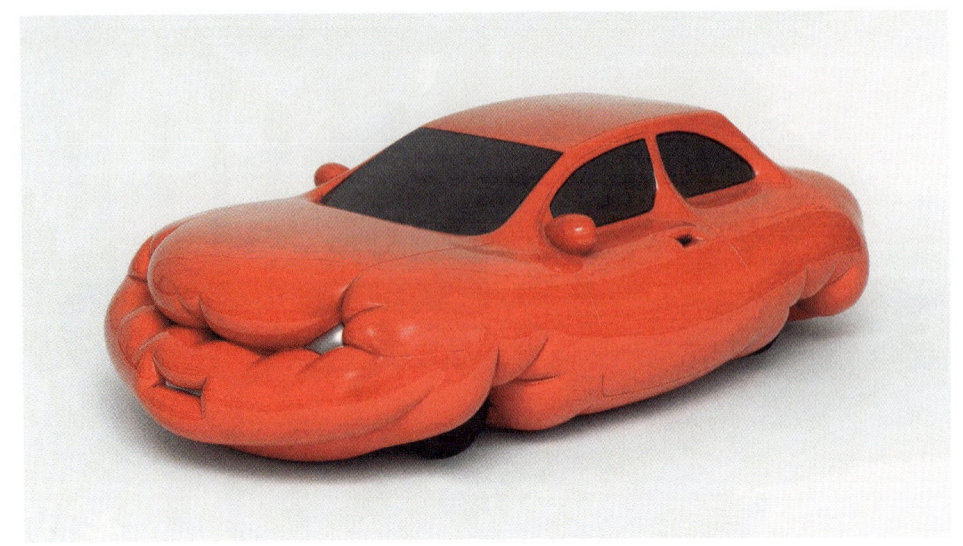

Erwin Wurm, *Fat Car*, metallic paint, styrofoam and polyester, 111 × 65 × 33cm. 2001–2004.

2001

The sprawling grassy area between the Los Angeles County Museum of Art and the La Brea Tar Pits is often littered with asphalt fissures big and small with a pungent viscous black substance oozing and sometimes bubbling from the ground. Some of the larger pools of exposed asphalt are cordoned off as they are sites of active excavation on view for park visitors from behind fences. Fossils dating from 11,000-50,000 years ago have been extracted from the pits over the decades, providing evidence of the region's climate and ecosystem change.

It is nearly irresistible to walk past one of these fissures without stopping to look at it or to poke at it with a small stick. The park's groundskeepers often create ad-hoc barriers, dams, and barricades to mitigate the spread of asphalt onto sidewalks and common areas cautioning park-goers who might otherwise step into the goo at the expense of their footwear. Sterling Ruby's 2003 work *Transient Bed of John* is a photographic readymade of one of these makeshift barricades—a human sized asphalt fissure surrounded by a teardrop perimeter of sandbags, the interior space littered with sticks ostensibly disposed of by people after having poked the ooze for a bit. The white sandbags are drizzled and dripped with asphalt and one of the sandbags shown in the lower left of Ruby's photo has the name "John" scrawled on it, the letters dripping down and touching the ground. The scene is nest-like, tomb-like, bed-like, the sticks are vaguely skeletal, and Ruby's photograph is composed so as to also include the nearby trash can, a public amenity for those who are consuming on the go. In a catalog essay for Ruby's 2015 "Vivids" exhibition, Eugene Y. Wang wrote of this work:

> Much is made of Ruby's insurrection against 1960s Minimalism. Less acknowledged is Ruby's continuation of a line of inquiry that Robert Smithson had launched: the exploration of matter and mind, geology and consciousness. Ruby's *Transient Bed of John* and *Refraction Bed of John*, for instance, are better seen as continuing a pedigree that goes back to Smithson's 1966 *Tar Pool and Gravel Pit*. But Smithson was more preoccupied with the "primordial ooze" that materializes the prototypical structure of human consciousness. In comparison, Ruby's basin epitomizes the transversal state of human subjectivity and identity. [1]

Existentially speaking, existence precedes essence in *Transient Bed of John* and, like much of Ruby's work, it exudes a rabid interiority that conflates the found and the made, the public and the personal, the future and the past. The La Brea Tar Pits asphalt is a transversal medium—a site of archeological threshold crossing through extraction, study, and display, as well as a site of continuous absorption and ingestion. ¶

NOTES

1. Eugene Y. Wang, *Posthuman Inscape: Sterling Ruby's VIVIDS Paintings and Subjectivity Without Subject*, Gagosian Gallery Hong Kong, 2015.

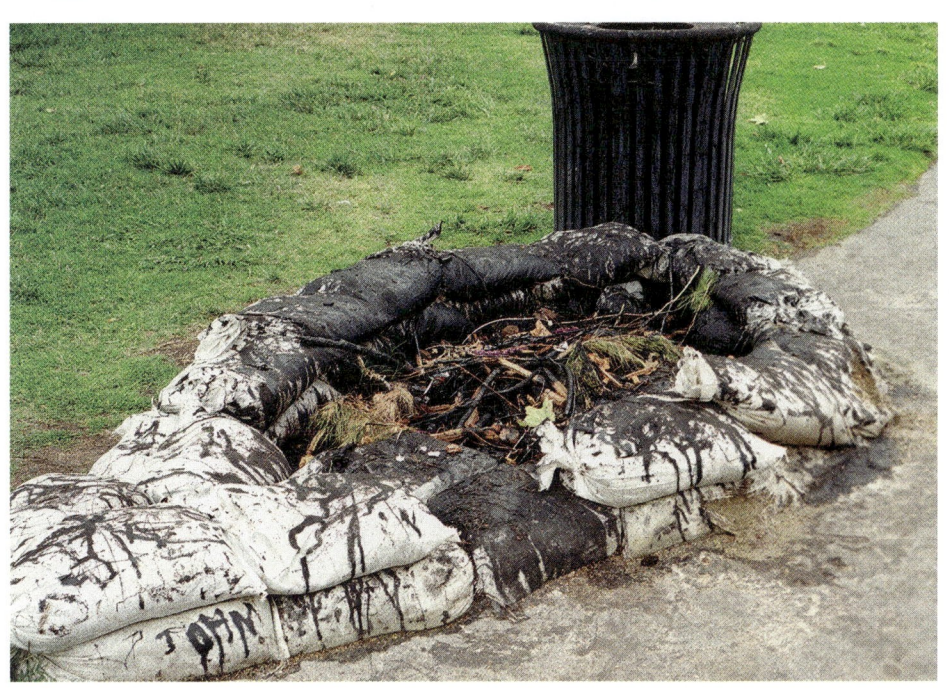

Sterling Ruby, *Transient Bed of John*, Lambda print, 15 ½ × 21 ¼, 2003.

Midway through Wayne Koestenbaum's book *Humiliation* is the chapter "The Blob," in which Koestenbaum unpacks an unambiguous tyrant/ victim/witness criteria trifecta required for humiliation to occur. Koestenbaum then opposes this condition to the internalized recognition of the imminent potential for humiliation on the part of a "witness," who might withhold completion of the triangle. Beginning with an acute account of a childhood awareness of the physical deformity of a schoolmate, Koestenbaum moves on to cite Annie Leibovitz's photographs of Susan Sontag's death as an example of humiliation being deferred through the medium of photography—deflecting from the deceased through the photograph and along to the viewer, a privatized circumvention. Albeit with Sontag's permission, among Leibovitz's several disarming and disorienting photographs of Sontag is *Leaving Seattle, November 15, 2004*:

> Susan's body unconscious on a stretcher. Her hair is short and white. The attendants cover her with a sheet. Leibovitz borrows a friend's plane to transport Susan to the Fred Hutchinson Research Center in Seattle where she receives a bone marrow transplant which eventually fails.[1]

This particular photograph is an emotionally charged symbolic multiplex, a film-still-like denouement—the plane's gullwing door open, Sontag's gurney at a slight diagonal, apparent wind blowing the sheet off her body, clouds churning in the background. Sontag's body alongside the plane is metaphorically ample, the photograph's scene suggesting a sudden acceleration of the death process. Koestenbaum's meditations in this chapter are largely death-centric and, in particular, his examples underline the way in which empathy clumsily functions as a kind of potential humiliation: "We use the word 'humiliation' sometimes merely rhetorically, to describe a potential for agony, even if the agony is not always, in that instant, an actual experience; in these cases, humiliation can't be touched, measured, visualized, or weighed."[2] The apparitional, formless quality of "potential" humiliation and the peculiar way in which a witness is implicated through still and moving images is aptly described by Sontag who once wrote, "Photographs state the innocence, the vulnerability of lives heading toward their own destruction, and this link between photography and death haunts all photographs of people."[3] The photograph as a posthumous communiqué is a special kind of slipperiness, slimy in its bilocational posture, lubricated in part by the latent potential for humiliation.

Autobiographically narrating the potential for one's enjoyment of another's humiliation to undo and even reverse itself via images, Koestenbaum describes his complicated enjoyment and subsequent feeling of personal humiliation resulting from watching a YouTube video of anti-gay rights activist Anita Bryant getting a pie in the face in 1977. (See page 132) During a press conference in Des Moines, Iowa, while reporters are questioning Anita Bryant about her national crusade against homosexuals, gay rights activist Tom Higgins throws a pie in Bryant's face prompting her to pray for Higgins' salvation, eventually breaking down and crying into her hands, squarely humiliated. "I may have momentarily hated her and wanted her to die, but when she cried, even if her sadness was mixed with rage, I believed that my misbehavior had ruined her, and I felt humiliated by that knowledge, dragged into the mucus and much of her tears, tears that I'd provoked, witnessed, relished, and rued."[4] Here is an account of the image again transmuting humiliation.

An age-old slapstick schtick, the pie that Bryant takes in the face pushes the entire press event in an unexpected, "unknowable" direction. Bataille carefully aligned laughter and the unknowable in his 1953 "Nonknowledge, Laughter, and Tears" where he writes:

> In sum, it makes us laugh to pass very abruptly, all of a sudden, from a world in which each thing is well qualified, in which each thing is given in its stability, generally in a stable order, to a world in which our assurance is suddenly overthrown, in which we perceive that this assurance is deceptive, and where we believed that everything was strictly anticipated, an unforeseeable and upsetting element appeared unexpectedly from the unforeseeable, that reveals to us in sum a final truth: that superficial appearances conceal a perfect lack of response to our anticipation.[5]

But it is Bryant's tears, momentarily obscured by pie filling, the sign of genuine sadness that pushes back at Koestenbaum.

Bryant's colleague immediately orders attendant authorities to "Let him stay" and then suggests, "Let's pray for him right now,"[6] a bizarre demonstration of weaponized passive-aggressive religiosity, oozing with guilt-trip. As with the comedic precedent of the pie-in-the-face, the maximum effect of this stunt is hinged on the accuracy of the impact of the pie itself on the victim's face, the particular way in which upon impact, an obliterated pie obscures facial features that might betray legible expression. It is not quite possible to gauge Bryant's facial expression, but her posture gives it away. Surprised for sure. Shocked perhaps. Displeased, mildly humored, threatened, matter of fact realization, confusion. The pie dispersed on Bryant's face prompts a reaction from the viewer before her own reaction is totally apparent, the delay between action and reaction the result of a face obscured by the amorphous coverage of pie filling. ¶

NOTES

1. Ann DeWitt, "Memento Mori," *Believer Magazine*, August 20, 2004.
2. Wayne Koestenbaum, "The Blob," *Humiliation*, (New York: Picador, 2011), pp. 68-80.
3. Susan Sontag, *On Photography*, (London: Penguin Books, 1979), p. 55.
4. Wayne Koestenbaum, "The Blob," *Humiliation*, (New York: Picador, 2011), pp. 68-80.
5. Bataille, "Nonknowledge, Laughter, and Tears," in *Unfinished System of Nonknowledge*, (University of Minnesota Press, 2001), p. 135.
6. "Anita Bryant's Pie to the Face." Youtube.com," NBCUniversal-Archives.com, Jun 9, 2014, https://www.youtube.com/watch?v=5tHGmSh7f-0.

In her 1986 book *Howl's Moving Castle*, Diana Wynne Jones vividly invokes the 'expression' of slime in her description of a conniption fit by one of the story's central characters, the preeminently vain Wizard Howl. Howl has a beauty-routine breakdown brought on by a hair catastrophe resulting from the unwanted cleaning of his bathroom and reorganization of his alchemical hair products. Following a verbal assault on his castle mates, Howl slumps speechless onto a stool where he then expresses his feelings with green slime. Jones writes, "He spread his arms out passionately. 'Despair!' he yelled. 'Anguish! Horror!'"[1] At other moments in the book, Howl's mood is gauged as on the brink of slime, locating the production of slime at the threshold of emotional regulation and verbal communication. Jones also describes the odor of Wizard Howl's slime as vile. Howl's slime is described as in "dollops" "glops" and "sticky strands" recalling the ontological crisis brough on by Sartre-esque slime, and its vile smell links up with qualities Julia Kristeva sometimes ascribes to abjected things.

> "Inside, Howl was still sitting on the stool. He sat in an attitude of utter despair. And he was covered all over in thick green slime. There were horrendous, dramatic, violent quantities of green slime—oodles of it. It covered Howl completely. It draped his head and shoulders in sticky dollops, heaping on his knees and hands, trickling in glops down his legs and dripping off the stool in sticky strands. It was in oozing ponds and crawling pools over most of the floor. Long fingers of it had crept into the hearth. It smelled vile."[2]

Slimy visuals are prominently featured in the animated films of Hayao Miyazaki, often standing to symbolize beings in flux and transference of mythical energy. In Studio Ghibli's adaptation of the above scene from Jones' book, the text is faithfully animated, with a dramatic addition of dialogue from Howl where he mutters, "I see no point in living if I can't be beautiful." ¶

NOTES

1.   Diana Wynne Jones, *Howl's Moving Castle*, 1986 (New York: HarperCollins Publishers, 2008), p. 117.
2.   Ibid. pp. 118–119.

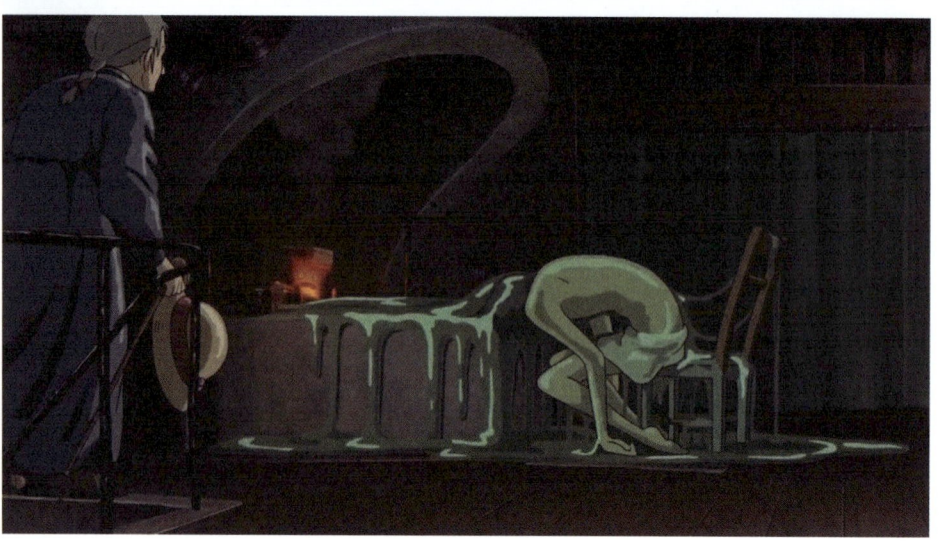

Film still from *Howl's Moving Castle*. Directed by Hayao Miyazaki. Studio Ghibli Inc., 2004.

In the days following Jason Rhoades' death, photographer Josh White discovered a large sealed garbage bag in the artist's studio.[1] Inside the bag was an early prototype batch of Rhoades' *PeaRoeFoam*, a "brand new product and revolutionary new material."[2] Opening the bag released a repugnant, noxious odor—this particular batch of *PeaRoeFoam* a rotten slurry, paralyzing in its stench having fermented for approximately 6 years.

The material, formulated by Rhoades and "manufactured" by his studio assistants and others in various interactive exhibition contexts, was a combination of peas, roe, and expanded polystyrene beads mixed together with liberal amounts of Elmer's glue that functioned as a stabilizer and binder allowing the material to be amorphously congellated, cast, applied, and sculpted. Rhoades packaged his *PeaRoeFoam* in reproductions of the notorious 1970s Ivory Snow detergent boxes featuring model and actress Marilyn Chambers holding an infant. Rhoades leaned conceptually on Chambers' situational iconoclasm, her image on the box a pop-cultural illustration of a conflated dirty/clean binary, further emphasized by the ostensive use of the detergent product itself.

Rhoades' *PeaRoeFoam* however replaces the white, snow-like detergent flakes with a dry mixture of *PeaRoeFoam's* three ingredients, along with a four-fluid-ounce bottle of Elmer's glue taped haphazardly to the back of each package. Whereas Proctor &

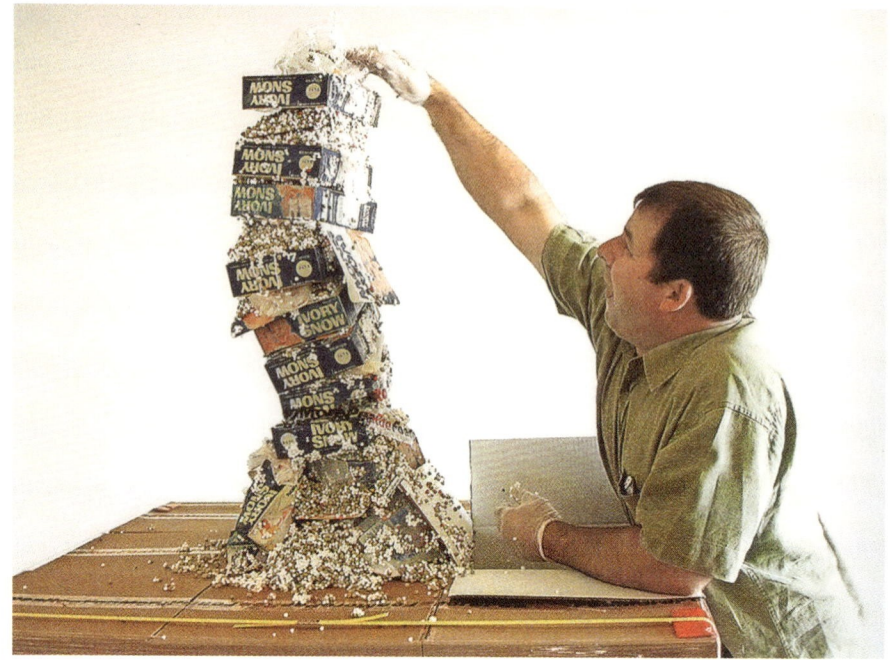

Jason Rhoades in the process of making *PeaRoeFoam Pallet with Sculpture from Liverpool-II*, 2002. "The first experience which the infant can have with the slimy enriches him psychologically and morally; he will not need to reach adulthood to discover the kind of sticky baseness which we figuratively name "slimy"; it is there near him in the very sliminess of honey or of glue."[1]

NOTES

1.   Jean-Paul Sartre, *Being and Nothingness: An Essay on Phenomenological Ontology*, trans. Hazel E. Barnes. 1943 (New York: Washington Square Press, 1956). p. 612.

2007

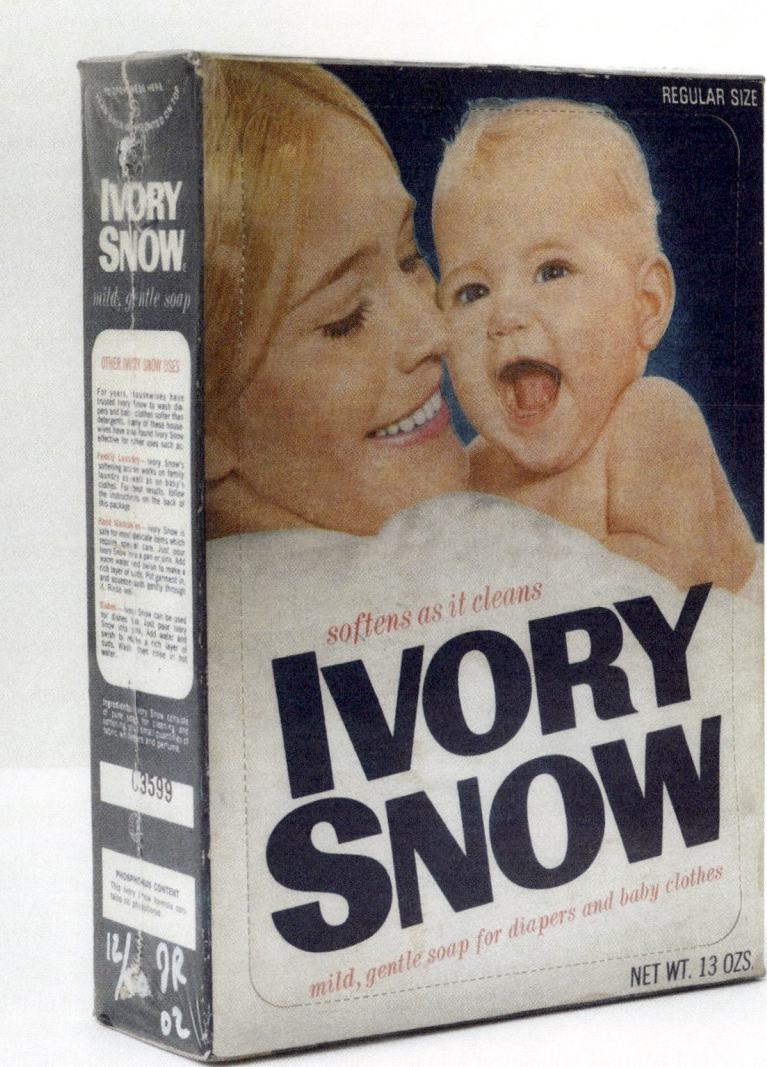

Jason Rhoades, *Ivory Snow Refrigerator Magnet*, Shrink-wrapped cardboard box with interior aluminum frame and magnet, 8 ½ × 6 x 2 inches, 2002.

2007

Gamble fired Chambers as the face of Ivory Snow immediately upon learning of her starring role in *Behind the Green Door*, Rhoades referentially rehired her, a symbolic gesture—litigiously transgressive, nostalgic, and emphatic in reenacting the messy cultural threshold crossing of Marilyn Chambers. Going so far as to install an actual free-standing green door in his studio through which he and others involved in *PeaRoeFoam* were encouraged to pass through, Rhoades' slimy infatuation with Chambers links together references and behaviors with a density that is at once dynamic, amorphous, and irreducibly elliptical. ¶

NOTES

1. Joshua White. Personal Communication. January 7, 2020.

2. *Jason Rhoades: PeaRoeFoam*, David Zwirner, Lucas Zwirner, Dylan Kenny, (David Zwirner Books, NY, 2005).

3. Jean-Paul Sartre, *Being and Nothingness: An Essay on Phenomenological Ontology*, trans. Hazel E. Barnes. 1943 (New York: Washington Square Press, 1956). p. 612.

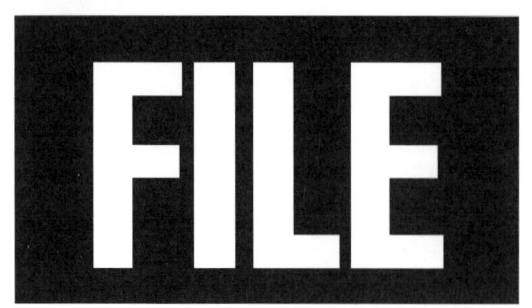

2010

2012

2015

2016

2017

2019

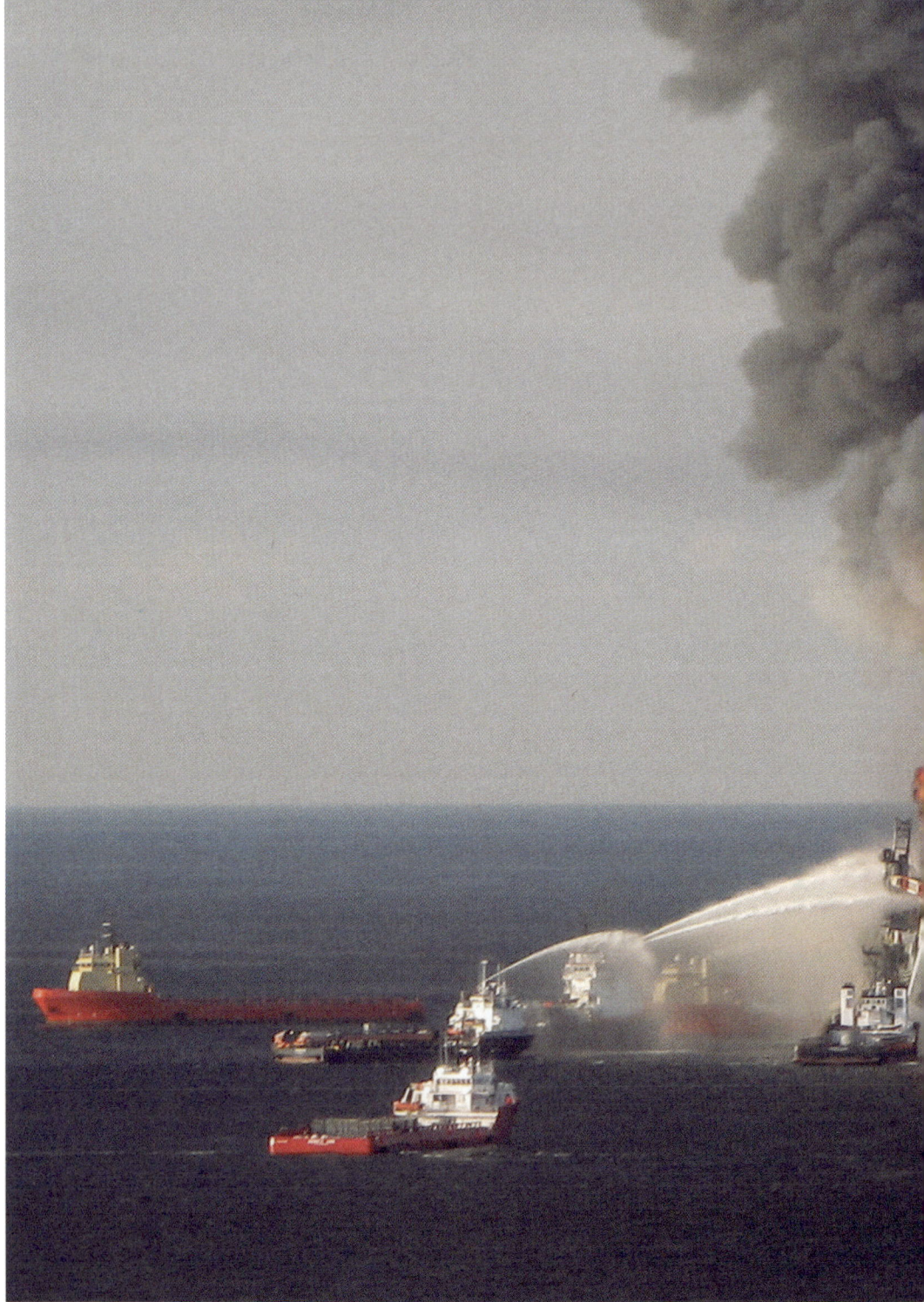

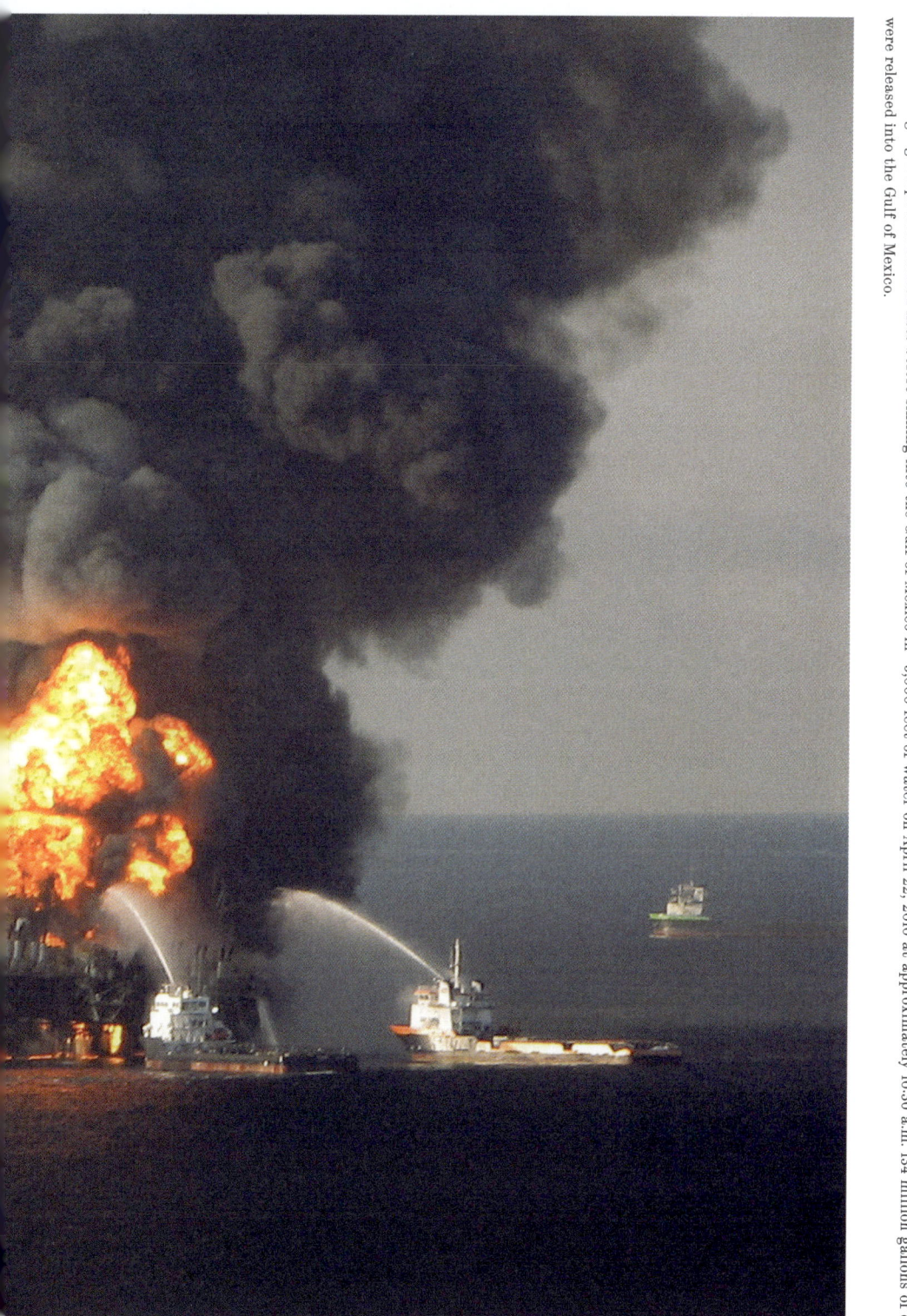

The oil drilling rig Deepwater Horizon lists before sinking into the Gulf of Mexico in ~5,000 feet of water on April 22, 2010 at approximately 10:30 a.m. 134 million gallons of oil were released into the Gulf of Mexico.

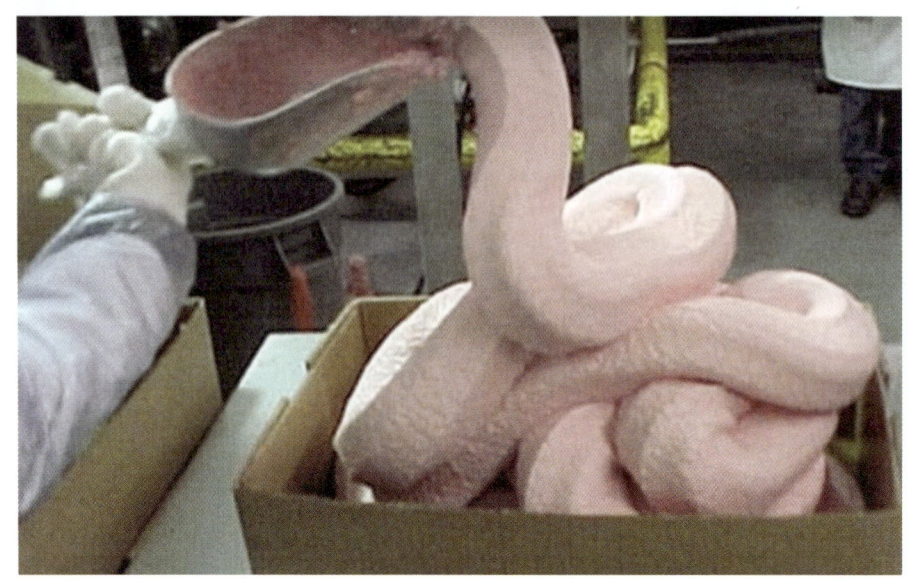

Pink Slime, 2012. Fatty proteins are centrifugally isolated from scrap meat and purified with gaseous ammonia to create a pink goo that is used to extend and augment ground beef products. Controversial and only recently accounted for on ingredient labels, pink slime is beef simulacrum processed to the point of near-total dissociation from the original animal. A waste product reconstituted back into edibility, pink slime represents the low end of industrialized food production as post-mortial ooze.

228

2012

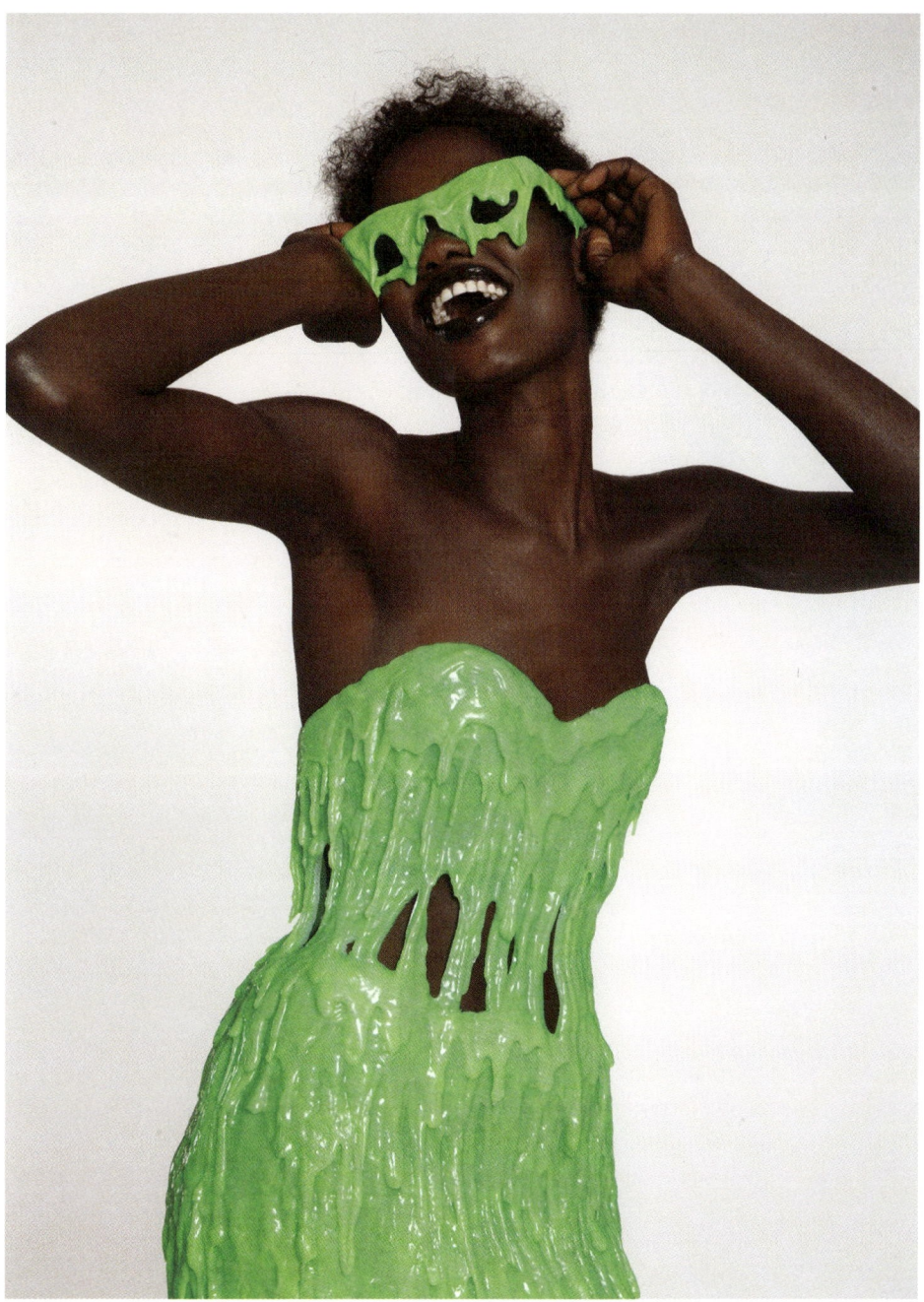

Rapper Young Thug's career trajectory can be described as sonically multivalent, prolific, and irreducible in its engagement with the elasticity of language, his relationship to referentiality expansive and generative. Notably Young Thug has been credited with an idiosyncratic introduction of "slime" into rap music's lyrical and visual multiversel — "Slime or get slimed" Young Thug raps on "Slime Shit," the fourth track on his 2016 album *Slime Season 3*. As a reviewer wrote of Young Thug's first *Slime Season* release in 2015, "Young Thug is a spectacle. His personal quirks — the tutu, his not-quite-there interview presence, and his fluid use of 'bae,' to name a few..." the writer continues, "Young Thug exists in Squigglevision. He flips common maxims into something extraterrestrial."[2]

In an interview from the same year, Young Thug was quoted insisting that he *is* from another planet, "And I'm ready to go back to it," he said "This shit petty. Like, earth. Close-minded people."[3] Young Thug's deployment of slime occurs repeatedly throughout his musical catalog in imagery, song names and lyrics, mix-tape and album titles. The slipperiness of his style is often attributed to a super saturation of content, the effect of his musical catalog being constantly flooded with leaks and unofficial releases. Music reviewers have an unproductive obsession with intra-catalog comparative analysis, questions of consistency, progression, and growth as metrics for evaluation, all of which are formally and conceptually

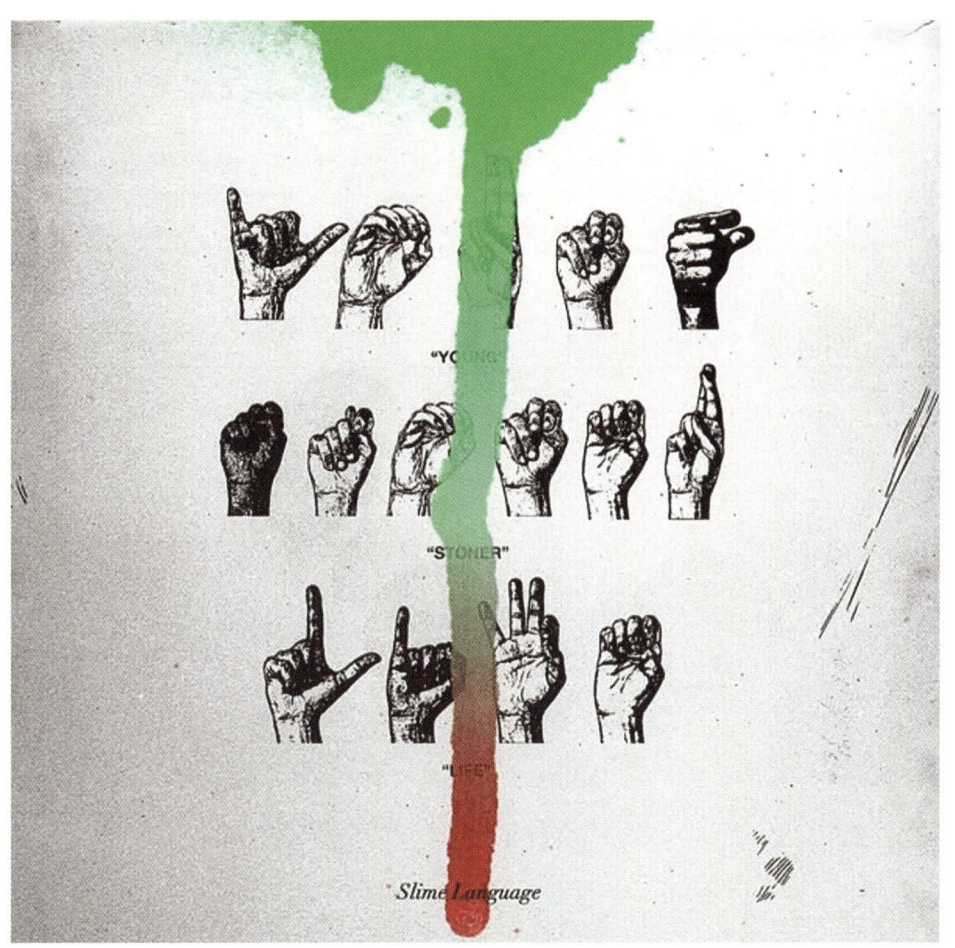

2015

foiled by Young Thug's creative output. As another reviewer put it, "*Slime Season* exists outside of space or time."[4] Young Thug has explicitly acknowledged an intentional use of slime as a term that previously did not really exist in rap music, his adoption of the word-concept a strategy simultaneously of differentiation and establishment, a threshold device that puts him at once uniquely in contact with and also just out of reach of rap music's regionally stratified expressive boundaries. ¶

NOTES

1. Slime is a somewhat un-trackable term within rap and hip-hop vernacular, its meaning ranging from a term of endearment, to a state of being, to underhandedness. Young Thug's use of slime is consistent with slime's historically restless relationship to signification.

2. Brian Josephs, "Album Review: Young Thug: Slime Season," *Consequence*, September 21, 2015

3. Davy Reed, "Young Thug: Slime Season," *Crack Magazine*, September 23, 2015

4. Paul Thompson, "Rap Report: Young Thug Slimes Us, Milo Takes Busdriver to School, Genre Reports," *Spin*, October 16, 2015

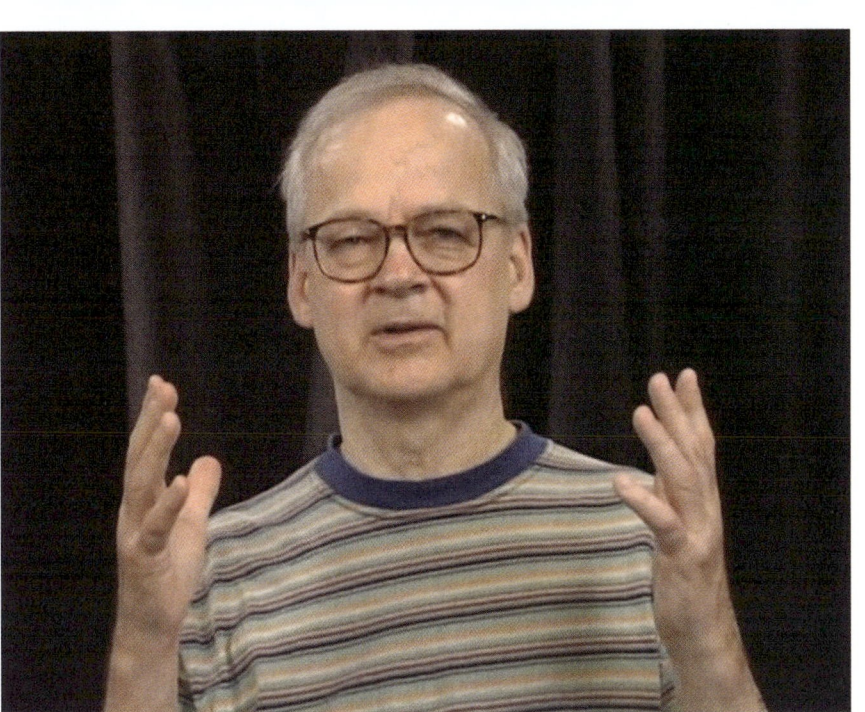

Tony Conrad, "Coming to terms with your own death," *Tony Conrad unedited pt 4*, Video, 2016. The staging of these posthumously released videos in which Conrad speaks plainly to the viewer in medium close-up, a heavy curtain as a backdrop are "strangely reminiscent of the initiation videos of the millenarian cult Heaven's Gate,"[1] some of which were released following the groups' mass suicide in 1997. Video produced with the intention to be watched online following one's death is a premeditated, threshold crossing, one-directional communiqué to the living.

So, you motherfuckers, you're out there watching me. And I'm dead. So, what do you think? How is it? Cause I feel fine and you're sitting on your asses watching me on video after I'm gone. Do I feel comfortable about this relationship to you? No. Why should I feel comfortable about it?[2]

–Tony Conrad

NOTES

1.   Yusef Sayed. "In Media Resistant: Tony Conrad." (1940–2016). Issue 7, LOLA, lolajournal.com

2.   Tony Conrad, "Coming to terms with your own death," *Tony Conrad unedited pt 4,* Video, 2016.

In dry sub-frozen weather conditions, the immense amount of steam emitted from nuclear power plant cooling towers can sometimes condense and freeze midair forming clouds and flurries of "nuclear snow," a collateral microclimate resulting from atom splitting. Ominous but not radioactive, the notion of nuclear snow nonetheless free-associatively precipitates the idea of a "nuclear winter," an abnormal period of cold and darkness predicted to follow a nuclear war, such a firestorm kicking dust and smoke into the atmosphere and blocking direct sunlight from reaching the surface of the earth.

Preserving the Cold War Russian villain stereotype while updating the fear of nuclear annihilation with a race for control of a bilocational portal, the Netflix series *Stranger Things* reaches backward and forward simultaneously. With a reverence for established horror clichés and special effects, the Duffer brothers feature slime prolifically and predictably. The substance is always denoting threshold crossing, generously coating each being who enters or exits the inconstant openings between the alternate dimension of the Upside Down and the right side up town of Hawkins. Within the space of the Upside Down and emanating from its varied entrances are floating white particles, spores, or snow-like flakes. The effect is achieved partially on set, though mostly in post-production, and is significant in that it provides an expanded representation of slime. The ominous flakes signify proximity to open bilocational portals, subtly spilling out and lingering in the air, a pre-slime atmospheric condition.

The accumulative silence of actual snow and its sound absorptive porousness creates a natural

anechoic chamber-like effect, amplifying an awareness of one's own sense of breathing, pulse, being
in space. The effect can be corporeally meditative.
Sound machines feature "white noise," a flat-spectral
density of frequencies that can be calming as well
as dangerous—a popular tool for those seeking to
eliminate or drown out ambient sound in the pursuit
of relaxation or distraction from their immediate
environment. The random pattern of electronic noise
displayed on an un-tuned television is sometimes
referred to as "snow," abrasive yet enthralling, it
draws attention to the flatness of the screen effectively breaking the fourth wall with abrasive effect.

In *Poltergeist,* Carol Anne is drawn to the snow on
the screen of the television at the foot of her parents'
bed, and it is there that she initially communicates
with the resident disturbance. In *Stranger Things*,
radio static features prominently as an un-tuned
space for communication between those inside and
outside of the Upside Down. Eleven, the psychoki-
netically and telepathically capable protagonist of
Stranger Things, achieves remote viewing through
sensory deprivation. Flashbacks show Eleven remote
viewing in a flotation tank, but she makes do post
escape with the white noise of a changing room
shower and duct tape covered safety goggles, a
kiddie pool with 1,500 pounds of dissolved salt, and
eventually remote viewing on-demand with only a
blindfold once her powers are honed. Boundary crossing as a not purely corporeal category of movement
is demonstrated with fluency in *Stranger Things* and
thresholds are interchangeably crossed physically
and psychically. ¶

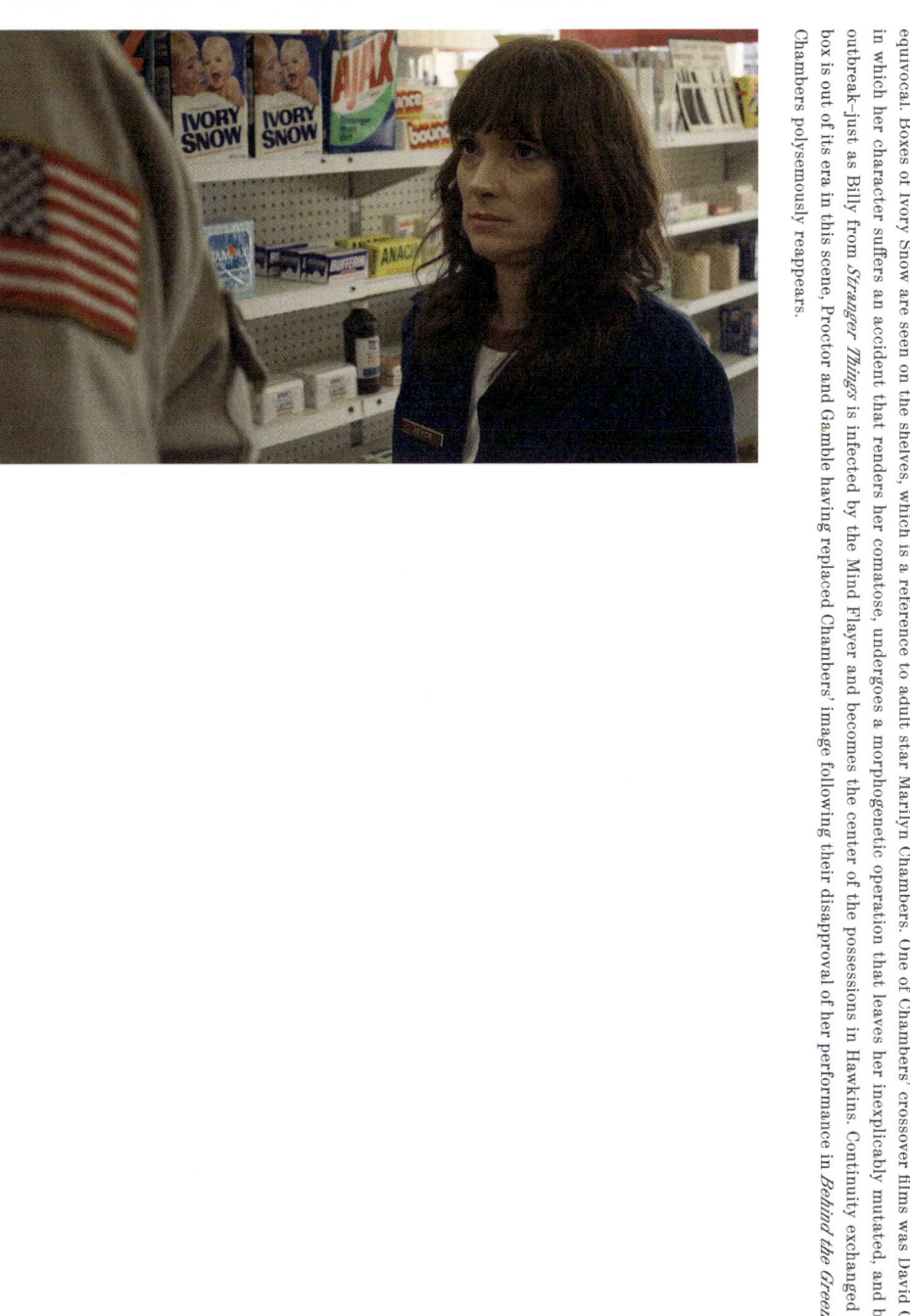

Film still from *Stranger Things*, Duffer Brothers, Netflix, 2016. Season 3 episode 1, "Suzie, Do You Copy?," 2019. Among *Stranger Things*' prodigious references this shot is rather equivocal. Boxes of Ivory Snow are seen on the shelves, which is a reference to adult star Marilyn Chambers. One of Chambers' crossover films was David Cronenberg's 1977 *Rabid*, in which her character suffers an accident that renders her comatose, undergoes a morphogenetic operation that leaves her inexplicably mutated, and brings about a "zombie" outbreak–just as Billy from *Stranger Things* is infected by the Mind Flayer and becomes the center of the possessions in Hawkins. Continuity exchanged for concept, Chambers' box is out of its era in this scene, Proctor and Gamble having replaced Chambers' image following their disapproval of her performance in *Behind the Green Door*, but in this scene Chambers polysemously reappears.

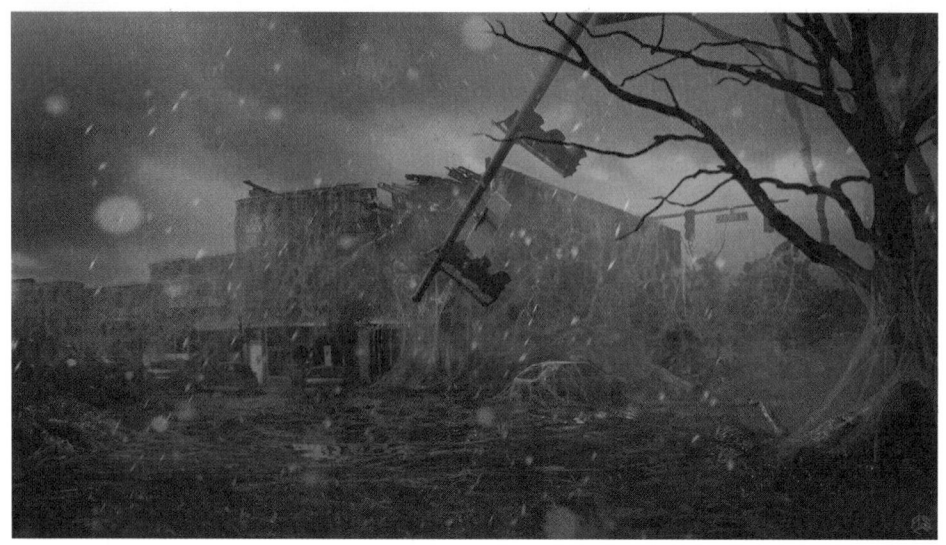

Aaron Sims, "Upside Down" concept art, *Stranger Things*. Duffer Brothers. Netflix, 2016.

2016

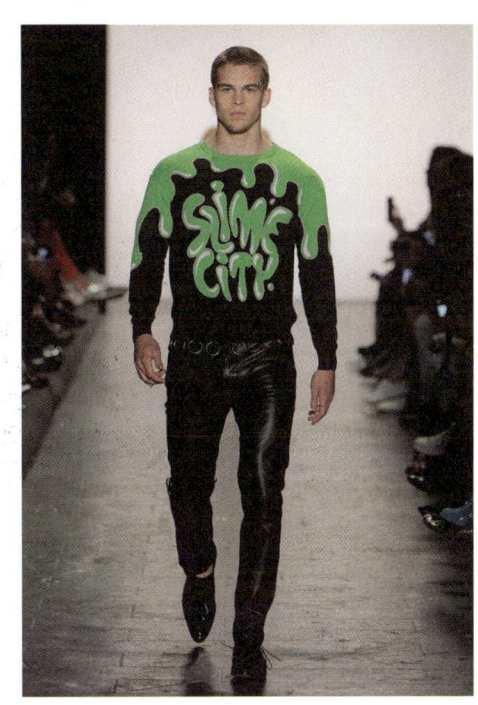

Jeremy Scott, Spring/Summer 2017 Slime City collection, New York Fashion Week, 2016.

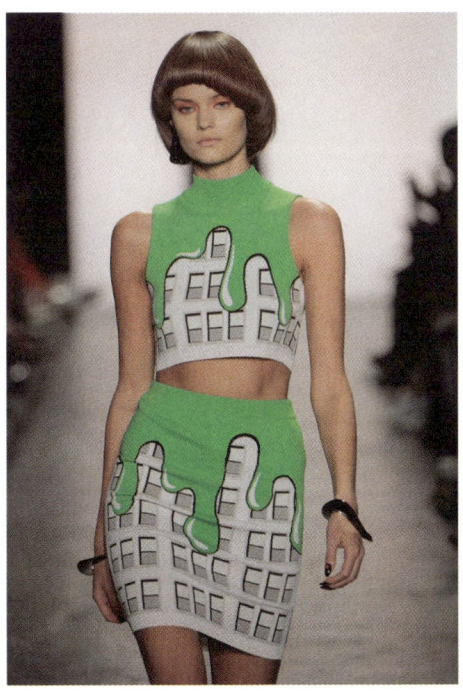

2017

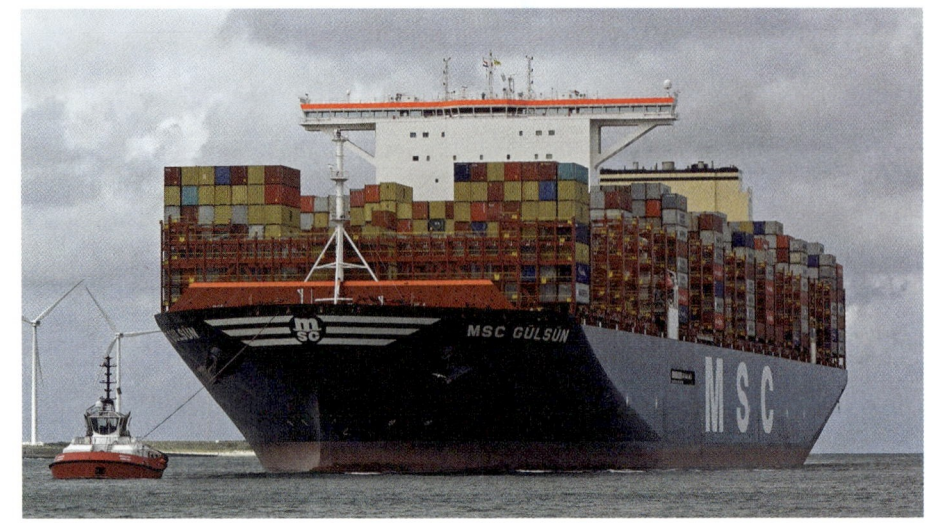

MSC Gülsün at the time of her launch in 2019 was the world's largest container ship with a total capacity of 23,756 TEU. Constructed by Samsung Heavy Industries in the Geoje shipyard in South Korea MSC Gülsün operates on MSC services between Asia and Europe.

2019

MSC Gülsün CO_2 Emission Calculation[1]

- 7.49g of CO2 emissions to move one ton of cargo one nautical mile
- 232,618 registered tonnage
- 26,000mi round trip from East Asia to Northern Europe
- 77 days round trip
- 26,000mi × 4.75 trips/year
- 123,500mi/year
- 7.49g × 232,618mt = 1,742,308g
- 1,742,308g x 123,500mi = 215,175,038,000g
- 215,175,038,000g = 237,190mt CO2/year
- MSC Gülsün = 50,465.96 cars/year
- One Car = emits 4.6mt CO2 /year[2]

NOTES

1. Calculation based on information from the "MSC Gülsün Fact Sheet." msc.com. Retrieved 11/16/20
2. Greenhouse Gas Emissions from a Typical Passenger Vehicle," *Green Vehicle Guide*. epa.gov. Retrieved 11/16/20.

Throughout this text I have cited and alluded to instances from the recent history of nuclear development in relation to the overarching discussion of slime. Fear and anxiety about the very real possibility of annihilation via nuclear warfare or power plant meltdowns is a relentless and ever-present feature of modernity, combined with, or recently superseded by, the stark fear of climate change and ecosystem collapse. In *Why We Can't Sleep*, Ada Calhoun elaborates on the mediatized fear of nuclear annihilation and the resulting effect on Gen X psychology:

> Until 1991, it was a major feature of our newscasts and our entertainment that with no warning we could all be incinerated. The partial meltdown at the Three Mile Island reactor in Pennsylvania in 1979 and the Chernobyl nuclear power plant explosion in 1986 helped make nuclear destruction feel plausible. Psychological studies in the 1980s found that the threat of nuclear war led to high anxiety in children. The silver lining according to one journal article, was that we didn't stew for long, because: "cynicism and apathy set in rapidly."[1,2]

While not exclusively illustrative of nuclear anxiety, slime in its referential capacity and material modulation seems at times to have absorbed and expressed the intergenerational evolution of this trepidation. Importantly, slime is more primordial than technological—slow not fast, an antidote to modernity rather than a sign of capitulation—and slime often seems to serve a metabolic function in the service of social consciousness in its semantic and behavioral modalities. Paul Virilio fleshes out the synthesized violence of speed and weapons in *The Speed of Politics,* where he writes, "In this paradoxical object, simultaneously explosive and implosive, the new war machine combines a double disappearance: the disappearance of matter in nuclear disintegration and the disappearance of places in vehicular extermination."[3] Notably Virilio later submits that, "There remains only a passive defense that consists less in reinforcing itself against the megaton powers of nuclear weapons than in a series of constant, unpredictable, aberrant movements, movements which are thus strategically effective for at least a little while longer, we hope."[4] Virilio's use of "aberrant" as the quality of the "constant, unpredictable" movement humanity must sustain to avoid nuclear holocaust "for at least a little while longer, we hope" suggests a slimy form. Factoring into this extrapolation the open-ended, global state of emergency in which we find ourselves, where resources and expenditures are disproportionately redirected toward the maintenance of a nuclear state, it isn't much of a stretch then to think of much of humanity itself as interned: "What else has the proletariat been since antiquity, if not an entirely domesticated category of bodies, a prolific, engine-towing class, the phantom presence in the historical narrative of a floating population linked to the satisfaction of logistical demands."[5]

What is at stake in this line of inquiry as it relates to slime? Nineteen years after Virilio's articulation that survival under a speed obsessed State is contingent upon aberrant movement, Rosalind Krauss extracted from Georges Bataille an earlier identification of "social abjection with a violent exclusionary force operating within modern State systems, one that strips the laboring masses of their human dignity and reproduces them as dehumanized social waste."[6] In this equation, life itself in its abjection is reduced to slime, violently separated from its form, an apropos metaphor for "naked life", albeit abject.

In his judicious *Form-of-Life*, Giorgio Agamben writes that human life "always retains the character of possibility,"[7] which he goes on to describe as "Irremediably and painfully assigned to happiness."[8] Agamben flatly criticizes the terminal condition of abjection in Bataille's elevated writing on the subject as an unproductive limit. "To have mistaken such a naked life separate from its form, in its abjection, for a superior principle–the sovereign or the sacred–is the limit of Bataille's thought, which makes it useless to us."[9] For Agamben thought itself as an individual and collective activity constitutes form-of-life: "Thought is form-of-life, life that cannot be segregated from its form; and anywhere the intimacy of this inseparable life appears, in the materiality of corporeal processes and of habitual ways of life no less than in theory, there and only there is there thought."[10] Semiotically unresolved, an ambiguous signifier pointing to ambling signifieds, slime retains its floating status, its openness and amorphousness inversely related to the number of precedents used to illustrate its peculiar physical qualities and conceptual character—slime is a restless thought.

It happens to be the case that the effects of climate change, at once measurable and unfathomable, is the existential fear du jour and slime's recent evolution of appearance has moved beyond its sticky green viscerality through manifestations as an aberrant, "asphaltic" black fluid and, most recently, to snow-like particulates, dust, spores, or flakes. In the final chapter of *Formless: A User's Guide,* Yve-Alain Bois recasts Bataille's own trepidation about the effect of overproduction of energy:

> Of course, Bataille is supremely optimistic: aware that, if we keep traveling down the same road in our race against the overproduction of energy, humanity one day will condemn itself (a fortiori if it sets the solution of war aside, as increasingly endangering its survival), he sees nothing less than a radical change of attitude that would force man to accede to sovereignty (voluntary renunciation of usefulness and of the accumulation of riches; propagation of nonproductive expenditures). But he doesn't exclude the possibility of failure.[11]

It is essentially snowing just outside the gateways to the Upside Down and very recently the producers of the superhero television series *The Umbrella Academy* illustrate the demonstrably apocalyptic almost-maximum powers of a central character by engulfing them in a self-generated blizzard. Looping back finally to Sartre, notorious Frankfurt School professor-slash-activist Herbert Marcuse wrote an analysis of *Being and Nothingness* in 1948 that highlighted the way in which Sartre's philosophy "exposes the danger zones of society, but transforms them into structures."[12] Global ecosystem collapse, like fascism creates a feedback loop where, "thought is thrown back upon itself by a reality which contradicts all promises and ideas."[13]

Compelling Marcuse's dive into *Being and Nothingness* however is a characterization of thought as relentlessly enduring in its clear and lucid fixation on freedom and happiness, despite whatever concrete reality. In his reliably liberative voice, Marcuse offers, "This life is nothing but 'consciousness and revolt,' and defiance is its only truth."[14] Extracting a line from Albert Camus' *Le Mythe de Sisyphe*, "L'homme absurde entrevoit un univers brûlant et glacé, transparent et limité, où rien n'est possible mais tout est donné, passé lequel c'est l'effondrement et le néant."[15] Marcuse evocatively notes, "Thought moves in the night, but it is the night."[16] Like the night, early descriptions of slime are described as asphaltic, a preeminently metabolic primordial substance whose existence and extraction is depended upon and which is also the entropic destination of much biologic life. Like the night, thinking about slime is enthralling and boundaryless, our location within it based on the number of reference points we can use to orient ourselves in an increasingly open-ended and evolving network of relations. ¶

1. S.J. Kiraly, "Psychological Effects of the Threat of Nuclear War," *Canada Family Physician*, v. 32

2. Ada Calhoun, *Why We Can't Sleep: Women's New Midlife Crisis*, (New York: Grove Press, 2020), pp. 35-36. (January 1986): 170-74.

3. Paul Virilio, *Speed and Politics*, (California: Semiotext(e), 2006), pp. 150-154.

4. Ibid.

5. Ibid.

6. Rosalind Krauss, "Informe" without Conclusion," *October*, Vol. 78, Autumn, 1996, pp. 89-105.

7. Giorgio Agamben, "Form-of-Life," *Means Without End*, University of Minnesota Press, Theory Out of Bounds v. 20, London, 2000, pp. 1-11.

8. Ibid.

9. Ibid.

10. Ibid.

11. Yve-Alain Bois and Rosalind Krauss, *Formless: A User's Guide* (New York: Zone Books, 1996), p. 224.

12. Herbert Marcuse, "Existentialism: Remarks on Jean-Paul Sartre's L'Être et le Néant," *Philosophy and Phenomenological Research*, Mar., 1948, Vol. 8, No. 3 (Mar., 1948), pp. 309-336.

13. Ibid.

14. Ibid.

15. Ibid.

16. Ibid.

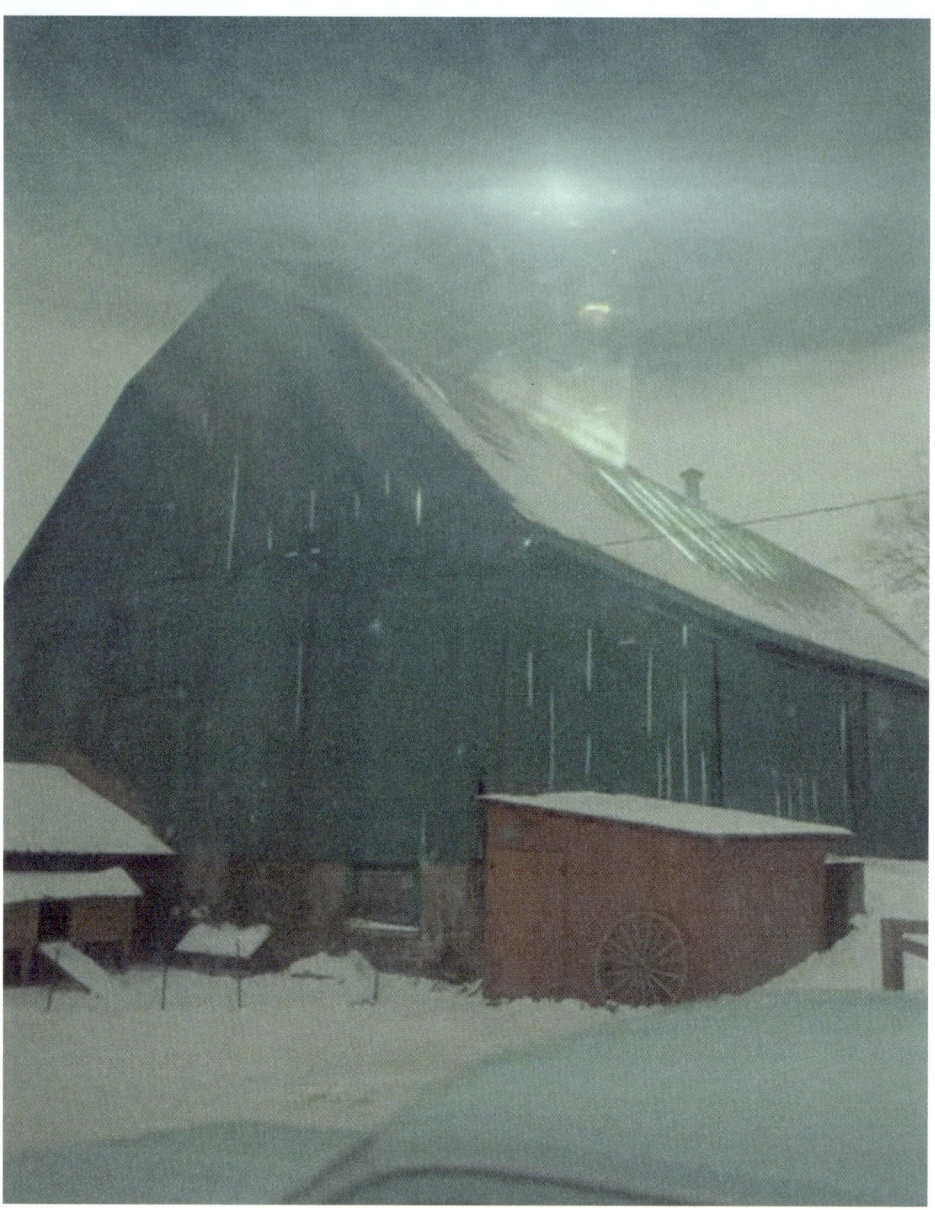

Steve Blackman , "Harlan's Farm," *Umbrella Academy,* Season 2 Episode 10, NBC Universal Television Distribution, Netflix, 2020.

REPRODUCTION CREDITS

p. 16. Ernst Haeckel, Mycetozoa Illustration (Slime Mold). Kunstformen der Natur (Artforms of Nature). (1899-1904), Plate 93.

p. 33. A wide-angle photograph of the medium Mary Marshall with a tele-plasmic mass enveloping her head during a séance at the home of Dr. Thomas Glendenning Hamilton on February 22, 1931. Photo credit: University of Manitoba Archives/Hamilton Family Fonds.

p. 37. Howard V. Brown, Illustration for "At the Mountains of Madness: Part 2," H.P. Lovecraft, Astounding Stories of Super Science. Street and Smith Publications, Inc. March, 1936.

p. 41. Buster Keaton rehearsing a skit for the Salute to Stan Laurel TV show, 1965. Photo credit: Don Cravens.

p. 45. A Manhattan Project team poses with "Jumbo" or "Big Brother" prior to its detonation on July 16, 1945 in Alamagordo, New Mexico. Photo credit: Los Alamos National Laboratory.

p. 47. Theodore Geisel (Dr. Seuss), Bartholomew and The Oobleck, 1949. © Dr. Seuss Enterprises, L.P./Licensed by Penguin Random House LLC Permissions Department.

p. 53. Promotional image for Lolita. Directed by Stanley Kubrick. Metro-Goldwyn-Mayer, 1962.

p. 57. Operation Plumbbob, Fizeau, 1957. Photo credit: Everett Collection.

p. 61. Promotional poster for *The Blob*. Directed by Irvin Yeaworth and Russell Doughten. Paramount Pictures, 1958.

p. 66. Film still from *The Twilight Zone* opening graphic. Created by Rod Serling. CBS, 1959-1964.

p. 68. Various Mathmos Lava Lamps, 1960s.

p. 69. Gunnar Aagaard Andersen, *Portrait of My Mother's Chesterfield*, Dansk Polyether Industri, Denmark, Poured polyurethane, 29 ½ × 44 ¼ × 35 ¼ inches, 1964.

p. 71. Basil Wolverton and Norman Saunders, Ugly Stickers, 1965, Topps Trading Cards.

p. 74. Mark Boyle in the first performance of Bodily Fluids and Functions with Aldis projection of stained catarrh, Bluecoats Art Center, Liverpool, 1966. Image source: J. L. Locher, *Mark Boyle's Journey to the Surface of the Earth*. Stuttgart (Engelhornweg 11, 7 Stuttgart 1): Hansjörg Mayer, 1978. Print.

p. 81. Wes Wilson, The Association, Quicksilver Messenger Service, Grassroots, Sopwith Camel; Fillmore Auditorium, July 22-23, 1966.

p. 84. Robert Smithson, *Glue Pour*, 1969. Photo credit: Christos Dikeakos. © 2020 Holt/Smithson Foundation/Licensed by Artists Rights Society (ARS), New York

p. 88-89. Richard Serra, *Gutter Corner Splash*, 1969. © 2021 Richard Serra / Artists Rights Society (ARS), NY

p. 92. Lynda Benglis pouring *Adhesive Products* at the Walker Art Center, 1971. Image credit: Video still from "Walker Art Center; Art Speaks; Lynda Benglis Discusses Adhesive Products (1971)."

p. 95. Slimey the worm. Still from Sesame Street, Episode 262: "Pet Show." May 11, 1971.

p. 98. Marilyn Chambers posing with an Ivory Snow detergent box featuring an image of her holding a baby. Procter & Gamble, 1970. Licensed by Newscom.

p. 100. Film still from *Behind the Green Door*, directed by Artie Mitchell and Jim Mitchell, starring Marilyn Chambers, Mitchell Brothers Film Group, 1972.

p. 103. Film still from the launch of the Saturn I SA-5 during NASA's Apollo program on January 26, 1964. Image credit: NASA.

p. 105. Francesca Woodman, *Self-portrait talking to Vince*, Gelatin silver print, Sheet: 8 × 10 in. (20.3 × 25.4 cm), 1975/78. Collection Museum of Contemporary Art Chicago, Gift from The Howard and Donna Stone Collection, 2002.76

p. 106. During an October 14, 1977 press conference in Des Moines, Iowa, while reporters are questioning Anita Bryant about her national crusade against homosexuals, gay rights activist Tom Higgins throws a pie in Bryant's face prompting her to pray for Higgins' salvation. Photo credit: Associated Press.

p. 108. Mike Kelley & David Askevold, *The Poltergeist*, 1978. © 2021 The Mike Kelley Foundation for the Arts. All rights Reserved. / VAGA at Artists Rights Society (ARS), NY

p. 112–113. Production still from *You Can't Do That On Television*. Nickelodeon, 1979.

p. 115. Film still from *Alien*. Directed by Ridley Scott. 20th Century Fox, 1979.

p. 121. Video still from Mountain Dew's 2020 Super Bowl commercial. Created by TBWA\Chiat\Day New York and directed by Tom Kuntz. 2020.

p. 125. "TCBY®" The Country's Best Yogurt logo, 1981–1996.

p. 132. The destruction of Pruitt-Igoe, March 16, 1972. Photo credit: St. Louis Post-Dispatch.

p. 135. Film still from *Poltergeist*. Directed by Tobe Hooper. Metro-Goldwyn-Mayer, 1982.

p. 138. Brinks guards in Toronto escort a Cabbage Patch Kid to its new owners, who paid $5,600 in an auction to help the Hospital for Sick Children, 1983. Photo credit: Boris Spremo/Toronto Star.

p. 144–145. Special effects artist Steve Johnson's "Slimer" models for *Ghostbusters*. Columbia Pictures, 1984. Photo credit: Virgil Morano, courtesy of Richard Edlund and Boss Film Corporation.

p. 152. Jim Phillips, *Slime Balls* sticker design, Santa Cruz Skateboards, 1985. Licensed by NHS, Inc.

p. 154. John Pound, Le*aky Lindsay*, Garbage Pail Kids, Second Series, 1985, Topps Trading Cards.

p. 157. Film still from *Better Off Dead*, Savage Steve Holland, A&M Films/CBS Theatrical Films, 1985.

p. 159. Film still from *The Stuff*. Directed by Larry Cohen. New World Pictures. 1985.

p. 163. Film still from *The Toxic Avenger*. Troma Entertainment, 1984.

p. 164. The Elephant Foot, Chernobyl. Photo credit: Alexander Sich. 1986.

p. 167. James Groman, "Slobulus" illustration from The Madballs Handbook, AmToy. 1986.

p. 168. Ron Wilson, Cover illustration for "The Garden of Evil," Masters of the Universe, Volume 1, Issue 3, Star Comics. September, 1986.

p. 171. Cindy Sherman. *Untitled #175*, Chromogenic color print, 46 ⅞ × 71 ½, 1987. Courtesy of the artist and Metro Pictures, New York.

p. 172. Andrew Probert, Armus concept art, Skin of Evil, Season 1, Episode 23, Star Trek: The Next Generation, Paramount Domestic Television, 1988.

p. 177. Fugazi, *Margin Walker*, EP cover, 1988. Photograph by Tomas Squip. Courtesy of Ian MacKaye.

p. 179. Fugitive Exxon Captain Joseph Hazelwood (R) listens as his attorney Thomas Russo addresses the court on April 5 after Hazelwood surrendered to the Suffolk County District Attorney. Hazelwood was arraigned in state Supreme Court where he was taken to the County Jail in Riverhead, New York, 1989. Photo credit: Reuter/cc POOL, Dick Yarwood, Newsday.

p. 182–183. John Martin, Bridge Over Chaos, Mezzotint print, 1826.

p. 186. Film still from Wee*kend at Bernie's*, Directed by Ted Kotcheff. 20th Century Fox, 1989. A ghost house that can only be experienced through the phantasmagoria of film. Bernie Lomax's House, 1610 Fort Fisher Blvd, Kure Beach, NC, Fort Fisher State Recreation Area. Built specifically for the film and torn down immediately after production.

p. 187. Film still from *Weekend at Bernie's*, Directed by Ted Kotcheff. 20th Century Fox, 1989.

p. 191. Black Lodge map, *Twin Peaks*, Mark Frost, David Lynch, American Broadcasting Company, 1990. Black Lodge entrance, Glastonberry Grove. Episode 27, "The Path to the Black Lodge," 1991.

p. 192. Film still from *Twin Peaks*, Mark Frost, David Lynch, American Broadcasting Company, 1990. Black Lodge entrance, Glastonberry

Grove. Episode 27, "The Path to the Black Lodge," 1991.

p. 194. Blinky the fish from "Two Cars in Every Garage and Three Eyes on Every Fish," *The Simpsons*. Season 2, Episode 4. November 1, 1990.

p. 197. Mark Quinn, *Self, Blood* (artist's), stainless steel, Perspex and refrigeration equipment, 208h × 63w × 63d cm, 1991.

p. 200. Film still from *Encino Man*, Directed by Les Mayfield, Hollywood Pictures/Touchwood Pacific Partners I, 1992.

p. 203. Heaven's Gate crime scene photograph, 1997. Photo credit: San Diego Police Department.

p. 206. Erwin Wurm, *Fat Car*, metallic paint, styrofoam and polyester, 44 × 25 × 13 inches. 2001–2004.

p. 209. Sterling Ruby, *Transient Bed of John*, Lambda print, 15 ½ × 21 ¼, 2003. Courtesy of Sterling Ruby Studio.

p. 216. Film still from *Howl's Moving Castle*. Directed by Hayao Miyazaki. Studio Ghibli Inc., 2004.

p. 218–219. Jason Rhoades in the process of making *PeaRoeFoam Pallet with Sculpture from Liverpool-II*, 2002.

p. 221. Jason Rhoades, *Ivory Snow Refrigerator Magnet*, Shrink-wrapped cardboard box with interior aluminum frame and magnet, 8 ½ × 6 × 2 inches, 2002.

p. 225. The oil drilling rig Deepwater Horizon lists before sinking into the Gulf of Mexico in ~5,000 feet of water on April 22, 2010 at approximately 10:30 a.m. 134 million gallons of oil were released into the Gulf of Mexico. Photo credit: U.S. Coast Guard/Files/Handout/Reuters.

p. 226. Pink Slime, 2012. Photo credit: KSDK-TV. F

p. 227. Gerlan Marcel, Slime Dress, Spring/Summer 2012.

p. 229. Young Thug, *Slime Language* album cover, 2018, YSL/300.

p. 231. Tony Conrad, "Coming to terms with your own death," *Tony Conrad unedited pt 4*, Video, 2016.

p. 235. Film still from *Stranger Things*, Duffer Brothers, Netflix, 2016. Season 3 episode 1, "Suzie, Do You Copy?," 2019.

p. 236. Aaron Sims, "Upside Down" concept art, *Stranger Things*. Duffer Brothers. Netflix, 2016.

p. 237. Jeremy Scott, Spring/Summer 2017 Slime City collection, New York Fashion Week, 2016.

p. 238. MSC Gülsün, msc.com.

p. 246. Steve Blackman , "Harlan's Farm," Umbrella Academy, Season 2 Episode 10, NBC Universal Television Distribution, Netflix, 2020.

FILE UNDER SLIME
BY CHRISTOPHER MICHLIG

FIRST NORTH AMERICAN EDITION, 2022

Copyright © 2022 by Hat & Beard Press, Los Angeles

Design by Brian Roettinger (Perron-Roettinger)
Edited by Christopher Michlig
Senior Editors: J.C. Gabel & Sybil Perez

ISBN 978-1-955125-20-8

10 9 8 7 6 5 4 3 2 1

Hat & Beard Press books are published by
Hat & Beard, LLC713 N La Fayette Park Place
Los Angeles, CA 90026

www.hatandbeard.com